LEADERSHIP EXCELLENCE

LEADERSHIP EXCELLENCE

Empower Your Leadership with
The Model for Sustained Leadership Success

Philip A. Iannuzzi, Jr.

BHP

An Imprint of Bunker Hollow Press
Doylestown, Pennsylvania

BUNKER HOLLOW PRESS

Copyright © 2025 by Philip A. Iannuzzi, Jr. All rights reserved.
Published by Bunker Hollow Press, Doylestown, Pennsylvania

Cataloging
    Leadership excellence : empower your leadership with the model for sustained leadership success / by Philip A. Iannuzzi, Jr.
    - 1st ed.
        p. cm.
        Includes bibliographical references and index
        ISBN: 979-8-9924534-2-3 (hardcover)
        ISBN: 979-8-9924534-0-9 (pbk)
        ISBN: 979-8-9924534-1-6 (ebk)

1. Leadership. 2. Leadership development. 4. Organizational leadership. 5. Business administration. 8. Education. I. Title: Leadership Excellence.

BISAC codes: BUS071000, EDU032000, EDU046000

Book cover design by *Philip A. Iannuzzi III*

LEADERSHIP EXCELLENCE. Printed in the United States of America. Except as permitted under the United States Copyright Act of 1976, no part of this publication may be reproduced or distributed in any form whatsoever, by any means, or stored in a database or retrieval system without the publisher's prior written permission except in the case of brief quotations embodied in critical articles and reviews. Neither the publisher nor the author shall be liable for any loss of profit or any other commercial damages. Readers should be aware that internet websites offered as citations and/or sources for further information may have changed or disappeared between the time this was written and when it is read. Requests to the publisher for permission to use material from the book should be addressed to bunkerhollowpress@gmail.com.

To current and aspiring leaders

May you lead with purpose, empower your team with integrity,
and strive for excellence that endures.

Contents

AUTHOR'S NOTE XI
INTRODUCTION 1
    Leadership Development 4
    The Study of Leadership 5
    Nature and Nurture 8
    The Leadership Role 9
    Team-Member Perspective 10
    Leading-Up Perspective 11
    Leadership Capabilities 11
    Leadership Styles 12
    Leadership Priorities and Focus Areas 13
    Sustained Leadership Excellence 13
    Model for Sustained Leadership Excellence 14
    Looking Ahead 18

PART I: ON LEADERSHIP 21

CHAPTER ONE: EVOLUTION OF LEADERSHIP THEORY
.... 23
    Leadership . . . a Human Endeavor 23
    Industrial Revolution 25
    Scientific Management 26
    Maslow's Theory of Human Motivation 29
    McGregor's Theory X and Theory Y 33
    Herzberg's Motivator-Hygiene Theory 35
    The Hawthorne Effect 38
    Evolving Management and Leadership Practices 39
    Quality Management 41
    Artificial Intelligence 49

CHAPTER TWO: LEADERSHIP 55
    The Leader Role 56

LEADERSHIP LEVELS	59
MANAGERS AND LEADERS	60
NATURE AND NURTURE	66

CHAPTER THREE: LEADERSHIP CAPABILITIES AND STYLES 69

LEADERSHIP CAPABILITIES	70
LEADERSHIP STYLES	78

CHAPTER FOUR: LEADERSHIP PRIORITIES 93

LEADERSHIP FOCUS AREAS	94
PEOPLE FOCUS AREAS	96
MISSION FOCUS AREAS	108
OPERATING RHYTHM	116
THE WAY AHEAD	124

PART II: A FRAMEWORK FOR SUSTAINED LEADERSHIP SUCCESS 125

THE LEADERSHIP PROCESS	129
UNIFYING FORCES OF THE LEADERSHIP PROCESS	133

CHAPTER FIVE: ENABLING ATTRIBUTES OF LEADERSHIP EXCELLENCE 139

ENABLING ATTRIBUTE OF TRUST	141
TRUST ENABLES LEADERSHIP CAPABILITIES	146
BUILDING TRUST	155
ENABLING ATTRIBUTE OF CONCERN	160
CONCERN ENABLES LEADERSHIP CAPABILITIES	162
EXERCISING CONCERN	174
ENABLING ATTRIBUTE OF THE WILL TO LEAD	175
THE WILL TO LEAD ENABLES LEADERSHIP CAPABILITIES	176
A WILLINGNESS TO LEAD	188

CHAPTER SIX: CORE VALUES OF LEADERSHIP EXCELLENCE 191

CHARACTER SHAPED BY INTEGRITY	193

A Service Mindset 201
The Continuous Pursuit of Excellence 207

**CHAPTER SEVEN: EMPOWER YOUR LEADERSHIP—
TURN PRINCIPLES INTO SUSTAINED PERFORMANCE 219**
Review of The Leadership Excellence Model 220
Integrated Framework 226
Operationalize the Model 232
Strategic Planning Workshop 238

MOVING FORWARD 249

ACKNOWLEDGMENTS 251

REFERENCES 255

INDEX 274

ABOUT THE AUTHOR 279

Author's Note

*

The world needs skilled, capable, and ready leaders at every level—from entry-level to the top. Fortunately, the need can be met through learning, training, and development. All leaders are learners . . . constantly observing, assessing, examining, and identifying ways to improve their leadership capability. They learn from doing, learn from others, learn from failures, and learn from accomplishments. This book was written with a singular purpose: to help develop, empower, and sustain the leadership capability of current and aspiring leaders across all fields.

My interest in the study and practice of leadership began as a college student at Temple University in Philadelphia, Pennsylvania. I planned to earn a bachelor's degree in computer science, followed by a career in management, leading teams in the business world. That plan unexpectedly turned into a lifelong journey of study, learning, service, and leadership experiences shaped by challenges and opportunities.

While at Temple, my motivation to learn about leadership led me to consider accepting an invitation from the university's Army Reserve Officer Training Corps (ROTC) detachment to attend officer field training at Fort Knox, Kentucky. At that time, the Army allowed students to enroll in field training without committing to serving as an officer until the training was completed, providing the flexibility to decide afterward. Having this option encouraged me to accept the invitation to learn about leadership as a military officer.

The six-week training program was both demanding and rewarding. It sparked my interest in becoming a military officer and reignited a childhood dream of flying jets—an aspiration that led me to pursue a commission as an officer and serve as a pilot in the Air Force. However, Temple did not have an Air Force ROTC detachment, so I transferred to Penn State University. There, I went on to complete another six-week officer field training program—this time with the Air Force at McConnell Air Force Base in Wichita, Kansas.

After field training at McConnell, I returned to Penn State and joined the Air Force ROTC program as a cadet, committing to serve as an Air Force officer and pilot for at least eight years after earning my degree. I graduated from Penn State and, on the same day, was commissioned as a second lieutenant in the Air Force. I then relocated to Lubbock, Texas, where I spent a year in pilot training at Reese Air Force Base, earned my wings, and went on to serve on active duty as an officer and pilot.

These formative experiences marked the beginning of a 24-year career on active duty in the Air Force, followed by a business career in the aerospace industry with The Boeing Company, serving in a wide range of leadership roles across the military and business sectors, from entry-level to executive. In tandem with these career experiences, I embarked on a lifelong journey of learning, researching, writing, and teaching about leadership. This journey led to a doctoral degree in educational leadership along with masters' degrees in systems management, international strategic studies, global air mobility logistics, and joint military operations.

As an adjunct faculty member at Embry-Riddle Aeronautical University, I taught courses on leadership. During the 10-week semester, students often asked about the differences between leading in the military and in business. Aside from differences in organizational missions, I explained that the leadership role remains fundamentally the same because, at its core, all leaders share a common aim: to safely and effectively achieve the correct mission results with their team over the long term.

This premise led to the central question shaping the content of the book: Is there a framework that can empower and sustain leadership success over the long term, regardless of the team one leads, the environment one operates in, or the mission one performs? The Model for Sustained Leadership Excellence introduced in this book is designed to help leaders achieve that objective.

Drawing from literature, research, and leadership best practices in business, education, government, the military, and multinational organizations, this comprehensive and integrated model underscores the impact of core values, enabling attributes, and unifying forces in shaping a leader's decisions, communication, and actions—referred to as the instruments of leadership. The model emphasizes the pivotal role these instruments play in generating the motivation, influence, and inspiration essential for leaders to consistently achieve the correct mission results with their teams over the long term.

My students' curiosity about the differences between leadership in the military and business, combined with my dedication to the study and practice of leadership and my desire to help empower current and aspiring leaders to sustain their success over the long term, inspired me to research, write, and publish this book.

The book is organized into two parts. Part I, On Leadership, explores leadership from research and experiential practice lenses. Part II, A Framework for Sustained Leadership Success, introduces the Model for Sustained Leadership Excellence, including strategies to implement and operationalize its principles.

Whether you are an experienced leader or stepping into a leadership role for the first time, I hope this book inspires you to reflect, grow, and lead with excellence. Leadership is not about perfection but about continuous growth—learning from successes and failures while inspiring those around you to reach their full potential. No matter the size or type of organization you lead—small or large business, multinational team, government agency, military unit, educational department, nonprofit, or any other team—I hope the insights shared in the pages ahead not only empower and sustain your leadership journey but also deepen your appreciation of the profound responsibility and honor inherent in leading others.

I'll close with some wisdom from Willie Mays, one of the greatest baseball players of all time. When praised as the best player ever during an interview, Mays responded, "I didn't play baseball to be number one. I played to make the guys around me number one."[1] This sentiment applies to sustained leadership as well: Don't lead to be number one. Lead to make your team number one while helping your team members reach their full potential.

Phil Iannuzzi
www.philiannuzzi.com

Introduction

> Personally, I am always ready to learn, although I
> do not always like being taught.
> — Sir Winston Churchill[2]

In our rapidly changing world, the demand for effective leadership has never been greater. At the same time, global and national challenges—including dynamic world events, globalization, and advancements in artificial intelligence—are placing increasing pressure on leaders at all levels.

In the largest study of its kind, Development Dimensions International (DDI) *Global Leadership Forecast 2025* revealed that leaders are struggling to succeed precisely when strong leadership is needed most.[3] As the longest-running global research initiative examining current and future leadership best practices, DDI's eleventh edition builds on 24 years of insights, analyzing 10,796 leaders from 2,014 organizations across 50 countries and 24 major sectors. The report underscores the need for today's leaders to be agile—capable of navigating rapid change, adapting strategies, and guiding their teams through uncertainty. They must also foster growth, drive innovation, and build genuine human connections—all while delivering results.[4]

Among the study's most notable findings, trust and leadership development emerged as critical concerns. "Trust is the currency of organizational success, yet it is rapidly deteriorating in today's volatile global landscape. From 2022 to 2024, trust in immediate managers took a dramatic nosedive from 46% to 29%," researchers found.[5] The 17-point decline exposed an increasing skepticism toward organizational leaders. In addition to concerns about trust, the study found that high-potential leaders and individual contributors were 3.7 times more likely to leave their organization within the next year if their leaders failed to provide opportunities for growth and development.[6]

In a separate study assessing the importance of leadership to an organization's success, Ann Howard, Ph.D., and Richard S. Wellins, Ph.D., surveyed 12,208 executives from 76 countries. They found that 75% of these leaders identified effective leadership as a top priority for organizational success.[7] Supporting this finding, Deloitte's *2023 Global Human Capital Trends* surveyed 10,000 global leaders across every industry, with 105 countries participating, revealing that 94% considered leadership capabilities and effectiveness important or very important to their organization's success.[8] Previously, Deloitte's *2021 Global Human Capital Trends* reported that 60% of surveyed leaders ranked leadership as the top priority for sustaining organizational success and preparedness for unknown futures.[9] Collectively, these findings underscore the growing recognition of leadership as a critical factor in organizational success.

Leveraging advanced technologies such as artificial intelligence, automation, machine learning, and robotics is essential for organizations to thrive and adapt in unpredictable environments. These innovations significantly enhance productivity and efficiency.

Yet, despite these advancements, the cornerstone of sustained success remains unchanged: effective leadership.

Effective leadership is widely recognized as vital to a team's success. Nevertheless, research highlights a significant shortage of leaders prepared to meet expanding organizational demands, with many organizations struggling to develop their future leaders.[10,11] Studies indicate that 50% to 75% of current leaders are underperforming—a troubling trend reflected in the declining tenure of senior leaders over the past two decades.[12,13,14]

Several factors contribute to this leadership shortfall, including shifting workforce demographics, intensified competition driven by globalization, frequent organizational restructuring, the rise of flattened or distributed leadership models, and significant changes in the nature of work, such as the growth of remote work.[15] For example, according to the U.S. Department of Labor, over 20 million Americans are employed in organizational leadership roles in the United States.[16] With the population growth projected to reach 417 million by 2060, the need for organizational leaders is expected to exceed 27 million.[17] The demand to backfill these positions is even more pressing due to the aging *baby boomer* workforce, those born between 1946 and 1964. With more baby boomers approaching retirement age and fewer workers currently prepared to fill the void, the result is a predicted shortage of talent.[18] Further, as the shift toward economic, political, and social globalization continues, more leaders are needed in the complex and diverse international work environment characterized by various language and cultural differences.[19]

The growing demand for leaders across all fields and levels has spurred considerable growth in leadership research and literature. In an exhaustive study on leadership, Mitchell Rothstein and Ronald Burke reported that "leadership is, arguably, the subject of more research and writing than any other topic in management literature."[20] Underscoring this view, a search of the Amazon.com database revealed over 60,000 books on leadership.[21]

Studies confirm that developing leadership capabilities is essential for long-term organizational success, regardless of mission, work scope, or size. A survey by the American Society for Training and Development highlighted this need, revealing that 45% of respondents identified a leadership skills gap as a top concern among talent management professionals.[22] Similarly, a study assessing the importance and value of leadership development training for college and university department chairs found that higher education leaders considered such training highly important and valuable. Yet, despite this recognition, only 20% of these leaders had received leadership development training before or after assuming their roles as department leaders.[23]

Leadership Development

Why is preparing and developing leaders a top priority for organizational success? Research indicates a clear link between the quality of leadership and team member motivation, performance, and mission results. Effective leadership drives productivity, retention, customer satisfaction, and profitability.[24] A study by Brandon Hall Group, a global leader in research and advisory services on leadership, highlights a growing gap in leadership preparedness and the need for organizations to prioritize leadership development for current and aspiring leaders. Brandon Hall's research found that 71% of organizational leaders believed their team members were not prepared to lead their organizations into the future. Even more concerning, only 25% of leaders said they had a successor ready and willing to step into even one of their ten most critical leadership roles.[25]

Indeed, the greatest demand for leaders is at the first and middle levels. Typically, they make up 50% to 60% of an organization's leadership and directly supervise as much as 80% of the workforce.[26] Noel M. Tichy, in his award-winning book *The Leadership Engine*, recommends that organizations should cultivate a *leadership engine* designed to systematically develop, grow, and prepare leaders to meet this demand.[27] Tichy uses the term to illustrate the process of educating and training leaders through a systematic leadership development track. The aim for aspiring leaders is to get on this track. Regrettably, however, it is estimated that 40% of leaders veer off track, unable to sustain their effectiveness.[28]

Even more daunting, advancing from one level of leadership responsibility to the next often presents significant challenges for leaders. According to Howard and Wellins, "Leaders who move up the management ladder face special challenges as they make the transition from one level of responsibility to the next. Leaders indicated that with each step up the ladder the transition became more difficult. Still, 46% of organizations provide no development support at all for leaders making transitions. If transitions—especially to the highest levels—are that difficult, organizations are remiss in not helping their leaders understand the challenges of the next step up and develop the knowledge and skills they need to meet those challenges."[29]

The Study of Leadership

> Study the past if you would define the future.
> — Confucius[30]

The historical roots of the study of leadership can be traced to government and military institutions dating back to the Egyptian empire over 5,000 years ago, when kings, queens, pharaohs, and military leaders exercised power and dominion over the known world. Writings on the philosophical principles of leadership emerged during this period. As seen in Figure 1, archaeologists uncovered records of ancient Egyptian hieroglyphics for leadership (seshemet), leader (seshemu), and follower (shemsu).[31] Centuries later, during the Greek empire, leadership concepts were also personified by heroes in Homer's *Iliad*.[32]

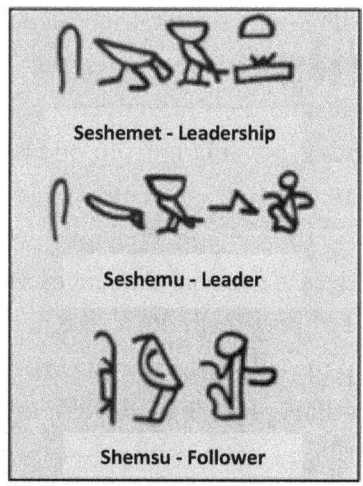

Figure 1. Egyptian Hieroglyphics for Leadership, Leader, and Follower

Throughout early history, rulers and military leaders commanded fighting forces in land and naval battles, enabling the security and expansion of regional territories and nation-states. The formal study and practice of military leadership can be found in the writings of political leaders and warriors dating back millennia. Sun Tzu, for example, the revered Chinese military strategist whose work influenced both Eastern and Western military philosophy, presented his theories on leadership over 2,500 years ago in a series of essays. His warfighting doctrine, *The Art of War*, remains part of today's global military, political, academic, and business education systems.[33]

From the ancient world to the post-modern world, leadership has been vital to human progress. "It's always about leadership . . . always," exhorts prize-winning author of *The One Minute Manager* and leadership consultant Ken Blanchard.[34,35] Despite Blanchard's affirmation, however, apart from a narrow range of formal military and paramilitary field training programs throughout history, the educational approach to developing and preparing leaders is a young academic discipline. *Merriam-Webster* reports that the first known use of the word *leader* was in the fourteenth century, and the first known use of the word *leadership* was in 1821.[36]

The formal study of leadership with a codified body of knowledge stemming from quantitative and qualitative research, along with disciplined peer-reviewed studies, can be traced to more recent years, during the last half of the nineteenth century. The scientific study of leadership was further propelled through the twentieth century as the world moved into the post-modern industrial age. During this period, for example, social scientists began conducting field research inside industrial manufacturing settings to understand the impact of working conditions on productivity. Their studies, analyses, and findings eventually led to scientific examinations of how leadership affects work performance and productivity.

Throughout the twenty-first century, the study of leadership and its associated body of knowledge expanded significantly, advancing our understanding of leadership as an academic discipline and field of study. It is now closely examined as an art and science. "Today, leadership is such a gripping subject that once it is given center stage it draws attention away from everything else," according to John W. Gardner, prize-winning author, leadership scholar, and Presidential Medal of Freedom award-winner.[37]

Nature and Nurture

For years, it was believed that leaders were born, not made. Today, however, research studies consistently find that genetic factors have much less influence than previously thought. "The answer to the question 'Can leadership be learned?' is an emphatic but qualified yes," contends Gardner.[38] Leaders learn to lead through study, observation, and practice. "It is a myth that leaders are born and not made," conclude Warren G. Bennis and Burt Nanus, noted research scholars in the fields of management and leadership.[39] Most people have the potential to lead, and leadership capabilities can be learned, assert Bennis and Nanus.[40]

Author Edgar F. Puryear's findings in a comparative study of the leadership qualities of World War II Generals George Marshall, Douglas MacArthur, Dwight Eisenhower, and George Patton underpin the views of Bennis and Nanus. Puryear's study concluded that the key characteristics of leadership are not innate but developed over many years.[41]

"Most of what leaders have that enables them to lead is learned. If effectiveness were a gift people were born with, the way they are born with a gift for music or an eye for painting, we would be in bad shape," professes Peter F. Drucker, one of the leading management consultants of the twentieth century and author of over 30 books on management and leadership.[42]

Yes, extraordinary leaders emerge at times, and their leadership capability, often attributed to genetic factors, is essential to the success of struggling organizations. In most organizations, however, the enduring requirement is for leaders to be effective, not extraordinary.

During World War II, the United States Army published its *Officer's Guide*, describing an effective leader as "one fitted by force of ideas, character, intellect, or by strength of will. The leader is deemed effective when able to arouse, incite, and direct others in conduct and achievement."[43]

Not long ago, leadership trait theory—the belief that only a select few are genetically born to lead—was considered the primary determinant of successful leadership. What we have come to learn, however, is that leadership effectiveness is not solely a function of nature. Effective leaders learn to lead, leveraging their natural abilities while at the same time developing, refining, and strengthening their leadership capability through inquiry, study, practice, experience, mentoring, and observing other leaders. The path to leadership excellence is paved with learning, and learning to lead begins with understanding the roles, responsibilities, and expectations of leadership.

The Leadership Role

Organizations have a wide range of titles for people serving in leadership roles: manager, supervisor, owner, boss, head, chief executive, governor, senator, mayor, director, commander, sergeant, dean, coach, principal, minister, imam, pastor, and president, for example. Despite one's title, however, a person responsible and accountable for the performance of others is serving in a leadership role, regardless of the type of organization or mission they support.

In the field of science, there is an axiom: If a thing cannot be measured, then it cannot be assessed. How, then, do we evaluate a leader's performance? The answer to this question begins with defining the terms leader and leadership. In this book, the term leader is defined as a person responsible and accountable for the performance of one or more team members as the team pursues an organization's mission, goals, objectives, priorities, and long-term vision. Leaders are expected to consistently achieve the correct mission results with their team members, regardless of the type of organization, mission, or team they lead. A leader's effectiveness, therefore, is assessed based on their ability to consistently achieve the correct mission results with their team. Correspondingly, the term leadership is defined as the process leaders employ through their decisions, communication, and actions—referred to as the *instruments of leadership* throughout this book—to motivate, influence, and inspire team members to consistently achieve the correct mission results.

Team-Member Perspective

A key premise of this book is that a leader's success depends not only on their own performance but also on the performance of their team members. Therefore, understanding what motivates, influences, and inspires others to excel requires examining these factors from the team's perspective. Author Donald T. Phillips, in his chronicle of Dr. Martin Luther King, Jr.'s views on leadership, recounts that Dr. King prepared to lead by first listening to understand the perspective and views of those he led.[44]

A team's performance is influenced, in part, by their perceptions and attitudes about the leader, which are shaped by ongoing assessments of the leader's verbal and non-verbal communication, decisions, and actions. These perceptions are also influenced by how team members perceive they are being treated, which affects their long-term commitment to the leader, their teammates, and the team's mission.

Research suggests that while financial compensation does have a positive impact on performance, money alone does not sustain motivation among dissatisfied team members over the long term.[45] Dissatisfied workers eventually become less productive and often seek other job opportunities. A growing body of evidence indicates that employees do not leave organizations—they leave their leaders.[46]

Leading-Up Perspective

Leading up refers to a leader's responsibility to align their team's goals, objectives, and priorities with those of the leadership chain above them and the organization as a whole. It requires staying engaged, involved, and in regular communication with immediate supervisors to understand, clarify expectations, and ensure the team meets or exceeds them.

Leadership Capabilities

Leadership capabilities are cultivated through learning, training, observation, practice, and real-world experience. A common goal of leadership and management books, courses, conferences, and formal development programs is to empower current and aspiring leaders by equipping them with the knowledge, capabilities, and practices demonstrated by successful leaders, including a leader's ability to:

> ➤ Cultivate and promote an environment of trust, teamwork, professionalism, communication, and goodwill through a set of shared values.
> ➤ Collaborate with team members and team leaders to establish challenging and achievable goals and objectives to sustain a team's pursuit of a shared vision.
> ➤ Model leadership behaviors and set an example for others by acting with integrity, showing respect, and valuing the diversity of people, ideas, and proposed solutions within the team.
> ➤ Solicit inputs and suggestions from team members and team leaders on decisions that have an impact on the team's mission.

- Listen, restate, and consider team members' concerns, feedback, and recommendations.
- Recognize team members' contributions and performance.
- Nurture a work environment that encourages safe, prudent risk-taking and empowers team members to speak up about safety, ethical, or legal concerns without fear of reprisal or retaliation.
- Coach, mentor, and encourage team members and team leaders to further develop their functional expertise and leadership capabilities.
- Identify, develop, and grow the organization's next generation of leaders through succession planning, education, and leadership development.
- Organize, train, equip, and provide resources for team members to accomplish the organization's mission.

Leadership Styles

Leaders interact with their teams through a leadership style shaped by their personality and evident in their communication, behavior, performance, and presence. When thinking about a leader's style or persona, people often envision extraordinary, heroic figures and personalities, especially in the context of political and military history. However, research shows that successful leaders employ a range of styles, and no single style fits all situations.

Some leaders are extroverts and some are introverts; some are loud and some are quiet; some micromanage while others macromanage; some are relaxed and others restless; some are charismatic and others pragmatic; some are comfortable in the public spotlight while others prefer less attention; some are analytical and others instinctive. Sustained leadership excellence often requires leaders to adapt their style to varying situations, circumstances, missions, cultures, and phases in an organization's life cycle.

Leadership Priorities and Focus Areas

Effective leaders sustain their team's performance by cultivating a work environment where team members feel valued and express pride and enthusiasm for being part of the team. They foster a commitment to the team's mission and support the development of their team members. Leaders create this environment by focusing on responsibilities aligned with two overarching leadership priorities: people and mission.

Leadership focus areas include activities, events, processes, systems, procedures, policies, management, and operating practices requiring ongoing leadership awareness, engagement, and involvement. A leader's attention to these focus areas promotes an environment in which team members see the leader as trusted and trusting, concerned about team members' success, welfare, and development, and committed to the success of the team's mission. Establishing an organizational operating rhythm gives leaders a structured framework to monitor progress, review mission performance, adjust course, and maintain situational awareness of these priorities.

Sustained Leadership Excellence

What is sustained leadership excellence? Sustained leadership excellence is a leader's ability to safely and effectively achieve the correct mission results with their team over the long term. What does it take to achieve this level of excellence? Consistently effective leaders develop and sustain their leadership capability through continuous study, education, training, observation, practice, and experience. This ongoing development process yields valuable learning and prepares leaders to take on additional leadership responsibilities.

Despite the level of preparation, however, the demands of leadership are challenging, time-consuming, unpredictable, unique, and wide-ranging. The key to sustained leadership excellence, regardless of uncertainties and challenges, is to lead from a foundation of core values and enabling attributes that inform and shape leadership decisions, communication, and actions—the instruments of leadership. This premise leads to the central question shaping the content of this book: Is there a development framework that can empower and sustain leadership excellence over the long term, regardless of the team one leads, the environment one operates in, or the mission one performs? The Model for Sustained Leadership Excellence is designed to help leaders achieve that objective.

Sustained Leadership Excellence

A leader's ability to safely and effectively achieve the correct mission results with their team over the long term. The key to sustained leadership excellence, regardless of uncertainties and challenges, is to lead from a foundation of core values and enabling attributes that inform and shape leadership decisions, communication, and actions—the instruments of leadership.

Model for Sustained Leadership Excellence

As outlined in Figure 2, the Model for Sustained Leadership Excellence is framed around three dimensions of leadership: a foundation of core values, pillars of enabling attributes, and a gabled capstone representing the leadership process. Figure 3 illustrates the model's core components. The foundation represents three core values of leadership: character shaped by integrity, a service mindset, and the continuous pursuit of excellence. Three pillars symbolize the model's enabling attributes of leadership: trust, concern, and the will to lead. The gabled capstone illustrates the inputs, outputs, and outcomes of the leadership process.

The inputs of the process comprise a leader's decisions, communication, and actions. The outputs reflect the motivation, influence, and inspiration generated by these inputs, and the outcomes represent the results achieved by the leader and their team.

The leadership process requires unity of effort, which is achieved by steering a team's performance through an aligned set of unifying forces, including the team's mission, vision, values, goals, objectives, priorities, and strategy. Figure 4 highlights the inputs, outputs, outcomes, and unifying forces of the leadership process.

This comprehensive and integrated model underscores the essential role the core values, attributes, and unifying forces play in consistently achieving the correct mission results.

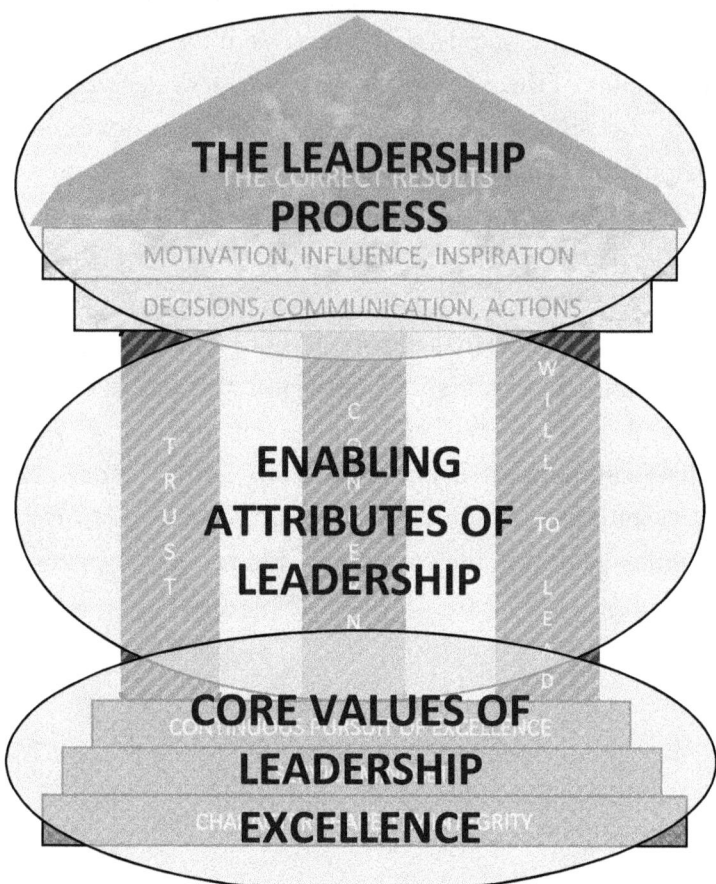

Figure 2. Three Dimensions of the Model for Sustained Leadership Excellence

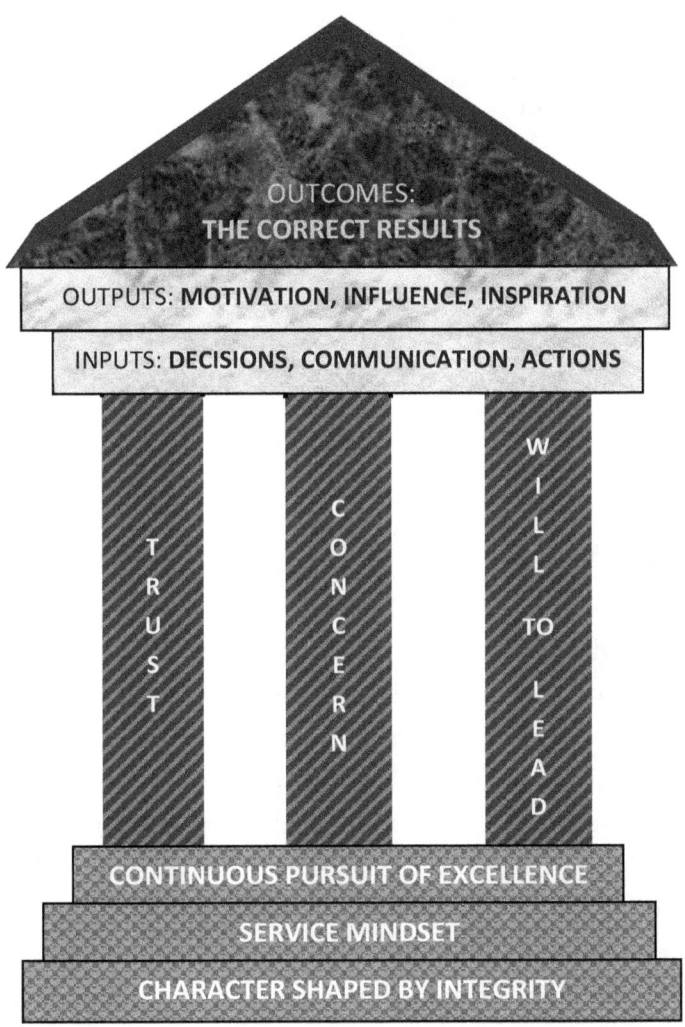

Figure 3. Model for Sustained Leadership Excellence

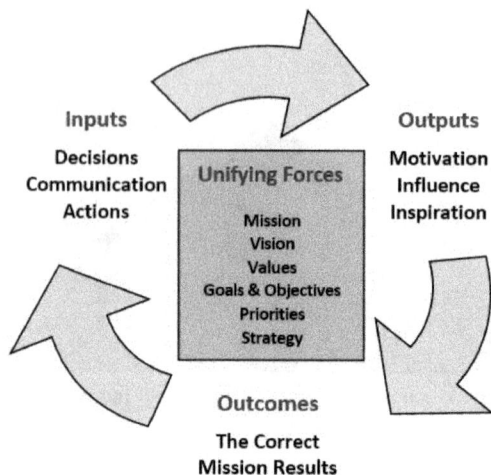

Figure 4. The Leadership Process

Looking Ahead

All leadership roles have one common aim . . . to consistently achieve the correct mission results with team members, regardless of the type of organization, mission, or team one leads. The Model for Sustained Leadership Excellence offers leaders a framework to achieve this objective. The model establishes a comprehensive and integrated view of leadership, affirming that sustained leadership excellence is rooted in core values, enabling attributes, and unifying forces that inform and shape a leader's decisions, communication, and actions to consistently achieve the correct mission results.

All leaders are learners . . . constantly observing, assessing, studying, and identifying methods to sustain their leadership effectiveness. The pages ahead support a leader's journey of learning and development.

Part I, On Leadership, is divided into four chapters. Chapter One, Evolution of Leadership Theory, traces the development of leadership as a distinct field of knowledge and scholarly discipline. Chapter Two, Leadership, explores key topics, including the differences between leaders and managers, the ongoing question of whether leaders are born or made, and the growing impact of artificial intelligence on the practice of leadership. Chapter Three, Leadership Capabilities and Styles, draws on the insights of prominent leadership practitioners and scholars to highlight effective leadership capabilities and styles. Chapter Four, Leadership Priorities, examines leadership focus areas crucial to a leader's two most important priorities: people and mission.

Part II, A Framework for Sustained Leadership Success, introduces the Model for Sustained Leadership Excellence, a framework designed to develop, empower, and sustain long-term leadership success. Rooted in the literature and leadership best practices examined in Part I, the model is intended for both current and aspiring leaders across all professions.

Part II begins with a discussion of the leadership process, followed by Chapter Five, which explores the Enabling Attributes of Leadership Excellence, and Chapter Six, which examines the Core Values of Leadership Excellence. The final chapter, Empower Your Leadership—Turn Principles Into Sustained Performance, recaps the holistic model and presents workplace scenarios illustrating the relationship between the model's components. The chapter offers a strategy to help leaders apply the model's principles in practice. It then concludes with a scenario depicting a strategic planning workshop designed to establish or revise a team's mission, vision, values, goals, objectives, priorities, and strategy—the unifying forces of the leadership process.

Part I: On Leadership

> Leadership is one of the most observed and least
> understood phenomena on earth.
> — James MacGregor Burns[47]

Leaders are required in all fields. They come from diverse backgrounds and cultures and are vital to all organizations. They hold a variety of titles across the spectrum of professions, occupations, and vocations—president, vice president, executive, chief executive, director, dean, provost, manager, general, sergeant, commander, division chief, foreman, minister, pastor, and imam, for example. Despite their titles, however, all leaders share the same primary role in their organizations: they are responsible and accountable for the performance of their team members as the team pursues its mission, guided by the organization's goals, objectives, priorities, and long-term vision.

The four chapters ahead explore a range of subjects related to leadership, beginning with the evolution of leadership theory and an examination of key themes. Part I concludes with a review of literature on leadership capabilities and styles from notable leaders and scholars, followed by a discussion of leadership priorities.

Chapter One: Evolution of Leadership Theory

The supreme purpose of history is a better world.
— Herbert Hoover
31st President of the United States of America[48]

When looking to the future, it is important to understand the past. Leadership development and the body of literature associated with leadership theory are relatively young educational disciplines, as viewed through the arc of educational history. "We have barely scratched the surface in our efforts toward leadership development," reports Gardner. "In the mid-twenty-first century, people will look back on our present practices as primitive."[49]

Leadership . . . a Human Endeavor

Some of the earliest documented records of leadership are rooted in political, military, and religious movements. Throughout history, religious leadership has played a central role in guiding communities and shaping societies. More than 5,000 years ago, spiritual figures such as Noah, Abraham, and Moses were recognized for their leadership. The *Bible* portrays Noah as organizing an escape by ark to lead his followers to safety, and Abraham as guiding the Jewish people to the land of Canaan. Moses is later depicted leading the Jewish people out of bondage in Egypt.[50]

Similarly, for over a millennium, leadership in the Islamic faith has been grounded in religious law from the Qur'an and exercised by imams, who serve not only as spiritual leaders but also as moral and community authorities within their congregations.[51]

The Hindu tradition also reflects a synthesis of religious, social, and moral leadership. Kings (*rajahs*) and sages (*rishis*) served as moral and spiritual leaders, guided by principles of *dharma* (duty) and wisdom. Ancient texts like the *Bhagavad Gita* emphasize righteous leadership rooted in selfless action, spiritual insight, and service to the greater good.[52]

Ancient hieroglyphics, artifacts, and papyrus scrolls uncovered from the Old Kingdom reveal how Egyptian government and military leaders wielded power and dominion over the known world. The pharaoh, as the absolute sovereign, served as both supreme military commander and head of government, relying on a bureaucracy of officials to manage the affairs of the state. In charge of administration was the vizier, the king's second-in-command, who acted as the king's representative and coordinated land surveys, the treasury, building projects, the legal system, and the archives. At the regional level, the Egyptian empire was divided into administrative regions governed and led by monarchs who were accountable to the vizier for their jurisdictions.[53]

For millennia, literature has chronicled the wars, campaigns, battles, and strategies of military leaders and commanders, offering insight into principles of leadership. Over 2,500 years ago, Sun Tzu, the Chinese military strategist whose contributions are revered in the canon of Chinese military literature, outlined his theories on strategy, operations, and leadership in a series of essays. Compiled into a modern tome entitled *The Art of War*, Sun Tzu identified command, or leadership, as one of five fundamental factors vital to battlefield success.[54]

During the nineteenth century, Napoleon Bonaparte outlined his ideas on military leadership in a list of 115 qualities. He articulated critical battlefield attributes—decisiveness, mental agility, communication, boldness, and the power of reward and recognition.[55] He famously quipped, "Give me enough medals and I'll win you any war."[56] His list also included perseverance, adaptability, moral courage, and a relentless focus on speed and surprise.[57] Together, these qualities formed the backbone of what he saw as the art and science of military leadership.

From the ancient world to the post-modern world, leaders have been essential to humanity's evolution, direction, and progress. Their influence has shaped societies, nations, and entire civilizations. Yet, despite the critical role leadership has played throughout history, the formal study of leadership and leadership development remains a relatively young academic discipline. While historical texts like *The Art of War* and Napoleon's leadership principles reflect efforts to codify the practice of military leadership, it wasn't until the latter half of the nineteenth century, with the rise of the Industrial Revolution, that significant academic inquiry and scientific research into leadership formally began. This period marked a shift from practical, experience-based leadership to a more systematic, scholarly exploration, setting the stage for the development of leadership as an academic field in the modern era.

Industrial Revolution

The dawn of the Industrial Revolution in the 1700s changed the nature of work and the need for leaders to direct and control the human resources employed in production, assembly, and manufacturing processes. Workers performed industrial jobs that required training, instruction, direction, and supervision. During the early stages of the Industrial Revolution, many owners and leaders of the means of production resorted to using the raw power and authority of their position in an autocratic way to drive work performance. This transactional approach to motivating performance often resulted in leaders abusing their power and authority, instigating protests from workers and their labor representatives. Over time, government agencies were compelled to intervene and protect workers from employers who neglected to address poor and unsafe working conditions or imposed excessive work hours without adequate compensation.

Acting on behalf of their political constituents, government legislators stepped in to protect non-management employees by regulating work hours, establishing minimum wage rates, and instituting minimum safety standards to ensure safe working conditions. The imposition of these regulatory measures set the stage for frequent disputes between employers and employees. Often, leaders and managers, aligned with the owners of production, were perceived as untrustworthy and unconcerned about employee safety and welfare, resulting in divisive and confrontational working relationships.

Scientific Management

As the Industrial Revolution expanded globally through the twentieth century, the impact of management practices on employee work performance eventually captured the attention of social and behavioral scientists. Researchers were interested in understanding the effects of environmental factors and working conditions on employee morale and work performance, setting the stage for developing scientific management as a formal academic discipline.

Social scientists began conducting field studies at industrial factories to examine how management decisions influenced productivity. This research evolved into empirical studies exploring the impact of different management styles on worker performance. Management science pioneers Frederick Winslow Taylor (1856–1915), Abraham Harold Maslow (1908–1970), Douglas M. McGregor (1906–1964), and Frederick Irving Herzberg (1923–2000) are credited with spearheading the first formal management studies in the United States, laying the foundation for the modern effort to better understand the dynamics of the leader–follower relationship.

The father of scientific management. Frederick W. Taylor, a mechanical engineer who sought to improve industrial efficiency, is considered the father of scientific management. Taylor, referred to as the Isaac Newton of the science of work, laid the foundation for codifying the art and science of management. In 1975, Peter Drucker, regarded as one of the most influential thinkers and widely read writers on modern organizations and leadership, described Frederick Taylor as "the first man in recorded history who deemed 'work' deserving of systematic observation and study," declaring that "Taylor's scientific management rests, above all, on the tremendous surge of affluence in the last 75 years which has lifted the working masses in the developed countries well above any level recorded before, even for the well-to-do."[58]

Taylor believed the industrial management practices of his day were amateurish. He believed management could be formulated as a functional discipline and that the best results would come from a partnership between trained and qualified managers and cooperative and motivated workers. Each side needed the other, theorized Taylor, so there would be no need for organized labor unions. Taylor espoused a management approach whereby managers made themselves functional experts, divided work processes into simple repetitive tasks, and treated workers as interchangeable parts.[59]

Taylor professed that by analyzing work, the best way to do it could be found. He is most remembered for developing the time and motion study, an analytical approach that reduced each job down to its basic component parts and measured each task to a hundredth of a minute. Taylor's scientific management consisted of four principles:

1. Replace rule-of-thumb work methods with methods based on a scientific study of a job's basic tasks.
2. Scientifically select, train, and develop each employee rather than passively leaving them to train themselves.
3. Provide detailed instruction and supervise workers in the performance of discrete tasks.
4. Divide work nearly equally between managers and workers so that managers can apply scientific management principles to planning the work and the workers who perform the tasks.[60]

Taylor had very precise ideas about how to introduce his system. According to Taylor, employees were supposed to be incapable of understanding what they were doing, and he maintained that this was true even for simple tasks. Thus, the introduction of his methodology was often resented by workers and provoked numerous protests, walkouts, and strikes.

The strike at Watertown Arsenal on the northern shore of the Charles River in Watertown, Massachusetts, led to a congressional investigation in 1912, one of the first of its kind. The arsenal, a U.S. Army weapons manufacturing facility, was implementing scientific management principles developed by Taylor. Taylor's system aimed to improve efficiency by using time-and-motion studies to standardize tasks, set performance benchmarks, and incentivize workers based on productivity.

Workers at the arsenal strongly resisted Taylor's methods, particularly the piece-rate wage system and rigorous time studies conducted by supervisors using stopwatches. They felt that the new system placed excessive pressure on them, eliminated autonomy in skilled work, and prioritized efficiency over worker well-being. The strike and worker complaints attracted the attention of the House Committee on Labor, leading to a formal investigation into scientific management practices at the arsenal. The investigation led to a ban on stopwatches in federal workplaces, slowed the adoption of Taylorism in government-run facilities, and fueled the broader scientific management debate, influencing labor policies and union activism.[61]

In political and sociological terms, "Taylorism," as it was coined, was criticized as the division of labor pushed to its logical extreme, with a consequent deskilling of the worker and dehumanization of the workplace.[62] Despite these concerns, Taylor's seminal work would go on to shape generations of academic research and business practices in the field of management. After Taylor's death, however, it would be decades before further scientific research resumed to examine the practice of management. Unfortunately, "not much had been added to his work—even though he had been dead for over sixty years," claimed Drucker.[63]

Maslow's Theory of Human Motivation

In 1943, Abraham Harold Maslow introduced one of the first scientific studies of human behavior in the workplace in his paper, "A Theory of Human Motivation." The study concluded that a hierarchy of needs motivates people to accomplish tasks.[64]

Maslow's hierarchy of needs is visually depicted as a pyramid consisting of five levels. The three lower levels are grouped together and are associated with *physiological* needs, while the top two levels are associated with *psychological* needs. Figure 1.1 depicts Maslow's Hierarchy of Needs.

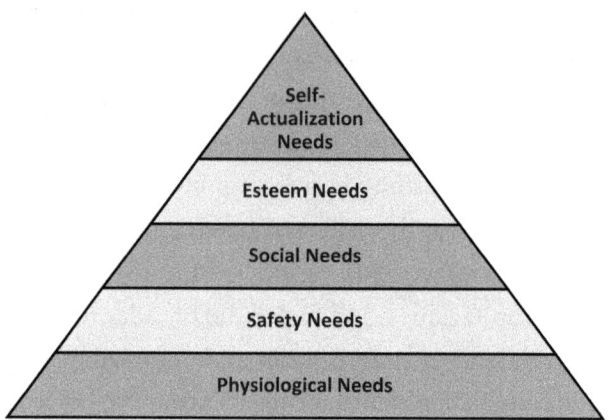

Figure 1.1. Maslow's Hierarchy of Needs

Maslow's study concluded that deficient needs at lower levels of the pyramid must first be met before seeking to satisfy higher-level psychological or personal growth needs. Once an individual moved up to the next level, claimed Maslow, lower-level needs were no longer priorities. However, if a lower set of needs were no longer being met, workers would temporarily reprioritize their needs by focusing on the unfulfilled lower-level needs.[65]

Maslow referred to the bottom three layers of the pyramid as *deficiency needs*, which include physiological, safety, and social needs. According to Maslow, workers feel anxious if these needs are not met. He identified the top two levels of the pyramid as *growth needs*, focused on self-esteem and the desire to reach one's full potential, which he termed self-actualization. The following sections summarize each element of Maslow's hierarchy of needs.

Deficiency needs. Deficiency needs are considered requirements for the basic human condition. They include:

> *Physiological needs.* These are the basic human needs for food, warmth, shelter, sex, water, and other physiological needs.

> *Safety needs.* With one's physical needs satisfied, an individual's safety needs become a priority and govern one's behavior. In addition to one's safety, these needs concern a person's yearning for a predictable, orderly world in which injustice and inconsistency are under control, the familiar frequent, and the unfamiliar rare. In the world of work, safety needs manifest themselves in such things as a preference for job security and access to grievance procedures to protect oneself from unchecked authority.

> *Social needs.* After physiological and safety needs are fulfilled, the third layer of human needs, social needs, becomes a priority. Social need is also called belongingness. These needs involve emotion-based relationships. Humans need to feel a sense of love, belonging, and acceptance. Social needs can be met by involvement in large social groups such as clubs, spiritual groups, professional organizations, and sports teams, or small social connections, including family members, intimate partners, mentors, close colleagues, and confidants. If human social needs are not fulfilled, then one becomes susceptible to loneliness, social anxiety, and depression.[66]

Growth needs. While deficiency needs address basic human needs, such as food, safety, and sleep, Maslow identified growth needs as a person's need to fulfill their human potential. Growth needs, according to Maslow, are motivated by a person's need for esteem and self-actualization, including:

- *Esteem needs.* All humans have a need for self-esteem ... to respect themselves, to be respected, and to respect others. After social needs are met, people need to connect with others to gain recognition and engage in activities that give them a sense of contribution and to feel accepted and valued in a profession or hobby. To one degree or another, an individual's ego values status, self-respect, recognition, prestige, and feelings of self-confidence. An imbalance at this level can result in low self-esteem and a sense of inferiority, according to Maslow.

- *Self-actualization needs.* In Maslow's behavioral model, the final stage of psychological development, self-actualization, comes after a person feels assured that their physiological, safety, social, and self-esteem needs have been satisfied. As these needs are met, a person becomes filled with a desire to realize their potential for being effective, creative, mature, and successful. A concept Maslow attributed to Kurt Goldstein, one of his mentors, is the instinctual human need to strive to be the best one can be. To do so, individuals seek growth, achievement, and advancement. 'What a man can be, he must be,' declared Maslow.[67]

Maslow's work was criticized because it did not consider the numerous human factors that impact an individual's priorities and values. Detractors claimed that Maslow's model oversimplified complex human behavior, suggesting that the universal application of a sequential hierarchical model to predict human behavior was unreliable.

Despite criticism of his theory, Maslow's ground-breaking work made a significant contribution to the formative body of literature on management and leadership. His work is credited with influencing modern leadership theory, as well as scholars such as Douglas McGregor, Rensis Likert, and Peter Drucker.[68]

McGregor's Theory X and Theory Y

In 1960, Douglas M. McGregor, an American social psychologist and professor at the Massachusetts Institute of Technology School of Management, introduced the Theory X and Theory Y management model in *The Human Side of Enterprise*.[69] McGregor's model outlines two fundamental approaches to leadership: Theory X, which aligns with an authoritarian approach, and Theory Y, which emphasizes a participative style.[70]

Theory X leaders. According to McGregor, Theory X leaders believe their team members dislike work and try to avoid it when possible. These leaders also think that most people prefer to be directed and must be forced to work with the threat of punishment for not achieving expected results. Most workers, according to the theory, avoid responsibility and are unambitious. Their primary motivation is job security. Typically, the following characteristics are associated with Theory X leaders:

> ➢ Results-driven and deadline-driven, to the exclusion of everything else.
> ➢ Intolerant.

- Issue ultimatums.
- Distant and detached.
- Short-tempered and impatient.
- Issue threats to make people follow instructions.
- Demand, do not ask.
- Do not team-build.
- Unconcerned about team members' welfare or morale.
- One-way communicators.
- Poor listeners.
- Do not thank or praise.
- Seek to apportion blame instead of focusing on learning from experiences and preventing recurrence.
- Think giving orders is delegating.
- Unconcerned about investing in future improvements.[71]

Theory Y leaders. Theory Y leaders treat people with respect and foster motivation without resorting to threats or punishment. Theory Y leaders prefer to use rewards as a motivator and believe team members usually accept and seek responsibility and professional development opportunities. Theory Y leaders allow team members to use their creativity to solve problems. According to McGregor, the following characteristics are associated with Theory Y leaders:

- Concerned about team members' welfare, morale, and the mission.
- Tolerant and allow team members to learn from their mistakes.
- Active listeners.
- Engaged and involved.

- Assume people are self-motivated and seek responsibility.
- Involve team members in decision-making.
- Establish clear expectations, define outcomes, and allow team members to achieve those outcomes.
- Give rewards, recognition, and constructive feedback.
- Give employees opportunities for professional development.
- Team builders.
- Delegate authority along with responsibility.
- Invest time and money in process improvements.[72]

Despite more recent studies questioning the rigidity of McGregor's model, the terms Theory X and Theory Y remain widely used in management and leadership literature, continuing to serve as key reference points in the historical development of leadership theory.

Herzberg's Motivator-Hygiene Theory

Noted psychologist Frederick Irving Herzberg joined Taylor, Maslow, and McGregor in their pursuit to better understand human motivation theory. Herzberg rapidly became one of the most influential names in business management and is most famous for introducing job enrichment and motivator-hygiene theory. His 1968 publication, *One More Time, How Do You Motivate Employees?* sold 1.2 million copies by 1987 and was the most requested article from the Harvard Business Review.[73]

Herzberg attended City College of New York but left to enlist in the United States Army before completing his studies. As a patrol sergeant, Herzberg witnessed firsthand the German Dachau concentration camp. He believed this experience, as well as the talks he had with other Germans living in the area, was what triggered his interest in motivation theory.

After serving in the Army, Herzberg graduated from City College in 1946 and began graduate studies in science and public health at the University of Pittsburgh. Herzberg introduced his Motivation-Hygiene Theory in 1959, also known as the *two-factor theory* of job satisfaction. According to the theory, two factors, hygiene and motivators, influence people.

Hygiene factors. Herzberg identified hygiene as the first set of factors associated with performance and job satisfaction. He describes hygiene factors as working conditions, pay and benefits, company policies and administration, relationships with co-workers, physical environment, supervision, personal life, status, and job security. According to Herzberg, hygiene factors do not motivate, but failure to meet these needs causes job dissatisfaction and poor performance.[74]

Motivator factors. The second of Herzberg's two factors is a set of motivators that drive people to achieve. Motivator factors are described as achievement, status, recognition, work itself, responsibility, promotion, and growth. These factors contribute to high levels of motivation and job satisfaction. Motivators are built around obtaining growth and self-actualization from task and mission accomplishment. The greater the responsibility and success with that responsibility, the more a person feels the satisfaction of a job well done.[75] Figure 1.2 illustrates Herzberg's hygiene and motivator factors and their impact on job satisfaction.

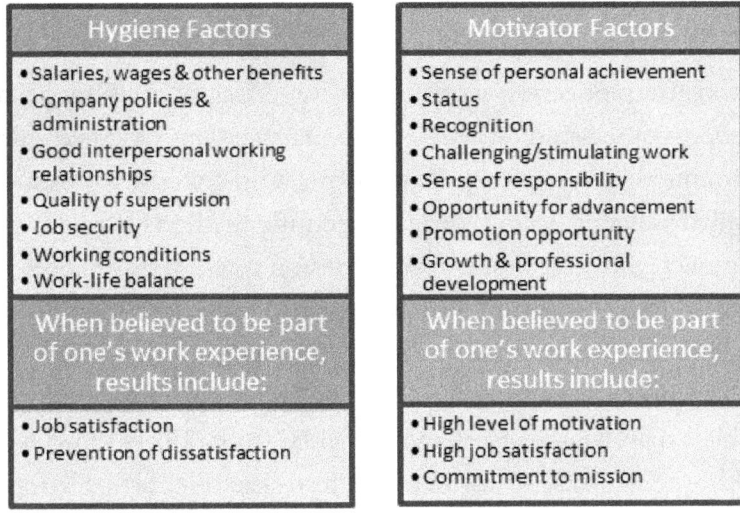

Figure 1.2. Herzberg's Motivation-Hygiene Factors

Herzberg's Motivator-Hygiene Theory has faced criticism for its methodological limitations, particularly its reliance on the critical incident technique, which may introduce response bias. It assumes a universal application of motivators and hygiene factors, overlooking individual differences and variations across job types and cultures. Critics argued that it failed to account for the interaction between motivators and hygiene factors, as well as the impact of job context on satisfaction. Additionally, while Herzberg's framework advocated for job enrichment, implementing its principles in highly structured roles can be challenging, limiting its practical applicability in certain job roles.

Despite these criticisms, Herzberg's theory remains a foundational concept in motivational psychology, management, and leadership theory, influencing job design and employee engagement strategies.

The Hawthorne Effect

Beyond the pioneering work of Taylor, Maslow, McGregor, and Herzberg, other studies in scientific management emerged during the twentieth century. The Hawthorne Works study, for example, provided valuable insight into the scientific methods used to assess the impact of management approaches on work performance.

The Hawthorne study set out to analyze how working conditions affected worker productivity.[76] The Hawthorne Effect, as it became known, was coined in 1950 by Henry A. Landsberger during his analysis of earlier experiments from 1924–1932 at the Hawthorne Works, a former Western Electric factory outside Chicago, Illinois.

The Hawthorne Works commissioned a study to see if their workers would become more productive in higher or lower levels of light. During the study, employee productivity seemed to correlate with changes in lighting; that is, improved lighting led to improved productivity and decreased lighting led to decreased productivity. Unexpectedly, however, productivity decreased after the study ended—even though lighting levels remained optimal. This suggested that the productivity gains stemmed more from the motivational impact of the attention shown to workers during the study rather than from changes in lighting conditions.[77]

In the years that followed the study, researchers attempted to explain the effects with various interpretations. In several instances, social scientists claimed that it was not the special attention given to workers during the study per se that influenced their performance, but their interpretation of the study's purpose. Despite a wide range of alternative explanations, the Hawthorne Effect has been well established through follow-on studies that set out to validate the findings in the original research.

Collectively, interpretations and critiques of the study underscore the importance of recognizing how the design and administration of field research can shape outcomes and conclusions. The study also serves as a reminder that uncontrolled variables must be carefully considered when conducting research involving human participants.

The Hawthorne Works study had significant implications for leadership theory, shifting the focus from purely scientific management principles to the human and social aspects of work. It highlighted the importance of employee attention, recognition, and social dynamics in driving productivity, laying the foundation for human relations theory in leadership. The Hawthorne Effect demonstrates that workers are motivated not just by physical conditions but also by the psychological impact of being observed and valued. This led to a greater emphasis on employee engagement, participative leadership, and workplace culture in leadership practices. Additionally, the study reinforced the idea that leadership effectiveness depends on fostering strong interpersonal relationships, recognizing employees' intrinsic motivations, and creating a work environment that prioritizes trust, collaboration, and morale.

Evolving Management and Leadership Practices

Throughout the twentieth century, Taylor, Maslow, McGregor, and Herzberg made significant contributions to the scientific study of human motivation and performance in the workplace. Their legacy can be traced to investigating leadership and employee productivity as a scientific problem. Their groundbreaking research in management explored the impact of physical, physiological, psychological, environmental, and behavioral factors on employee performance and productivity. This formative work laid the foundation for modern, codified leadership theory and paved the way for further research into motivation theories centered on the leader-follower relationship.

With the rise of management as a science and the advancement of statistical measurement tools, interest in the analytical and empirical study of leadership expanded. Throughout the twentieth century, leaders in large industries and government organizations turned to data-driven, computer-based systems to address complex challenges and inform operating processes, management strategies, and leadership decisions. Notable approaches included operations research, systems management, and quality management.

Influence of statistical science on leadership practices. Dr. Walter Andrew Shewhart (1891-1967), a renowned physicist, engineer, and statistician, is known as the father of statistical quality control. Born in New Canton, Illinois, he attended the University of Illinois at Urbana–Champaign before being awarded his doctorate in physics from the University of California, Berkeley, in 1917. Shewhart's interests included industrial quality control and the application of statistical inference to manufacturing processes.

When Shewhart joined the Western Electric Company Inspection Engineering Department in 1918, industrial quality control was limited to inspecting finished products and removing defective items. That all changed on May 16, 1924, when Shewhart developed the schematic control chart. The chart set forth the key principles and considerations known today as process quality control.[78]

In 1938, Shewhart's work came to the attention of physicist Dr. W. Edwards Deming. Deming was deeply intrigued by the issue of measurement error in science. Absorbed by Shewhart's insights, Deming and his colleague, Raymond T. Birge, published a groundbreaking paper in *Reviews of Modern Physics* in 1934. They wrote to the journal to recast their approach in the terms that Shewhart advocated. Their work began a long collaboration centered on championing Shewhart's ideas. Deming developed some of

Shewhart's methodological proposals around scientific inference and named his synthesis the Shewhart cycle.[79] Shewhart's original notions of statistical control were the driving force behind Deming's subsequent development of Total Quality Management (TQM), leading to Shewhart's reputation as the grandfather of TQM.

Deming went on to pioneer and energize the quality management movement. His work highlights the need for organizations to pursue continuous product and service improvements by focusing on quality, leadership, and management principles.

Quality Management

W. Edwards Deming (1900-1993), an American statistician, was invited to Japan in 1947 by the U.S. government to assist with Japan's post-World War II census and economic recovery efforts. Recognized as a leading expert in quality management systems, Deming introduced statistical process control to leaders of prominent Japanese businesses. His work is credited with popularizing the process management approach best known as Total Quality Management.

Deming's philosophy begins with the responsibilities of top organizational leaders and maintains that a company must adopt quality control at all levels to achieve a high level of performance through continuous process improvement. Deming taught that 96% of variations in any process have common causes, and 4% have special causes. He developed what is known as the Deming chain reaction; that is, as quality improves, costs decrease, and productivity increases, resulting in more jobs, greater market share, and sustained growth for an organization. Deming's overall approach focused on the continuous improvement of work processes and the role of leaders, focusing on the system rather than the worker as the cause of process variation.[80]

In July 1950, at the request of the Japanese Union of Scientists and Engineers, Deming returned to Japan to provide business leaders with a lesson on quality control. He lectured daily, delivering an eight-day course on quality control.[81] After applying Deming's techniques, Japanese businesses like Toyota, Fuji, and Sony saw great success. Their quality was far superior to that of their global competitors and their costs were lower. The demand for Japanese products soared, and by the 1970s, many of Japan's manufacturing companies dominated the global market.

American and European companies realized they could no longer ignore the quality revolution, driving Western business leaders to embrace Deming's quality control system. The system's focus on the quality of products and services through incremental process improvements also required leaders to educate and train workers to understand quality management practices and principles.

Deming received little recognition for his work until 1982 when he published *Out of the Crisis*. In the book, he summarized his influential Fourteen-Point Management Philosophy. He maintained that his fourteen points of management apply to any type and size of business because service companies need to control quality just as much as manufacturing companies. His approach applies equally to large multinational corporations, small group operations, and different product and service divisions within an organization.[82]

Deming's philosophy focused on quality control of systems, processes, products, and services. It also recognized the central role and responsibility of leaders in motivating, influencing, and inspiring team members to pursue continuous improvement and decrease costs. His insights into the leader's role in an organization's sustained mission success are embedded throughout his fourteen points. The following summary outlines Deming's Fourteen-Point Management Philosophy.[83] According to Deming, leaders must:

1. Create and communicate a constant purpose toward improvement.
   - Plan for quality over the long term.
   - Resist reacting with short-term solutions.
   - Do not just do the same things better—find better things to do.
   - Predict and prepare for future challenges and always have the goal of getting better.
2. Adopt the new quality philosophy.
   - Embrace quality throughout the entire organization.
   - Put your customers' needs first, rather than react to competitive pressure, and design products and services to meet those needs.
   - Be prepared for a major change in the way business is done. It is about leading, not simply managing.
   - Create your quality vision, share it, and implement it.
3. Stop depending on inspections as the primary source of process improvement.
   - Inspections are costly and unreliable, and they do not improve quality; they merely find a lack of quality.
   - Build quality into the process from start to finish.
   - Do not just find what you did wrong – eliminate the "wrongs" altogether.
   - Use statistical control methods—not physical inspections alone—to prove a process is working.

4. Use a single supplier for any one item.
    - Quality relies on consistency; the less variation you have in the input, the less variation you will have in the output.
    - Look at suppliers as your partners in quality. Encourage them to spend time improving their own quality; they should not compete for your business based on price alone.
    - Analyze the total cost to you, not just the initial cost of the product.
    - Use quality statistics to ensure suppliers meet your quality standards.
5. Improve constantly and forever.
    - Continuously improve your systems and processes. Deming promoted the "Plan-Do-Check-Act" approach to process analysis and improvement. The four phases in the Plan-Do-Check-Act cycle involve:
        i. Plan: Identify and analyze the problem.
        ii. Do: Develop and test a potential solution.
        iii. Check: Measure the effectiveness of the test solution and analyze whether it could be improved.
        iv. Act: Implement the improved solution fully.
    - Emphasize training and education so everyone can do their jobs better.
    - Use "kaizen" as a model to reduce waste and improve productivity, effectiveness, and safety. The word kaizen translates to mean

change (kai) for the good (zen); an approach to continuous improvement based on the belief that everything can be improved.
6. Use training on the job.
    - Train for consistency to help reduce variation.
    - Build a foundation of common knowledge.
    - Allow workers to understand their roles in the "big picture."
    - Encourage staff to learn from one another and provide a culture and environment for effective teamwork.
7. Implement leadership.
    - Expect your supervisors and managers to understand their workers and the processes they use.
    - Do not simply supervise—provide support and resources so that each team member can do their best. Be a coach instead of a police officer.
    - Figure out what employees need to do their best.
    - Emphasize the importance of participative management and transformational leadership.
    - Find ways to reach your full potential, and do not just focus on meeting targets and quotas.
8. Eliminate fear.
    - Allow people to perform at their best by ensuring they are not afraid to express ideas or concerns.

- Let everyone know that the goal is to achieve high quality by doing more things right—and that you are not interested in blaming people when mistakes happen.
- Make workers feel valued and encourage them to look for better ways to do their jobs.
- Ensure your leaders are approachable and that they work with teams to act in the company's best interest.
- Use open and honest communication to remove fear from the organization.

9. Break down barriers between departments.
   - Build the "internal customer" concept, which recognizes that each department or function serves other departments that use their output.
   - Build a shared vision.
   - Use cross-functional teamwork to build understanding and reduce adversarial relationships.
   - Focus on collaboration and consensus instead of compromise.

10. Get rid of unclear slogans.
    - Let people know exactly what you want—do not make them guess. "Excellence in service" is short and memorable, but what does it mean? How is it achieved? The message is clearer in a statement like "You can do better if you try."
    - Do not let words and nice-sounding phrases replace effective leadership. Outline your

expectations and then praise people face-to-face for doing good work.

11. Eliminate management by objectives.
    - Look at how the process is carried out, not just aiming for numerical targets, because production targets encourage high output and low quality.
    - Provide support and resources so production levels and quality are high and achievable.
    - Measure the process rather than the people behind the process.
12. Remove barriers to pride in work.
    - Allow everyone to take pride in their work without being rated or compared.
    - Treat workers the same and do not make them compete with other workers for monetary or other rewards. Over time, the quality system will naturally raise the level of everyone's work to an equally high level.
13. Implement education and self-improvement.
    - Improve the current skills of workers.
    - Encourage people to learn new skills to prepare for future changes and challenges.
    - Build skills to make your workforce more adaptable to change and better able to find and achieve improvements.
14. Make "transformation" everyone's job.
    - Improve your overall organization by having each person take a step toward quality.
    - Analyze each small step and understand how it fits into the larger picture.

Taken as a whole, Deming's Fourteen-Point Management Philosophy defined a new paradigm for leaders. Leaders were instructed to add clarity, awareness, and focus to reduce variation, lower costs, and improve product and service quality. Notably, his approach called out the need to *implement leadership*. According to Deming, leaders are expected to understand their team members and the processes they use, provide support and resources, coach, remain engaged, be approachable and involved, and eliminate fear to allow team members to perform at their best and express ideas and concerns.

Deming's philosophy has been widely praised, but it has also been criticized for lacking specificity in its implementation. While he provided broad principles for quality management and leadership, critics argue that he did not offer concrete, step-by-step guidance on how organizations should apply these principles across different industries and operational contexts.

Another criticism is that his philosophy is better suited to production environments and may not fully translate to service-oriented businesses or rapidly evolving industries, despite his claim of universal applicability. Some service-based organizations find it difficult to measure and control quality in the same structured way as manufacturing organizations.

Additionally, some critics argue that Deming underemphasized financial and short-term performance metrics, which are crucial for organizations in competitive markets. Furthermore, resistance to cultural change poses a significant challenge to implementing his philosophy, which requires a fundamental transformation of organizational culture, leadership mindset, and employee engagement. Many organizations struggle with this shift, particularly in environments where hierarchical leadership styles and cost-cutting measures are deeply ingrained.[84,85,86]

Despite these criticisms, Deming's philosophy has had a lasting impact on leadership theory. It encourages leaders to adopt systematic, data-driven, and people-focused approaches to sustaining organizational excellence.

Artificial Intelligence

Artificial intelligence (AI), machine learning, automation, and robotics are reshaping the practice of leadership, with their influence expected to grow significantly in the coming years. These innovations will reduce administrative demands, allowing leaders to focus more on activities that require emotional intelligence, personal engagement, and customer support. The impact on leaders and their teams will vary depending on their role within an organization, ranging from entry-level to executive leadership. The following sections explore how AI can enhance leadership effectiveness when these systems are applied in a responsible and ethical manner to augment decisions, communication, and actions.

Enhanced decision-making. AI systems can analyze vast amounts of data quickly and provide leaders with actionable insights. This enables better-informed decisions by highlighting trends, risks, and opportunities that might not be immediately visible to human leaders. For example:

- ➢ Predictive analytics can help leaders anticipate challenges and opportunities in markets, workforce trends, or customer behaviors.
- ➢ AI-powered dashboards provide real-time metrics for monitoring performance and adapting strategies.

Streamlined operations. Automation of repetitive, time-consuming administrative tasks allows leaders to focus on high-value strategic and operational initiatives. Leaders can leverage AI to enhance:

> ➢ Workflow optimization.
> ➢ Resource allocation.
> ➢ Customer service.
> ➢ Budgets.

Data-driven leadership. AI systems can enhance leadership effectiveness by analyzing employee engagement, performance, and well-being. AI tools that track workforce analytics can help leaders:

> ➢ Personalize team members' professional development based on individual strengths and goals.
> ➢ Predict team dynamics and optimize collaboration.
> ➢ Identify burnout risks and promote well-being.
> ➢ Assess performance.

Enhanced communication and collaboration. AI-powered tools, such as natural language processing and real-time translation models, can significantly improve communication by helping leaders deliver clear, context-sensitive messages across languages and cultures. These tools foster stronger collaboration among geographically dispersed and culturally diverse team members, making them especially valuable for leaders managing international teams. AI communication tools help leaders:

> ➢ Translate messages across languages and cultures.

➤ Facilitate collaboration in virtual and hybrid environments with enhanced workflows and project management.

Increased focus on human-centric leadership. As AI systems take on more analytical and operational tasks, leaders must increasingly rely on emotional intelligence, creativity, and relationship-building to drive innovation, foster collaboration, and inspire their teams. AI can help leaders:

➤ Guide their teams through change.
➤ Build trust and rapport with their teams by providing insights that enable personalized support and a better understanding of individual and team needs.
➤ Empower teams to adapt and innovate by providing AI-driven insights that enable leaders and their teams to anticipate, stay ahead of, and respond effectively to change.

Ethical leadership and accountability. AI introduces complex ethical challenges, such as data privacy, algorithmic bias, and decision-making transparency. Leaders must model responsible AI use by setting clear expectations, establishing accountability measures, and ensuring alignment with organizational values. These values should guide the creation of ethical frameworks that address key areas, including fairness, inclusivity, data governance, and the transparent use of AI in decision-making. Leaders must consider:

➤ Promoting ethical AI practices and policies that protect the rights and interests of team members, customers, and stakeholders.

- Ensuring fairness and minimizing bias in AI systems through transparent design, testing, and oversight.
- Balancing the pursuit of efficiency and speed with thoughtful implementation, aligning AI solutions with organizational values and long-term goals.

Leadership development and learning. AI is revolutionizing how leaders and their teams develop their skills by personalizing learning experiences. AI-enabled learning and development systems can:

- Provide customized leadership development and learning programs.
- Offer adaptive learning paths and on-the-job learning opportunities.
- Generate simulations that allow leaders and their teams to practice decision-making in complex scenarios.

Long-term strategic thinking. AI is prompting leaders to think more strategically about their organization's future. As AI reshapes organizations, leaders must:

- Continuously monitor emerging trends and future opportunities.
- Foster a culture of lifelong learning and adaptability within their teams.
- Drive innovation and transformation to ensure relevance and competitiveness.

While AI can significantly enhance many aspects of leadership, it must not substitute the uniquely human qualities of empathy, sound judgment, and ethical decision-making. As Henry A. Kissinger, Craig Mundie, and Eric Schmidt emphasize in *Genesis: Artificial Intelligence, Hope, and the Human Spirit*, society must carefully define the boundaries of AI's authority over these human-centric qualities.[87] The goal for leaders is to integrate AI into their decisions, communication, and actions—while upholding essential human values—to motivate, influence, and inspire their teams effectively and ethically toward long-term mission success.

As the study and practice of leadership evolve and technology continues to enhance team productivity and efficiency, one constant remains: long-term team success depends on effective leadership. The Model for Sustained Leadership Excellence, introduced in Part II, was developed to meet this enduring need by empowering current and aspiring leaders with the values, attributes, and best practices essential for sustaining leadership success.

The next chapters explore key leadership themes, examine leadership capabilities and styles through the lens of notable leaders and scholars, and introduce a set of focus areas aligned with a leader's top priorities: people and mission.

Chapter Two: Leadership

> There is nothing exalted about being an effective executive. It is simply doing one's job like thousands of others.
> — Peter F. Drucker[88]

Modern leadership theory traces its origins to Frederick Taylor's early study of management as a science. Over time, research and literature shifted from examining environmental influences on human behavior to the impact of leadership behavior on team performance. Despite major advances in management science throughout the twentieth century, leadership remained underexplored as both a distinct field of study and an academic discipline.

In 1978, Pulitzer Prize-winning author James MacGregor Burns published his highly acclaimed book, *Leadership*. Through his research, Burns concluded that despite the immense reservoir of data and analysis regarding management that had been developed up to that point, there was no formal field of academic study for leadership. This was attributed, he contended, to scholars working in separate disciplines and sub-disciplines in pursuit of different and often unrelated questions and problems regarding leadership. "No central concept of leadership has yet emerged," declared Burns.[89]

While management emerged as a formal academic discipline in the early twentieth century, leadership was often treated as a subtopic within management, psychology, or military science rather than as a distinct academic field. Over time, however, interest in leadership as a unique and essential area of study has steadily increased. In recent years, the volume of leadership literature—books, journals, reports, articles, and studies—has grown significantly, offering valuable insights, theories, and lessons. Much of this literature presents research and analysis on the skills, competencies, capabilities, characteristics, behaviors, and traits that define successful leaders. The findings contribute to the evolving understanding of leadership as both an art and a science.

This chapter explores key leadership themes from the growing body of literature, including the leader's role, the distinction between managers and leaders, and the ongoing debate over whether leaders are born or made.

The Leader Role

Leaders come from diverse backgrounds, they serve in all fields, and they hold a wide variety of titles. Their personalities and leadership styles are equally diverse. Despite these differences, however, their role and function in an organization are the same. Whether a leader works in the manufacturing industry or law enforcement, health care or government, university or military, a leader is responsible, first of all, for influencing others to get things done—"the right things," asserts Peter Drucker.[90] Effective leaders, therefore, make decisions, communicate, and act in ways to motivate, influence, and inspire team members to accomplish the correct job(s), task(s), and mission(s) in pursuit of an organization's goals, objectives, priorities, and long-term vision. Drucker expresses his view on effective leadership:

> The foundation of effective leadership is thinking through the organization's mission, defining it and establishing it, clearly and visibly. The leader sets the goals, sets the priorities, and sets and maintains the standards. He makes compromises, of course; indeed, effective leaders are painfully aware that they are not in control of the universe. But before accepting a compromise, the effective leader has thought through what is right and desirable. The leader's first task is to be the trumpet that sounds a clear sound.
>
> The second requirement is that the leader sees leadership as responsibility rather than as rank and privilege. When things go wrong—and they always do—they do not blame others. Winston Churchill is an example of leadership through clearly defining a mission and goals. General George Marshall, America's chief of staff in World War II, is an example of leadership through responsibility. Harry Truman's folksy 'the buck stops here' is still as good a definition as any.
>
> But precisely because an effective leader knows that he, and no one else, is ultimately responsible, he is not afraid of strength in associates and subordinates. An effective leader wants strong associates; he encourages them, pushes them, and indeed champions them. Because he holds himself ultimately responsible for the mis-

takes of his associates and subordinates, he also sees the triumphs of his associates and subordinates as his triumphs rather than as threats.

A leader may be personally vain—as General MacArthur was to an almost pathological degree. Or he may be personally humble—both Lincoln and Truman were almost to the point of having inferiority complexes. But all three wanted able, independent, self-assured people around them; they encouraged their associates and subordinates, praising and promoting them.

An effective leader knows, of course, that there is a risk: able people tend to be ambitious. But he realizes that it is a much smaller risk than to be served by mediocrity. He also knows that the gravest indictment of a leader is for the organization to collapse as soon as he leaves or dies, as happened in Russia the moment Stalin died and as happens all too often in companies. An effective leader knows that the ultimate task of leadership is to create human energies and human vision.[91]

Drucker emphasizes that effective leadership begins with clearly defining the organization's mission, setting priorities, and maintaining standards. Leadership is ultimately a responsibility, requiring leaders to accept accountability for both successes and failures.

The essence of effective leadership lies in the ability to build relationships that foster support and commitment, and to communicate what is needed in a way that helps others understand why specific actions are essential to advancing the team's mission. Consistently effective leaders offer sound reasoning and a compelling rationale for their decisions. They inspire team members through encouragement and persistence, articulate both risks and opportunities, and motivate others to achieve mission objectives.

In *Leadership*, Burns defined the leadership role as "leaders inducing followers to act for certain goals that represent the values and the motivations—the wants and needs, the aspirations and expectations—of both leaders and followers. And the genius of leadership lies in the manner in which leaders see and act on their own and their followers' values and motivations."[92]

As defined in the United States Air Force doctrine on leadership and force development, leadership is the art and science of influencing and directing people to accomplish an assigned mission. The aim is to transform human potential into effective performance in the present and prepare the most capable leaders for the future.[93]

Leadership Levels

Regardless of level, leaders perform crucial day-to-day leadership responsibilities with their team members, clients, customers, internal and external business partners, and a myriad of other stakeholders. According to Gardner, "Leaders at every level must take action to make their piece of the system work."[94] Senior executives are often the focus of discussions about leadership; however, it is important to note that first-level and middle-level leaders have a more direct and influential impact on most team members within an organization. On average, first-level leaders make up 50% to 60% of the leadership ranks and directly supervise at least 80% of the workforce.[95] These leaders are central to the daily execution of an organization's strategy, highlighting the need for effective leaders at all levels, not just the top.

Research indicates that the leadership capabilities required for effectiveness vary by organizational level. One study identified three core skill categories associated with these levels: technical, interpersonal, and decision-making. The findings suggest that top-level leaders rely more on interpersonal and decision-making skills than on technical expertise. Middle-level leaders require a balanced mix of all three, while first-level leaders depend more on technical and interpersonal skills.[96]

Leadership levels introduce the concept of leading other leaders—a responsibility that requires balancing guidance and direction with empowerment. Success in this endeavor depends on a leader's ability to foster trust, alignment, and collaboration. The Unifying Forces of the Leadership Process, discussed in Part II, support this by uniting the team around a shared set of goals, priorities, values, and vision that strengthen the leadership team's collective efforts.

Managers and Leaders

What does it mean to be a manager, and what does it mean to be a leader? Are managers leaders? Are leaders managers? Can one be a manager and a leader at the same time? Are leadership skills a subcomponent of management, or are management skills a subcomponent of leadership?

In the fields of management and leadership, scholars and practitioners continue to examine the similarities and differences between managers and leaders, often equating the two and using the terms interchangeably. While debates over their definitions persist, a growing body of literature distinguishes the two roles, treating management and leadership as separate and distinct roles.

What differentiates managers from leaders? Warren Bennis and Burt Nanus argue that managers and leaders serve fundamentally different organizational purposes. Managers concentrate on doing things right—ensuring efficiency and order—while leaders focus on doing the right things—setting direction and inspiring progress.[97]

"Leaders have a unique perspective and set of responsibilities, and they require a different set of aptitudes and skills" than managers.[98] As Bennis puts it, "Managers administer; leaders innovate. Managers maintain; leaders develop. Managers focus on systems and structure; leaders focus on people. Managers rely on control; leaders inspire trust. Managers have a short-range view; leaders have a long-range perspective. Managers ask how and when; leaders ask what and why."[99]

Yes, "there is a distinction between a manager and a leader," declares Ross Bernstein in his book about coach Herbert Paul "Herb" Brooks, Jr.[100] Coach Brooks is best known for leading the United States hockey team to a gold medal during the 1980 Winter Olympics against the veteran Soviet Union players. In *America's Coach: Life Lessons and Wisdom for Gold Medal Success: A Biographical Journey of the Late Hockey Icon Herb Brooks*, Bernstein examines Brooks' leadership and concludes, "Leadership is about implementing changes. It's about transforming organizations so that creativity and innovation are encouraged and can thrive. Management is not enough by itself. Managing is taking care of what has already been created. Leaders tell us not only what is, but what can be."[101]

Born in 1909 and often referred to as the dean of American business and management studies, Peter Drucker established himself as a trenchant, unorthodox, and independent analyst of economics and society. Tom Peters, co-author of *In Search of Excellence*, called Drucker "the creator and inventor of modern management."[102] Drucker maintains that most managers are leaders, but not all. Many people supervise others, sometimes in large numbers, yet have little impact on the organization's overall performance. He explains, "Managers oversee the work of others, but they have neither the responsibility for, nor authority over, the direction, the content, and the quality of the work or the methods of its performance. The leader sets the goals, sets the priorities, and sets and maintains the standards.

Managers can still be measured and appraised very largely in terms of efficiency and quality."[103]

Leading, on the other hand, involves determining the correct things to do. It requires motivating, influencing, and inspiring team members by creating a safe, cohesive, and positive work environment free from discrimination or harassment. An environment that inspires others to excel at accomplishing the right things by shaping attitudes, behaviors, values, and norms. Successful leaders communicate a vision of their team's future and articulate a path to get there. "Leaders provide the vision and managers carry it out; leaders make it better and managers make it run," contends General Bill Creech, former Commander of the United States Air Force Tactical Air Command.[104] Effective leaders envision the future and clearly communicate the path forward. Team members expect their leaders to articulate the team's goals, objectives, priorities, vision, and strategy—the what, why, and how behind the team's mission.

According to Gardner, "Even though it has become conventional to contrast leaders and managers, I am inclined to use slightly different categories, lumping leaders and leader-managers into one category and placing in the other category those numerous managers whom one would not normally describe as leaders."[105] He distinguishes leaders and leader-managers from managers in at least six ways:

1. They think longer term—beyond the day's crises, beyond the horizon.
2. In thinking about the group and where they are heading, they grasp its relationship to larger realities—the larger organization of which they are a part.
3. They reach and influence constituents beyond their jurisdictions and beyond boundaries.

4. They put heavy emphasis on the intangibles of vision, values, and motivation and understand intuitively the unconscious elements in the leader-constituent interaction.
5. They have the political skills to cope with the conflicting requirements of multiple constituencies.
6. They think in terms of renewal. The routine manager tends to accept organizational structure and process as it exists. The leader seeks the revisions of process and structure required by ever-changing reality.[106]

After four decades of studying business and leadership, John P. Kotter, Konosuke Matsushita Professor of Leadership and Emeritus at Harvard Business School, suggests that people make three mistakes when they equate management with leadership:

> **Mistake #1**: People use the terms management and leadership interchangeably. This shows that they do not see the crucial difference between the two and the vital functions that each role plays.
> **Mistake #2**: People use the term leadership to refer to the people at the very top of hierarchies. They then call people in the layers below them in the organization management. And all the rest are workers, employees, specialists, and individual contributors. This is a mistake and very misleading.
> **Mistake #3**: People often think of leadership in terms of personality characteristics, usually as something they call charisma. Since few people have great charisma, this leads logically to the

conclusion that few people can provide leadership, which gets us into increasing trouble.[107]

Kotter contends that "management is a set of well-known processes, like planning, budgeting, structuring jobs, staffing jobs, measuring system performance and problem-solving, which help an organization to predictably do what it knows how to do well."[108] Kotter refutes the argument that we should replace management with leadership. "This is obviously not so: they serve different, yet essential, functions. We need superb management. And we need more superb leadership. Management is crucial, but it's not leadership," asserts Kotter.[109]

Leader. With few exceptions, most individuals report directly to an organizational leader and are accountable to that person for their job performance. Organizations assign various titles to these roles, such as supervisor, manager, director, chief, head, president, vice president, lead, commander, sergeant, dean, principal, coach, minister, owner, executive, governor, senator, mayor, and more.

This book defines organizational leaders, regardless of title, as individuals responsible and accountable for the performance of one or more team members who report directly to them, as they work together to accomplish the organization's mission. These responsibilities may include interviewing, hiring, onboarding, evaluating, promoting, adjusting salaries, and rewarding team members. Leaders are also responsible for organizing, training, resourcing, coaching, developing, and mentoring. When necessary, they administer corrective actions and, in cases of serious legal or ethical breaches, take appropriate steps to separate team members from the organization. Additionally, they make critical decisions regarding furloughs or layoffs during organizational restructuring or downsizing.

Leadership. In line with the leader's role, this book defines leadership as the process by which leaders motivate, influence, and inspire team members to consistently achieve mission success safely, efficiently, and effectively through their decisions, communication, and actions. This process is guided by the team's shared commitment to a clear set of goals, objectives, priorities, values, strategy, and long-term vision.

Manager. Many organizations use the term *manager* synonymously with *leader*. In this book, however, the leader role is defined less by title and more by the responsibilities tied to the role. Since leadership is inherently people-focused, this definition emphasizes human resource responsibilities over job titles.

In this book, the term leader applies to managers who are responsible and accountable for the performance of one or more team members, what Gardner referred to as "leader-managers." Other managers may have no such responsibilities and instead oversee non-human resources such as systems, assets, schedules, projects, or budgets.

Management. This book defines management as the process by which managers, leaders, and individual contributors operate, control, communicate, solve problems, innovate, and make decisions about resources, planning, strategy, and execution. This process includes overseeing systems, processes, projects, programs, budgets, and schedules—among other essential work requirements—for successfully achieving a team's mission, vision, values, goals, objectives, priorities, and overall strategy.

Leaders manage. In addition to motivating, influencing, and inspiring team members to achieve the desired mission results, leaders are responsible for managing various work requirements such as projects, systems, programs, processes, budgets, schedules, operations, and other non-human resources. One of the most important resources leaders manage is time. Effective time management is crucial for sustaining leadership effectiveness. While office administrators and assistants can support time management, the ultimate responsibility lies with the leader to ensure their time is managed effectively.

Shaping team-member performance. Leaders are responsible and accountable for the performance of their team. This responsibility includes evaluating, assessing, recognizing, rewarding, and improving team member performance through regular reviews, such as quarterly performance assessments.

To achieve these outcomes, leaders must ensure that team members clearly understand the expectations for both individual and team performance. They do this by engaging in collaborative and candid conversations, both one-on-one and in group settings, to communicate the expected outcomes aligned with the team's mission, vision, values, goals, objectives, priorities, and strategy. Leaders also provide timely feedback to recognize when performance is on track or to address when it is off track. Performance management systems equip leaders with tools to communicate, collaborate, guide, coach, assess, evaluate, seek feedback, document, develop, reshape, and, when necessary, correct team member performance.

Nature and Nurture

Among the most successful leaders, some are assertive and others reserved. Some micromanage, while others macromanage. Some are relaxed and others restless. Some are hot-headed and others level-headed. Some are overweight and some are lean. Some are charismatic and others pragmatic. Some are short and some are tall. Some are personable, others detached. Some are studious and others informal. Some welcome the spotlight while others avoid it. Some are analytical and others are spontaneous. Some are serious, others casual. Effective leaders, in other words, vary. They differ in personality, physical appearance, gender, race, and skills. Effective leaders come from many backgrounds and employ a variety of leadership styles. What, then, determines if one will be an effective leader? Are leaders born or made?

Throughout the modern and postmodern periods, it was widely believed that effective leaders were born, not made. Numerous trait-based studies conducted during the nineteenth and twentieth centuries sought to identify the physical characteristics, personality traits, and innate abilities thought to define natural-born leaders. Commonly cited traits included high energy levels, stress tolerance, self-confidence, internal locus of control, emotional maturity, and intelligence. However, current research reveals that no single set of traits consistently predicts long-term leadership effectiveness.[110]

Recent studies consistently show that genetic factors play a much smaller role in leadership than once believed. The idea that only individuals born with unique genetic traits, special abilities, or charismatic personalities can motivate, influence, and inspire others has not been validated. There is no universally agreed-upon list of traits required for leadership success.[111] As Bennis and Nanus contend, "Nurture is far more important than nature in determining who becomes a successful leader."[112] Contemporary research emphasizes that sustained leadership excellence is learned and developed through experience, practice, observation, and education.

Learning to lead. While leadership trait theory once dominated thinking, suggesting that only those with certain inborn characteristics could lead effectively, this view has since evolved. Contemporary research and real-world experience show that successful leaders are not merely born; they are made. Across all sectors—business, government, education, nonprofit organizations, the military, and others—effective leaders develop their capabilities through systematic study, inquiry, observation, experience, and practice. As Bennis and Nanus argue, "Everyone has leadership potential, and leadership opportunities are within the reach of most people. Major capacities and competencies of leadership can be learned, at least if there's a basic desire to learn and one does not suffer from a [significant] learning disorder. Nurture is far more important than nature in determining who becomes a successful leader."[113]

These insights reinforce a growing consensus: leadership effectiveness is not predetermined by birthright but shaped over time through learning and experience. Edgar Puryear's comparative study of World War II generals George Marshall, Douglas MacArthur, Dwight Eisenhower, and George Patton underscores this point, revealing that the vital elements of their leadership success were not innate but developed gradually over the course of their careers.[114]

Gardner echoes this conclusion in *On Leadership*, dismissing the idea that leaders are simply born. "Leaders are born not made. Nonsense!" he proclaimed. "Most of what leaders have that enables them to lead is learned."[115] While Gardner acknowledged that certain traits, such as energy level, may be genetically influenced, he maintains that "the notion that all the attributes of a leader are innate is demonstrably false . . . the individual's hereditary gifts, however notable, leave the issue of future leadership performance undecided."[116]

Similarly, Drucker, drawing on more than four decades of consulting with leaders across industries, sectors, and continents, observed that he had never encountered a natural-born leader, one who was innately effective. "All the effective ones," he contends, "had to learn to be effective."[117]

Together, these perspectives affirm the central message of this chapter: sustained leadership success is not the result of a rare genetic gift—it is the outcome of intentional development. With this foundation established, the next chapter turns to an examination of the leadership capabilities and styles that empower leaders to achieve and sustain success.

Chapter Three: Leadership Capabilities and Styles

> Books are the carriers of civilization. Without books, history is silent, literature dumb, science crippled, thought and speculation at a standstill.
> — Barbara Tuchman[118]

Chapters One and Two traced the evolution of leadership theory and highlighted key leadership themes, laying the groundwork for this chapter's exploration of leadership capabilities and styles. Today, countless books, courses, conferences, and seminars aim to develop leaders by sharing knowledge of the capabilities and styles demonstrated by successful leaders.

Leadership capabilities refer to the qualities, competencies, attributes, skills, and functions that enable leaders to motivate, influence, and inspire team members to achieve mission success. Leadership styles, by contrast, reflect how leaders interact with team members, peers, senior leaders, and external stakeholders, such as clients, customers, partners, suppliers, regulators, and community groups. These styles often mirror a leader's personality and preferred approach to leadership.

Understanding leadership capabilities and styles bridges the gap between theory and practice. While the previous chapter examined key themes on leadership, this chapter focuses on the capabilities and styles that shape effective leadership. Drawing on key insights from notable scholars and practitioners, the following sections provide a research-based review of these critical elements.

Leadership Capabilities

Bennis's leadership qualities. In his highly acclaimed book, *On Becoming a Leader*, Warren Bennis—renowned scholar, organizational consultant, distinguished professor of business administration at the University of Southern California, and author of numerous books on contemporary leadership challenges—identifies nine qualities that define leadership. According to Bennis, successful leaders:

1. Master the context.
2. Understand the basics.
3. Know themselves.
4. Know the world.
5. Operate on instinct.
6. Deploy themselves; strike hard and try everything.
7. Move through chaos.
8. Get people on their side.
9. Know organizations can help or hinder leaders.[119]

Bennis's essential leadership competencies. In the introduction to his revised edition of *On Becoming a Leader*, Bennis added four essential competencies to his original nine leadership qualities, emphasizing that effective leaders:

1. Are able to engage others by creating shared meaning, have a vision, and can persuade others to make that vision their own.
2. Have a distinctive voice—a purpose, self-confidence, a sense of self, and the whole gestalt of abilities we now call emotional intelligence.
3. Have integrity.
4. Have adaptive capacity—what allows leaders to respond quickly and intelligently to relentless change.[120]

Drucker's essential leadership competencies. In a review of Peter Drucker's extensive research on executive leadership, he contends that five essential competencies must be acquired to be an effective leader, none of which require extraordinary intelligence or charismatic appeal. These competencies, he claims, are the same whether the leader works in a business or a government agency, as a hospital administrator or a university dean. Drucker's Five essential leadership competencies include:

1. Effective executives know where their time goes. They do not start with their tasks. They start with their time. They attempt to manage their time and cut back on unproductive demands on their time.
2. Effective executives focus on outward contribution. They gear their efforts to results rather than work. They start out with the question,

'What results are expected?' rather than with 'What work should be done?'

3. Effective executives build on strengths—their own strengths and the strengths of their superiors, colleagues, and subordinates. They do not build on weakness. They do not start out with the things they cannot do.
4. Effective executives concentrate on the few major areas where superior performance will produce outstanding results. They force themselves to set priorities and stay within their priority decisions, doing first things first.
5. Effective executives make effective decisions. They know that an effective decision is always a judgment based on 'dissenting opinions' rather than on 'consensus on the facts.' And they know that to make many decisions fast means to make the wrong decisions.[121]

Dr. Martin Luther King, Jr. on leadership. Few leaders exhibited more influential leadership during the twentieth century than Dr. Martin Luther King, Jr. In examining Dr. King's leadership principles, Donald T. Phillips chronicled the decisions Dr. King made, the people he trusted, and the leadership skills he applied to turn a small crusade into a movement. According to Phillips, Dr. King's inspiration and wisdom on leadership include the following tenets:

- First, listen; lead by being led.
- Learn, learn, learn.
- Encourage creativity and innovation.
- Involve everyone through alliances, teamwork, and diversity.

> Set goals and create a detailed plan of action.
> Be decisive.
> Have the courage to lead.
> Inspire people with your dream.[122]

Gardner's key leadership attributes. In drawing upon the writings of Ralph Stogdill, Bernard Bass, Edwin Hollander, and others, John Gardner identifies 14 key leadership capabilities exercised by effective leaders. He maintains that the significance of each attribute varies based on the situation and that not all attributes are present in every leader. With these caveats, Garnder identifies the following attributes of effective leaders:

1. Physical vitality and stamina.
2. Intelligence and judgment-in-action.
3. Willingness (eagerness) to accept responsibilities.
4. Task competence.
5. Understanding of followers/constituents and their needs.
6. Skill in dealing with people.
7. Need to achieve.
8. Capacity to motivate.
9. Courage, resolution, and steadiness.
10. Capacity to win and hold trust.
11. Capacity to manage, decide, and set priorities.
12. Confidence.
13. Ascendance, dominance, and assertiveness.
14. Adaptability and flexibility of approach.[123]

Harvard Business Publishing's Eight Capabilities. In *Leading Now: Critical Capabilities for a Complex World*, Harvard Business Publishing (HBP) identifies eight essential capabilities that leaders must possess to be effective. Ray Carvey, executive vice president of corporate learning at HBP, notes that as the world continues to evolve, the capabilities required for leadership success may also shift. According to HBP, effective leaders:

1. Manage complexity.
2. Manage global businesses.
3. Act strategically.
4. Foster innovation.
5. Leverage networks.
6. Inspire engagement.
7. Develop personal adaptability.
8. Cultivate learning agility.[124]

Lussier and Achua's essential skills for leadership success. In the fifth edition of *Leadership: Theory, Application, & Skill Development*, Robert Lussier and Christopher Achua identify three essential skills exercised by successful leaders.

1. Technical skills: skills that involve the ability to use methods and techniques to perform a task. Technical skills can also include business skills, such as computer skills.
2. Interpersonal skills: skills that involve the ability to understand, communicate, and work well with individuals and groups through developing effective relationships, often referred to as human, people, and soft skills.

3. Decision-making skills: skills that require the ability to conceptualize situations, select alternatives to solve problems, and take advantage of opportunities. It is about understanding 'what is going on.'[125]

Maxwell's 21 indispensable leadership qualities. John Maxwell, noted author and leadership expert, asserts that great leaders possess the 21 indispensable leadership qualities depicted in Table 3.1.

Table 3.1

Maxwell's 21 Indispensable Leadership Qualities[126]

1. Character	8. Focus	15. Relationships
2. Charisma	9. Generosity	16. Responsibility
3. Commitment	10. Initiative	17. Security
4. Communication	11. Listening	18. Self-Discipline
5. Competence	12. Passion	19. Servanthood
6. Courage	13. Positive Attitude	20. Teachability
7. Discernment	14. Problem Solving	21. Vision

United States Army leadership guidelines. The *United States Army Officer's Guide* provides leadership guidelines for military officers. According to the guide, a leader must:

➤ Know their job.
➤ Set the example.
➤ Instill pride: establish the value, purpose, and importance of the work being done. Develop pride in oneself, pride in the work one does, and pride in one's organization.

> Gain followers' confidence, self-respect, and cooperation.
> Foster morale: morale is confidence, courage, and zeal.
  - Confidence is obtained when soldiers are certain in their own minds they know their jobs well, their leaders are good leaders, and that in battle with the enemy they will win.
  - Courage is born of confidence.
  - Zeal comes with an appreciation of the worthwhileness of a cause accompanied by the resolution to get on with a task and end it.
  - Morale is high when team members think their organization is the best in the world, and their unit is the best unit.[127]

Yukl's leadership functions. In the fifth edition of *Leadership in Organizations*, Gary Yukl identifies 10 key leadership functions that enhance the collective performance of teams and organizations, including:

1. Help interpret the meaning of events.
2. Create alignment on objectives and strategies.
3. Build task commitment and optimism.
4. Build mutual trust and cooperation.
5. Strengthen collective identity.
6. Organize and coordinate activities.
7. Encourage and facilitate collective learning.
8. Obtain necessary resources and support.
9. Develop and empower people.
10. Promote social justice and morality.[128]

Zenger and Folkman's suggestions for developing leadership. In their research-based book, *The Extraordinary Leader, Turning Good Managers Into Great Leaders,* John Zenger and Joseph Folkman analyzed data from over 200,000 employees who rated more than 25,000 leaders to identify the competencies that drive leadership success. Based on this extensive empirical study, they offer 25 practical strategies leaders can use to strengthen the attributes and behaviors most critical to achieving impactful leadership results.

1. Decide to become a great leader.
2. Develop and display high personal character.
3. Develop new skills.
4. Find a coach.
5. Identify your strengths.
6. Identify your weaknesses and then find ways to make them irrelevant.
7. Fix fatal flaws.
8. Increase the scope of your assignment.
9. Connect with good role models.
10. Learn from mistakes and negative experiences.
11. Seek ways to give and receive productive feedback and learn to absorb it in an emotionally healthy way.
12. Learn from work experiences.
13. Study the current reality the organization faces.
14. Learn to think strategically.
15. Communicate with stories.
16. Infuse energy into every situation.
17. Allocate specific time to people development.
18. Weld your team together.
19. Build personal dashboards to monitor leadership effectiveness.

20. Plan and execute a change initiative.
21. Study the high performers and replicate their behavior with others.
22. Volunteer in your community.
23. Practice articulating your vision for the organization and your group.
24. Prepare for your next job.
25. Think ahead about the skills you will need.[129]

As highlighted by scholars and practitioners, effective leaders draw on a broad range of competencies, attributes, skills, and functions—expressed through their decisions, communication, and actions—to motivate, influence, and inspire their teams to achieve mission success. Research increasingly affirms that these capabilities are developed over time through observation, study, practice, and experience. While vital to sustained success, these capabilities are brought to life through a leader's personality and style, which shape how they engage with others and navigate their roles. Building on the discussion of leadership capabilities, the next section explores leadership styles—the distinctive approaches and personas leaders bring to their work.

Leadership Styles

Leadership is a human-centric process shaped by a leader's personality, which in turn influences their leadership approach or style. Research shows that leadership style plays a vital role in long-term effectiveness, affecting how team members experience a leader's decisions, communication, and actions—the core drivers of motivation, influence, and inspiration required to accomplish the organization's mission. Perceptions of fairness, opportunity, trust, concern, and respect are crucial to a team's sustained commitment to challenging goals. These perceptions are largely formed through team members' lived experiences with a leader's approach or style.

The word leader often generates images of a person who has a profound impact on the course of history during times of crisis. We read books about them, teach others about them, tell stories about them, watch movies about them, and learn from them. These leaders are frequently portrayed as possessing a mysterious blend of strength, bravery, and charisma as they accomplish heroic feats in the face of danger. This image, however, creates the perception that leadership success is reserved only for those born with a supernatural leadership style.

While extraordinary leaders do emerge and their abilities—often attributed to innate qualities—are crucial for the success of struggling organizations, this perspective can be misleading. In most organizations, the enduring requirement is for leaders to be effective, not extraordinary. During World War II, the United States Army published its *Officer's Guide*, describing an effective leader as "one fitted by force of ideas, character, intellect, and strength of will. The leader is deemed effective when he is able to arouse, incite, and direct others in conduct and achievement."[130]

In addition to heroic and gallant images often associated with leadership, it is commonly believed that successful leaders must possess an extroverted personality and charismatic appeal, especially in the context of political and military history. "A senior executive, we are told, should have extraordinary abilities as an analyst and as a decision-maker. He should be good at working with people and at understanding organization and power relations, be good at mathematics, and have artistic insights and creative imagination. What seems to be wanted is universal genius," says Drucker.[131] Yet, contrary to this idealized image, research studies affirm that there is no single leadership style that fits all situations, and that consistently effective leaders adapt their style to various situations, circumstances, missions, and stages of an organization's life cycle.[132]

Personas. Leadership practitioners and scholars continue to examine how a leader's persona—or personality—influences team performance. Research findings suggest that personality plays a significant role in determining a leader's effectiveness. This section highlights key elements of leadership related to personality, as outlined by Lussier and Achua in *Leadership: Theory, Application & Skill Development*.[133]

Personality is a combination of traits that influence behavior, relationships, and decision-making.[134] These traits are unique personal characteristics. Personality develops through a blend of genetic factors and environmental influences. Certain personality traits, ambivalence, for example, help explain why some people procrastinate or avoid making decisions.[135] Although it is difficult, people can change their behavior to be more effective leaders.[136] In applying trait theory, it is important to understand that there are traits that many successful leaders share, but "there is no agreed upon list of traits that leaders need to be successful. So, you don't need to have all of them to be a successful leader," stress Lussier and Achua.[137] For example, many successful leaders exhibit extrovert behaviors; however, 40% of corporate chief executives describe themselves as introverts, including former Microsoft chief Bill Gates, investors Warren Buffett and Charles Schwab, and Avon Company's Andrea Jung.[138] Dr. Martin Luther King, Jr. was described as "quiet, introspective, and introverted."[139]

Personality self-assessments like the Myers-Briggs Type Indicator and the Minnesota Multiphasic Personality Inventory help leaders understand their preferred behavioral styles and temperaments. For instance, the Myers-Briggs Type Indicator evaluates and compares four dimensions of behavior: extraversion versus introversion, sensing versus intuition, thinking versus feeling, and judging versus perceiving. The outcome of the assessment provides self-awareness. Understanding one's leadership persona and temperament is important because personality influences behavior, which in turn affects how team members perceive, experience, and respond to a leader's decisions, communication, and actions.

Big Five model of personality. Researchers conducted a major meta-analysis combining 73 prior studies to correlate personality dimensions with leadership effectiveness, dubbed the Big Five Model of Personality.[140] According to Lussier and Achua, "the Big Five Model of Personality is the most widely accepted way to classify personalities because of its strong research support."[141]

The purpose of the model is to reliably categorize most personality traits into one of five core dimensions. Each dimension includes multiple characteristics. The Big Five Model of Personality categorizes traits into surgency, agreeableness, adjustment, conscientiousness, and openness to experience.[142]

1. *Surgency*. Traits of assertiveness, extraversion, and high energy with determination.
2. *Agreeableness*. Traits of sociability, cooperation, and harmony.
3. *Adjustment.* Traits of emotional stability, narcissism, and self-confidence.
4. *Conscientiousness*. Traits of dependability and integrity.
5. *Openness to experience*. Traits of flexibility, intelligence, and internal locus of control or one's belief in control over one's destiny and performance.

The research suggests that certain personality traits are correlated with leadership effectiveness. However, "Not all effective leaders have all the traits associated with the Big Five," caution Lussier and Achua, "and, like all of us, are higher and lower in some than others."[143] Findings from the Big Five meta-analysis showed a strong correlation between effective leadership and the personality traits of surgency (0.31), conscientiousness (0.28), and openness to experience (0.24). Leaders high in surgency—characterized by assertiveness, energy, and social confidence—are perceived as leaderlike. Conscientious leaders are disciplined and dependable, while those high in openness to experience are intellectually curious and adaptable to change. These leaders are not overly preoccupied with being liked by everyone; they are emotionally stable, confident, and purposeful.[144]

In contrast, agreeableness showed only a weak correlation (0.08) with leadership effectiveness, and adjustment (emotional stability) had a negative correlation when measured as neuroticism (-0.24), suggesting these traits may play a lesser or more nuanced role in predicting leadership success. Could there be situations where traits of agreeableness and adjustment contribute to effective leadership? Yes, in certain contexts, traits like agreeableness and adjustment are particularly important. For example, in work environments that demand high levels of collaboration, empathy, and emotional intelligence—such as healthcare, education, or social services—leaders with high agreeableness often thrive. Their ability to build rapport, listen actively, and foster trust can greatly enhance team cohesion and morale. Likewise, in highly volatile or high-stress settings—such as emergency response, combat, or firefighting—leaders with high adjustment tend to maintain stability, composure, and clear judgment under pressure, making them highly effective in crisis situations.

In addition to the Big Five Model of Personality, the literature identifies leadership personas as autocratic, democratic/participatory, teaming, practical, charismatic, transformational, and situational. The following sections summarize these personalities.

Autocratic leaders. In the 1930s, before behavioral theory gained popularity, Kurt Lewin and his colleagues at the University of Iowa conducted studies to identify leadership styles.[145] Their research identified two basic styles: autocratic and democratic, or Theory X and Theory Y, as McGregor identified them. Autocratic leaders are job-centered, prioritizing task completion within a highly structured work environment. They give clear directives, closely supervise team members, and often dictate how tasks should be accomplished.[146] While they may care about their team members, their strong emphasis and control can create the impression of a taskmaster.

Certain situations call for an autocratic leadership approach, particularly during time-compressed emergencies or high-risk missions. Medical crises, fire rescue operations, and combat engagements, for example, demand swift, decisive action. In these contexts, autocratic leaders use their authority to direct and steer team members, delegating when necessary, providing coaching, and applying control measures to achieve outcomes and accomplish the mission. However, few leaders can sustain long-term influence, inspiration, and effectiveness by relying solely on an autocratic style to direct and control team performance.

Consistently effective leaders understand that mission success depends on the commitment and performance of their team members. They seek to earn and sustain trust and respect by listening, learning, and collaborating—not merely directing actions. Navigating the challenges of organizational change, restructuring, workforce expansion and contraction, evolving stakeholder expectations, and the shifting nature of work often calls for a democratic or more collaborative leadership approach.

Democratic/participatory leaders. Lewin's University of Iowa study identified what he termed the democratic leadership style, also known as the participatory style. The democratic leader encourages participation in decisions, works with team members to determine what to do, and does not closely supervise team members.[147] Democratic leadership is closely aligned with behaviors demonstrating high concern for people. People-centered behavior refers to the extent to which the leader focuses on addressing the human needs of team members while fostering relationships. A people-centered leader is attentive to team members, communicates effectively to build support and mutual respect, and prioritizes the welfare of their team members.

> *Consistently effective leaders understand that their success rests in the hands of their team members.*

Team leaders. Robert Blake and Jane Mouton, from the University of Texas, developed the Managerial Grid, first published in 1964. In 1991, it was updated and renamed the Leadership Grid, with Anne Adams McCanse continuing the research after Mouton died in 1987. Like Lewin's model, the Leadership Grid theory is based on two dimensions: concern for production and concern for people. During the study, leaders were asked to determine their leadership style through a questionnaire on a scale from 1 to 9. The results from the questionnaire were plotted on a chart that identified five leadership styles: impoverished (1,1), authoritative (9,1), country club (1,9), middle of the road (5,5), and team leader (9,9).

The team-leader style, according to Blake and Mouton, was consistently identified as the most effective leadership style. It characterizes leaders who demonstrate high concern for both production and people, striving to achieve strong team performance while ensuring employee satisfaction. Research showed that this style often led to improved performance, low absenteeism, reduced turnover, and high employee morale.[148] While other leadership styles proved effective in certain contexts, depending on the nature of the work, the team-leader style was generally preferred across most situations.[149]

Practical leaders. Many organizations experience turbulent periods of change and transformation. During these times, steady, persistent, and practical leadership is important to maintaining focus on safety, quality, and productivity. Practical leaders emphasize the organization's mission, policies, practices, processes, core functions, and people. This leadership style is particularly effective in guiding organizations through significant transitions.

Practical leaders make pragmatic decisions that serve both the organization and its team members. They consistently reinforce the importance of the team's mission, listen respectfully to concerns and suggestions, and uphold the team's values and culture. Practical leaders are especially effective at stabilizing performance during unsettled times or periods of change. They are also well-suited to guide organizations facing external pressures and challenges.

Charismatic leaders. Charismatic leaders provide their teams with a clear, inspirational vision and often make personal sacrifices to accomplish the mission. They instill a sense of urgency and work to earn the deep trust of their team. Rather than relying on force or majority consensus, charismatic leaders use persuasion to influence and inspire those they lead.

While the personalized power orientation of charismatic leaders can significantly boost team performance, its effects are not always positive. Some entrepreneurs who build successful businesses may evolve into tyrants or egomaniacs, exhibiting behaviors that are perceived as insensitive, manipulative, overbearing, or reckless—ultimately eroding trust. These leaders may prioritize personal loyalty and self-serving goals over the organization's long-term interests. In a *Wall Street Journal* article, Drucker shared his perspective on charismatic leaders who misuse their power.

Leadership is mundane, unromantic, and boring. Its essence is performance. Leadership is not by itself good or desirable. It is a means to an end. Leadership to what end is thus the crucial question. History knows no more charismatic leaders than last century's triad of Stalin, Hitler, and Mao—the misleaders who inflicted as much evil and suffering on humanity as have ever been recorded.

But effective leadership does not depend on charisma. Dwight Eisenhower, George Marshall, and Harry Truman were singularly effective leaders, yet none possessed any more charisma than a dead mackerel. Nor did Konrad Adenauer, the chancellor who rebuilt West Germany after World War II. No less charismatic personality could be imagined than Abe Lincoln of Illinois, the raw-boned, uncouth backwoodsman of 1860. And there was amazingly little charisma to the bitter, defeated, almost broken Churchill of the inter-war years.

Indeed, charisma can become the undoing of leaders. It makes them inflexible, convinced of their own infallibility, unable to change. This is what happened to Stalin, Hitler, and Mao, and it is commonplace in the study of ancient history that only Alexander the Great's early death saved him from becoming an ineffectual failure.

Charisma does not by itself guarantee effectiveness as a leader. John F. Kennedy may have been the most charismatic person ever to occupy the White House, yet few presidents got as little done.

What, then, is leadership if it is not charisma and not a set of personality traits? The first thing to say about it is that it is work—something stressed again and again by the most charismatic leaders: Julius Caesar, for instance, or General MacArthur and Field Marshal Montgomery, or, to use an example from business, Alfred Sloan, the man who built and led General Motors from 1920 to 1955.[150]

The most effective charismatic leaders inspire devotion to the organization's shared goals and objectives. Their influence tends to endure, often leaving a lasting positive impact on the organization long after they have moved on.

Transformational leaders. Transformational leaders trust and encourage their team members to meet or exceed the organization's goals and objectives. They achieve this by communicating a clear and compelling vision, presenting scenarios that outline rewarding paths to that vision, emphasizing the value and purpose of the organization's mission, promoting teamwork and collaboration, empowering team members, delegating authority with responsibility, and inspiring commitment to action. In describing transformational leadership, Burns says it "is moral in that it raises the level of human conduct and ethical aspiration of both leader and led, and thus it has a transforming effect on both."[151]

Transformational leaders articulate the importance and value of the team's mission, inspiring team members to rise above self-interest for the sake of the organization. They instill confidence by empowering individuals with greater responsibility and challenging them to achieve stretch goals, contributing to job enrichment, engagement, and overall satisfaction. In *Leaders: Strategies for Taking Charge*, Bennis and Nanus describe a transformational leader as "one who commits people to action, who converts followers into leaders, and who may convert leaders into agents of change"[152]

Transformational leaders also provide support and encouragement when needed to sustain momentum through exhausting challenges, setbacks, and failures. Because of this influence, team members develop trust in transformational leaders and are often motivated to exceed expectations. Former United States Air Force General Bill Creech serves as an example of a transformational leader. General Creech commanded the United States Air Force Tactical Air Command from May 1, 1978, to December 31, 1984. The now-inactive major command directed the combat fighting forces of more than 111,000 military and civilian personnel. When General Creech assumed command in 1978, he inherited an ailing organization with steadily declining flying hours and a correspondingly high flight accident rate.[153]

Drawing on the principles of W. Edward Deming's quality management system, General Creech transformed Tactical Air Command's combat air power capabilities by focusing on two organizational principles. First, he consistently articulated the need to organize combat units during peacetime as they would be organized and led during wartime. Second, he believed organizations should be structured in small teams oriented toward their products and services. For Tactical Air Command, the products and services were combat sortie missions, servicing targets in support of geographic combatant commanders worldwide.[154]

General Creech undertook other initiatives to instill pride, which he believed was related to productivity. The first was to establish a system of goals that cascaded down to the Air Force squadron level, the front-line fighting unit, which he believed had been lacking. Creech established a system of goals for squadrons so the troops in the unit could relate to them. For example, if the squadron were expected to fly 400 training sorties per month and they met their goal, squadron members would receive extra time off. They worked longer if they did not meet their sortie goals. "They understood that," maintained Creech.[155]

Many of the systems and organizational concepts Creech put in place saw a trial by fire during the 1991 Persian Gulf War. General Creech's transformational leadership style was responsible for committing people to action, converting followers into believers, converting leaders into agents of change, and ushering in a new generation of combat air power capability. His leadership style, strength of character, and inspirational vision earned him the respect and loyalty of senior leaders and front-line troops alike during the deployment of a new quality management system across a large, globally dispersed, and change-resistant organization.

At the end of his command tour, General Creech successfully reduced Tactical Air Command's aircraft mishap rate by 275% improvement.[156] "No organization could have been more difficult to install and to maintain total quality management because of the size of the organization, its diversity, its being widely scattered, and because of the resistance of a military organization to drastic changes in behavior, habits, and relationships," reported Drucker.[157]

Situational leaders. Why are some leaders highly effective in one organization but less so in another? Shouldn't strong leadership capabilities translate across all settings? Research suggests that long-term leadership effectiveness is often shaped by organizational context, which can determine whether a leader thrives or falters across different teams and environments.[158]

Zenger and Folkman found that leaders must fit their organizations rather than organizations having to fit leaders.[159] A leader who flourishes in one setting may struggle in another due to factors such as the nature of the work, the organization's stage in its life cycle, the leader's credibility, work experience, and the surrounding political landscape. A corporate finance officer, for example, may likely apply a different leadership style when directing their finance team than as head of a community's civic association. As Gardner notes, this is not to suggest that organizational context and external factors are everything while a leader's attributes and preferred style are insignificant; rather, leadership effectiveness often hinges on how well a leader's style aligns with the unique demands of the organization and its situation.[160]

A leader's effectiveness in different organizations or with different teams is affected by their situational awareness of the organization's mission, people, and life cycle, as well as their ability to adapt to the organizational context. Robert House developed the Path-Goal theory of leadership based on an early version of the theory by M. G. Evans. The Path-Goal leadership theory suggests that leaders select the leadership style (directive, participative, or achievement-oriented, for example) appropriate to the situation to maximize team member performance and job satisfaction.[161]

Situational leadership infers that no single style is always the right style, especially when considering an organization's mission, values, and team culture. Research by Zenger and Folkman reinforces this view.[162] Their findings indicate that successful leaders sustain their effectiveness by employing adaptive approaches based on changing situations.

The leadership style that best aligns with a team's mission often depends on the organization's stage in its life cycle, such as start-up, initial growth, expansion, periodic transformation, or ongoing evolution. Thomas Cronin, noted political scientist and educator, points out that it may take one leadership style to start a new enterprise and quite another to keep it going through its various phases.[163] This helps explain why some team members respond favorably or unfavorably to various leadership styles.

Situational leaders adapt their leadership style—ranging from autocratic to transformational—to effectively motivate, influence, and guide their teams in accomplishing the right tasks and missions over time. They align their approach with both the mission's demands and the nature of the team's work. For example, an autocratic style may be necessary during time-critical emergencies, where swift, decisive action is essential. In contrast, leading a team through a strategic planning session calls for a more collaborative approach—one that fosters open dialogue and shared commitment to the organization's goals, objectives, and priorities.

Leadership situational awareness. Enduring leaders demonstrate flexibility and innovation by maintaining situational awareness and adapting to changing circumstances. They strive to understand barriers, cultural differences, team-member diversity, organizational context, environmental factors, and interpersonal dynamics. By recognizing and leveraging the unique strengths of their team members, they drive performance and achieve results. As General H. Norman Schwarzkopf, the successful strategist and commander during the 1991 Gulf War, says: "To be an effective leader you have to figure out the people working for you and give each tasks that will take advantage of their strengths."[164]

Consistently effective leaders maintain a high level of situational awareness, enabling them to adjust their leadership approach based on feedback from superiors, team members, clients, customers, business partners, suppliers, and other stakeholders. As Gardner maintains, the interaction, communication, and influence between leaders and stakeholders flow in both directions—in the process, leaders shape and are shaped.[165] The most effective leaders, across a broad spectrum of organizations and life cycles, understand the structure of the organization, the nature of the mission, and the unique characteristics of their team members. They take time to get to know their team members in an authentic, meaningful way, and they remain attuned to the evolving needs of individuals as well as the shifting scope, demands, and pace of the mission.

Contemporary leadership theories acknowledge that no single leadership style fits all situations. Consistently effective leaders adapt their style to suit varying circumstances, missions, organizational contexts, and stages of the organizational life cycle. They apply a flexible approach to motivate, influence, and inspire team members to accomplish the right tasks, achieve mission objectives, and sustain long-term performance. Achieving sustained leadership excellence requires time, energy, effort, patience, perseverance, and commitment. To meet these demands, leaders must maintain situational awareness by focusing on two enduring priorities: people and mission.

Chapter Four: Leadership Priorities

> As we look ahead into the next century, leaders
> will be those who empower others.
> — William H. Gates III[166]

Effective leaders sustain their team's performance by cultivating a work environment where team members feel proud to be part of the team and find their contributions to its mission rewarding. They emphasize the importance and value of the team's mission and its impact on the organization's broader goals, objectives, priorities, and vision. This chapter explores two overarching leadership priorities—people and mission—along with key focus areas aligned to each priority. A leader's engagement, involvement, and attention to these priorities help foster an environment where team members view the leader as trusted and trusting, invested in their success and well-being, and committed to the team's mission. Figure 4.1 illustrates a leader's top priorities.

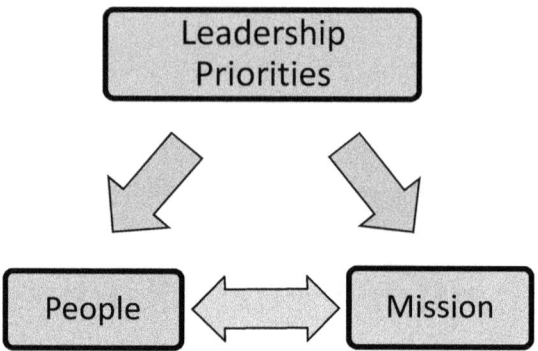

Figure 4.1. Leadership Priorities

Leadership Focus Areas

A set of focus areas is aligned with each leadership priority. These focus areas encompass activities, events, processes, procedures, policies, and practices requiring ongoing leadership awareness, attention, engagement, and involvement. Regular leadership team meetings, metrics, and reports help leaders manage the continuous flow of information and maintain situational awareness of these key areas. Through these review meetings, leaders can identify and communicate changes to a team's scope of work, staffing, budgets, customers, partners, stakeholders, goals, priorities, and strategy.

Establishing a structured cadence or operating rhythm for meetings, metrics, and reports ensures that leaders and their teams have the knowledge, information, and intelligence needed to adjust plans, anticipate changes, and address unintended consequences promptly. At the end of this chapter, an example of an operating rhythm schedule illustrates how this tool helps leaders and their teams maintain situational awareness and organizational health. Table 4.1 outlines the leadership focus areas aligned with each priority, explored in the following sections.

Table 4.1

Leadership Focus Areas

People	**Mission**
➢ Safety and security ➢ Engagement and involvement ➢ Culture ➢ Communication ➢ Organizing ➢ Hiring and staffing ➢ Learning, training, and development ➢ Equipment and resources ➢ Compensation and benefits ➢ Performance management ➢ Coaching ➢ Mentoring ➢ Team-building events ➢ Leading up ➢ Leading across ➢ Leading other leaders	➢ Mission execution ➢ Clients, customers, partners, and stakeholders ➢ Products and services ➢ Communication ➢ Organizational planning ➢ Financial planning and budgeting ➢ Controlling ➢ Innovating ➢ Community outreach

Leadership focus areas should be reviewed on a recurring schedule; nevertheless, there will be times when unplanned events, crises, or emergencies require immediate attention and action. Well-prepared teams—organized, trained, equipped, and properly resourced with robust operating practices, processes, procedures, and policies—enable leaders and their teams to respond effectively to unplanned events. The following sections highlight leadership focus areas related to people and mission priorities.

People Focus Areas

> Take care of your people and they will take care of the mission.
> — Lieutenant General Douglas Robb[167]

A leader's success rests not only in their own hands but in the hands of others. Mark Zuckerberg, one of the world's most recognized entrepreneurs and creator of the largest social media network, Facebook, knew he could not find success on his own. He needed others. "When I was getting started, I didn't want to build a company and I didn't know anything about building companies," claimed Zuckerberg. "The thing that got me through it and I think gets a lot of people through it is the people around them."[168]

Team members are the cornerstone of a leader's success because they are the ones who safely, effectively, and consistently accomplish, sustain, improve, and advance an organization's mission. This holds true for all organizations—small businesses, large corporations, government institutions, military units, educational systems, community service organizations, nonprofits, and not-for-profits, to name a few. It takes people to accomplish a mission. That is why team members should always be the first priority . . . people first.

Leaders, therefore, must prioritize team member safety, health, welfare, and development. This leadership mindset supports the perspective that if a leader takes care of their team members, their team members will take care of the mission . . . take care of your people, and they will take care of the mission. Simon Sinek, influential speaker and author on the topic of leadership, says the most important lesson of great leadership is that leaders always work for their people.[169,170] The following sections summarize the key focus areas associated with a leader's top priority: people.

Safety and security. Ensuring the safety and security of team members is a top priority. Maintaining a safe operating environment is a shared responsibility between leaders and team members; however, leaders are ultimately accountable for creating and sustaining a workplace where team members feel secure from both physical and psychological harm. Leaders are responsible for developing, maintaining, reinforcing, and promoting safety programs and practices that generate awareness and encourage proactive safety measures throughout the organization. Leaders must establish a work environment where team members are willing to identify unsafe operating practices, harassment, or discrimination without fear of reprisal.

Engagement and involvement. A leader's ongoing engagement, involvement, support, and interaction with team members, as well as internal and external stakeholders above, below, and laterally across an organization, is crucial for sustained leadership excellence. Leadership engagement and involvement occur through group discussions and one-on-one interactions. The benefits of leadership engagement and involvement are multifold. They include situational leadership awareness around opportunities, risks, challenges, successes, failures, and team-member contributions to the mission. Leadership engagement and involvement enable leaders to harness team members' ideas and solutions while also understanding their concerns, needs, and challenges. Engagement and involvement ensure that team members are informed about changes to the team's mission or scope of work. Engaged and involved leaders view their team members' challenges as their challenges; they provide help when needed; they see and are seen; they are available, accessible, and approachable. Engaged leaders cultivate a work environment that promotes team-member involvement in problem-solving and encourages ongoing product, service, and process improvements that tap into team members' talents and leadership capabilities.

> *Engaged and involved leaders view their team members' challenges as their challenges; they provide help when needed; they see and are seen; they are available, accessible, and approachable.*

Culture. A team's culture reflects who they are, their values, how they interact with each other, and how they engage with others both inside and outside the organization. Shared values, norms, behaviors, and beliefs shape a team's culture. A positive culture fosters shared responsibility, individual accountability, camaraderie, and ethical decision-making. Such a culture not only drives team performance but also communicates who we are is why we succeed.

A team's reputation is a direct reflection of its culture. For example, a team might be known for high performance, reliability, cooperation, cohesion, loyalty, professionalism, or high morale. Alternatively, it could have a reputation for poor performance, unreliability, lack of cooperation, unprofessionalism, low commitment, or dissatisfaction.

Sustained leadership excellence requires leaders to cultivate a work environment where integrity, respect, human dignity, ethical behavior, teamwork, performance, and job satisfaction are valued and expected. It is characterized by a work culture that encourages open and honest communication, where team members appreciate and understand the importance of adhering to the organization's expected standards of conduct and ethical behaviors. Effective leaders foster open communication and prompt action when safety practices, work policies, procedures, ethical standards, or legal requirements are compromised.

A team's culture is reflected in its self-identity. It reveals how team members feel about being part of the group and how proud and confident they feel about their membership in the group. A company, organization, division, department, or work unit with a positive self-concept is one in which people feel great about themselves, their fellow team members, their team's mission, and the quality of their products and services. With a positive self-concept, team members are productive, resilient, confident, and satisfied. Leadership consultant and best-selling author Brian Tracy explains that a team's self-identity comprises three basic ingredients: self-ideal, self-image, and self-esteem.

Self-ideal. The first ingredient is the self-ideal. "The self-ideal is a combination of the vision, values, ethics and mission of the organization. Wherever these are clear, positive, and committed to by top leadership, the people in the organization are happier, more positive and more confident about themselves and where they're going."[171]

Self-image. The second ingredient of a team's self-concept is its collective self-image. This is how leaders and team members see themselves and think about themselves. How well a team thinks they are doing their jobs and performing their jobs determines this self-image. Leadership coach Lolly Daskal emphasizes that it is especially affected by the quality of a team's products and services and how leaders and team members believe they are perceived both inside and outside the organization.[172]

Self-esteem. The third ingredient of a team's self-concept, self-esteem, is the sum of the ideals of an organization, the organization's current performance, and how well team members feel their superiors and coworkers are treating them. Leaders who regularly encourage, support, and praise team members for exceptional work help to build their self-esteem. High self-esteem is revealed in optimism, energy, creativity, cooperation, and commitment. It is the hardest ingredient of all to build and maintain, but people who like and respect themselves as part of a first-class team become a powerful force.[173]

Communication. Communication can be considered the lifeblood of an organization. As a focus area, verbal, nonverbal, and written communication are important leadership competencies. Leaders must communicate clearly, concisely, and coherently with team members, colleagues, junior and senior leaders, clients, customers, business partners, suppliers, and the full array of organizational stakeholders associated with their team's mission.

A crucial component of communication is listening. Sustained excellence in leadership requires active and engaged listening, responding both verbally and nonverbally, and providing interactive feedback that includes questions, answers, paraphrasing, and sometimes ideas or recommendations. Effective listening conveys to the sender that their message has been heard and understood. Recommending solutions to problems may be necessary at times, but "knowing when someone is seeking a solution versus wanting just to talk it out is important," says Dave Zimmer, strategic advisor for change management and business leadership. "In those situations, it is better to withhold advice and let the team member determine a solution. It builds self-confidence and esteem."[174]

One of the most consistent ways for leaders to motivate, influence, and inspire team members is to communicate regularly during team meetings and one-on-one discussions. Leaders should provide feedback on performance and clarify expectations regarding goals, objectives, priorities, and strategy. They should also encourage questions and promote two-way dialogue during these discussions.

Storytelling. Storytelling is a powerful tool for leaders to engage, connect, inspire, and motivate their teams. Well-crafted stories forge emotional bonds, fostering trust and rapport. Unlike facts and figures, stories are memorable and resonate deeply. Narratives of success, failure, resilience, and overcoming challenges help leaders provide vision and instill purpose. Personal stories, particularly those that reveal a leader's own experiences and vulnerabilities, build credibility and authenticity, amplifying their positive influence and impact.

In one case, for instance, a senior leader faced a tough decision—her team had missed a critical deadline, and morale was low. She could have pointed fingers, but instead, she shared a story from her own experience. She told her team about a time early in her career when she failed to meet a major goal and how she learned from it. That failure, she explained, taught her the importance of resilience, teamwork, and accountability. By sharing her vulnerability, the team felt empowered to learn from their setback rather than dwell on it. The next time they faced a challenge, they tackled it together with renewed commitment and trust. That story transformed the team's perspective—and their future performance.

Organizing. Leaders are responsible for structuring their team's roles, functions, and capabilities to accomplish the mission safely and successfully. Effective leaders ensure team members are properly trained, qualified, and aligned with mission requirements. A well-organized team facilitates efficient communication internally and externally across all levels of the organization to meet the needs of customers and partners. Typically represented in an organization chart, team structure should clearly define roles and illustrate both direct and indirect relationships.

Organizational structures are dynamic. Changes may emerge from shifts in mission, scope of work, organizational lifecycle, or evolving customer needs. Leaders must regularly assess the impact of internal and external factors affecting their team's composition and update their organizational charts accordingly.

Hiring and staffing. Leaders are responsible for hiring and onboarding the right talent to meet mission requirements. Emphasizing the importance of these decisions, Steve Jobs, co-founder, chief executive, and chairman of Apple, once said recruiting was the most important part of his job.[175] Hiring decisions carry significant consequences—both positive and negative—for team performance, making them a critical leadership responsibility.

Effective hiring requires leaders to consider multiple factors, including a candidate's experience, education, knowledge, skills, abilities, diversity, and interpersonal communication. To build a high-performing, diverse team, leaders must take an active role in defining roles, screening applicants, conducting interviews, selecting candidates, and onboarding new team members. This process may include contacting references to gain insight into a candidate's work history, qualifications, performance, potential, and ability to collaborate effectively.

Learning, training, and development. A team's mission determines the talent, skills, and capabilities required for success. Effective leaders seek out the right talent, then hire, onboard, align, leverage, and continuously develop team members to ensure excellence in delivering products and services to both internal and external customers and stakeholders.

Newly hired team members must be trained in organizational policies, procedures, processes, safety protocols, and ethical standards. In addition, leaders must provide ongoing learning and development opportunities to help team members maintain current skills, enhance performance, and acquire new capabilities essential to performing their roles safely and effectively.

On-the-job learning. Effective leaders leverage advancements in learning technologies and instructional strategies to enhance training. Technology continues to shift the learning paradigm from traditional classroom and instructor-led sessions to real-time, on-the-job learning.

Computer-based modules, virtual reality platforms, and artificial intelligence tools now offer on-demand learning at the point of need—whether at a workstation, on the shop floor, in the office, or out in the field.

Talent development. To sustain an organization's mission capability, effective leaders develop long-range talent development and succession plans aligned with their organization's mission. These plans focus on forecasting future needs, attracting and hiring top talent, developing and retaining high-performing team members, and preparing to backfill critical roles, ensuring the organization remains mission-ready.

Equipment and resources. In line with a leader's priority on people, equipping team members with the right tools, materials, supplies, budgets, and resources is essential to executing the mission safely, efficiently, and effectively. These resources include workspaces, safety equipment, office supplies, job-specific materials, computers, communication tools, and other information management systems. Leaders must also establish dependable supply and resupply systems to ensure resources are available when and where they are needed. Ongoing planning and forecasting help prevent disruptions in logistical supply chains, keeping product and service schedules on track.

Compensation and benefits. An organization's compensation and benefits package is shaped by its size, type, and applicable legal or government regulations. In addition to salary, common benefits include health and life insurance, paid time off, wellness days, retirement savings plans, and, in some cases, pensions. To attract and retain top talent, compensation and benefits must be equitable and competitively aligned with market standards and regional cost-of-living considerations. Competitive programs offer opportunities for salary increases, incentives, and promotions. For long-term financial sustainability, the overall value of compensation and benefits must remain aligned with the organization's budget.

Performance management. Leaders are responsible and accountable for the performance, productivity, training, and development of team members. Performance management systems, tools, and processes help leaders guide, develop, and evaluate team member contributions through a structured annual performance cycle. These systems foster communication and engagement by supporting a collaborative process that identifies, aligns, and documents individual goals, objectives, priorities, and values.

Performance management also facilitates ongoing professional development discussions, giving leaders a framework to coach, mentor, and support team members in achieving their development goals and career aspirations.

The process begins at the start of each performance cycle. Leaders meet individually with team members to establish clear expectations aligned with organizational goals, objectives, and strategy. These expectations should be specific, measurable, achievable, relevant, and time-bound—commonly known as SMART goals.

Performance feedback. According to Development Dimensions International *Global Leadership Forecast* 2025, a survey of 10,796 leaders from 2,014 organizations worldwide found that team members who receive feedback from their supervisor are nine times more likely to trust their leader.[176]

The annual performance management process includes periodic verbal and written feedback during structured review sessions. Ideally, these reviews incorporate input from team members, clients, customers, partners, and other stakeholders. While virtual reviews are acceptable, in-person meetings are generally more effective for building rapport and ensuring clarity.

Leaders should not wait until the end of the performance cycle to provide feedback. At a minimum, feedback should be delivered at three key points: the beginning of the cycle to establish goals, priorities, and expectations; the midpoint to assess progress; and at the end of the cycle to evaluate performance, recognize accomplishments, and identify areas for improvement. When performance is off track, timely and specific feedback is critical for course correction and growth.

Differentiating performance between team members in the same role and level helps leaders clarify expectations. Jack Welch, former Chairman and Chief Executive Officer of General Electric between 1981 and 2001, whose leadership is credited with increasing GE's value by 4,000%, stresses the importance of differentiating performance among team members. He argues that team members' contributions, like investments, are not equal, and leaders who lack the courage to differentiate performance are ineffective. "Leaders who don't differentiate usually do the most damage when it comes to people. Unwilling to deliver candid, rigorous performance reviews, they give every employee the same kind of bland, mushy, 'nice job' sign-off. And when rewards are doled out, they give star performers not much more than the laggards. Now, you can call this 'egalitarian' approach kind or fair—and these lousy leaders usually do—but it's really just weakness. And when it comes to building a thriving enterprise where people have an opportunity to grow and succeed, weakness just doesn't cut it, asserts Welch."[177]

Awards and recognition. Awards and recognition programs are vital components of performance management. The human need for appreciation—and its positive impact on motivation and performance—are well documented, from Maslow's Hierarchy of Needs to Saks' Employee Engagement Theory.[178] Timely recognition instills pride in job performance and demonstrates a leader's genuine appreciation for individual and team contributions. Publicly acknowledging outstanding achievements serves as a powerful motivator, inspiring both individuals and teams to excel in their roles.

Corrective action. Organizations must establish, communicate, and publish clear policies, procedures, and ethical guidelines to ensure team members understand expected behaviors and the consequences of violations. Effective leaders are responsible for administering progressive corrective actions, including potential dismissal, when breaches occur.

Addressing and correcting poor behavior or misconduct is a critical leadership responsibility. The goal of corrective action is to improve performance and behavior through a system of progressively consequential measures aligned with the severity of the infraction. This tiered review process begins by addressing issues at the lowest level and escalates as necessary through the leadership chain.

To promote fairness and consistency, an organizational review board should oversee the most serious corrective actions. This board typically consists of experienced leaders, human resource professionals, and, when necessary, legal counsel. Additionally, organizations should provide an independent reporting channel outside the direct leadership chain, allowing team members to report abuse, harassment, retaliation, or unfair corrective actions without fear of reprisal.

Coaching. Coaching team members offers leaders a proactive way to reinforce positive behaviors beyond the formal performance management process. It also enables leaders to address and redirect negative behaviors before they escalate into major issues. Leaders often invest significant time resolving disagreements and conflicts among team members, colleagues, and sometimes customers. Such challenges typically stem from misunderstandings, personality differences, and other human factors. Effective conflict resolution requires a systematic coaching approach that identifies root causes, addresses concerns, and implements solutions. A conflict resolution framework is presented in Chapter Five.

Mentoring. Leaders mentor team members and others beyond their immediate team by providing professional development guidance and encouraging them to realize their full potential. Often, leaders recognize a team member's or protégé's potential before they do themselves. In such cases, leaders should challenge them with stretch assignments that build confidence and enhance skills.

Candid conversations about career aspirations, growth opportunities, and development goals inspire individuals to pursue advancement aligned with their career stage. Through mentoring, leaders cultivate talent, foster growth, and empower others to achieve long-term success.

Team-building events. Effective leaders recognize that strong teams don't just happen—they're intentionally developed. Team-building activities provide opportunities to cultivate trust, enhance communication, and foster a sense of belonging among team members. These shared experiences break down barriers, encourage collaboration, and help individuals appreciate one another's strengths in new ways. When people feel connected and valued, they become more engaged, motivated, and aligned with the team's mission, goals, and shared vision.

Team-building events also allow leaders to lead by example. Whether through problem-solving exercises, service projects, or informal group challenges, leaders demonstrate key attributes such as adaptability, empathy, and accountability. These moments outside routine operations show a leader's genuine investment in people, not just performance. As trust deepens and camaraderie grows, the team becomes more resilient and better equipped to navigate complex challenges together—hallmarks of sustained leadership excellence.

Leading up. An important focus area for leaders is their engagement and interaction with the leader they report to. *Leading up* refers to a leader's responsibility to support and align their priorities with those of their supervisor, while also understanding their supervisor's leadership style and performance expectations. By aligning leadership priorities, leaders can leverage talent across the organization, creating a force multiplier that drives the organization toward its broader goals and objectives.

Leading across. In addition to leading up, leading across is essential for a leader's sustained success. Building strong partnerships with peer leaders and colleagues fosters positive working relationships that enable leaders and their teams to collaborate effectively and support one another in achieving their respective team goals.

Leading a leadership team. Leading other leaders involves guiding individuals who are capable, self-reliant, and responsible for leading their own teams. The Unifying Forces of the Leadership Process, introduced in Part II, provide an integrated framework for aligning the leadership team's efforts with the organization's mission, vision, values, goals, objectives, priorities, and strategies. This strategic alignment fosters cohesion, enabling leaders to collaborate effectively and drive collective success.

The focus areas discussed above center on a leader's highest priority: people. By maintaining situational awareness in these areas, alongside the mission-focused considerations addressed in the following sections, leaders can make informed decisions, communicate with clarity, and take purposeful actions that motivate, influence, and inspire their teams to excel over the long term.

Mission Focus Areas

> People first, mission always.
> — Reuben D. Jones, Major General, U.S. Army[179]

Leaders and their teams are responsible for accomplishing a mission, one of two overarching leadership priorities. A team's mission is driven by the organization's goals, objectives, priorities, strategies, and long-term vision. The following sections summarize key focus areas aligned with this priority.

Mission execution. A leader's focus on mission execution ensures the team achieves the right outcomes—safely, efficiently, and effectively—over the long term. Mission success depends on a clear understanding of the mission and well-defined criteria for success. By maintaining this focus, leaders align their team's time, energy, efforts, and resources toward mission accomplishment.

Clients, customers, partners, and stakeholders. Every organization serves both internal and external customers, as well as partners and stakeholders who are invested in the success of its mission. Leaders and their teams must identify and understand the individuals and groups their mission supports—and how the organization's products and services meet their needs. Adopting a customer-focused mindset, both internally and externally, fosters initiative, collaboration, and innovation in enhancing products and services.

Products and services. Regardless of a team's mission, leaders must first understand how their products and services fulfill the needs of both internal and external customers. They should continually seek improvements in products, services, and processes. This customer-focused approach not only enhances the team's value but also advances their customers' missions. By emphasizing quality, speed, reliability, and affordability, teams ensure they deliver maximum value to their customers.

Communication. An organization's mission depends on effective communication—verbal, nonverbal, visual, and written—flowing up, down, and across the organization, both internally and externally. As the symbolic lifeblood of organizational health, timely and purposeful communication keeps leaders, team members, partners, and stakeholders informed and situationally aware. Group and individual meetings, reports, metrics, and data serve as critical channels for sharing mission-critical information, enhancing awareness and insight, and supporting data-driven decision-making.

Meetings. Recurring and ad hoc meetings—in person, online, or via teleconference—offer leaders opportunities to collaborate and engage with team members, partners, and stakeholders involved in the mission. When well-organized and purpose-driven, meetings inform decisions and actions, align teams on goals, objectives, priorities, and strategies, and enhance situational awareness across programs, operations, budgets, projects, training, and staffing.

They also provide a platform to generate, coordinate, adjust, track, and close action items while assessing key performance indicators, metrics, and other success measures. In addition, meetings help resolve misunderstandings and reinforce clarity and cohesion.

In support of change management, meetings enable discussion of planned changes to the mission, scope, or staffing and offer a forum to address concerns and clarify expectations. They also strengthen team culture and provide opportunities to recognize exceptional performance in a group setting.

Virtual meetings. Digital and telecommunication platforms provide efficient, cost-effective solutions for meetings, conferences, and workshops with geographically dispersed team members, partners, customers, and stakeholders, as well as those working remotely or facing travel budget constraints. By eliminating expenses related to transportation, lodging, meals, and other travel costs, virtual meetings significantly reduce overall expenditures.

Despite their efficiencies and cost savings, however, participants may miss important nonverbal cues due to technological limitations such as camera angles, screen resolution, and lens apertures. Research suggests that more than half of communication is nonverbal, conveyed through facial expressions, gestures, and body language. According to Albert Mehrabian, a pioneer in body language research, face-to-face communication consists of 55% nonverbal cues, 38% vocal elements, and only 7% verbal content.[180]

Beyond the challenge of interpreting nonverbal communication, virtual meetings can also limit opportunities to build interpersonal relationships—connections that often develop more naturally through in-person interactions.

Reports. The primary purpose of reports is to provide leaders and team members with timely information and intelligence that supports decision-making, communication, and action. Reports can take many forms, including documents, memorandums, presentations, letters, data visualizations, performance metrics, and analytics. To ensure consistency and accountability, leaders and teams should establish a regular cadence for recurring reports. Reports containing sensitive, confidential, or classified information must be properly safeguarded to prevent compromise of the mission. The frequency and depth of reporting should reflect the significance of the information to the team's goals, objectives, priorities, and strategic direction.

Organizational planning. Organizational planning typically follows a cascading structure composed of three tiers: strategic, operational, and tactical.

Strategic planning. Strategic planning is a broad, high-level planning process. It is designed to steer a team toward achieving its goals over the long term, while pursuing a vision of its future. It synchronizes, unifies, and aligns teams and their missions across all levels of the organization—from top to bottom. Much like steering a large cruise ship, changing strategic direction takes time; as such, the planning horizon for most strategic plans extends five years or more.

For example, the United States government outlines its national security strategy through various strategic planning documents. These documents serve to guide and inform senior-level decisions across federal departments and agencies, influencing budgets, appropriations, foreign policy, diplomacy, national security, and military operations.

Operational planning. Operational plans are developed by leaders at all levels to define the actions needed to achieve their team's goals, objectives, priorities, and strategies aligned with the broader strategic plan. These plans identify the equipment, tools, systems, materials, supplies, personnel, and other resources required to execute the mission. The typical time horizon for operational planning spans one to five years, with adjustments made as needed to address evolving demands.

In the United States military, for example, a regional combat campaign plan is supported by operational plans—known as O Plans—developed by each branch of service supporting the campaign. An Air Force O Plan, for instance, provides aerospace combat units with guidance outlining aerospace goals and objectives in support of the broader campaign plan. These plans are derived from the geographic combatant commander's overarching military objectives, as directed by the President of the United States.

Exercises. A leader's ability to galvanize and sustain a team's performance when responding to unplanned or unexpected events is often a defining test of leadership effectiveness. To enhance readiness for both planned and unplanned missions, many organizations conduct exercises or rehearsals—known as war gaming in the military—to practice their response strategies.

For example, industrial production sites, police departments, fire units, hospitals, universities, military units, and government agencies conduct exercises to prepare for emergencies and contingencies. These rehearsals simulate scenarios, refine actions, and provide learning experiences that improve decision-making, communication, and execution during real-world events, especially under time constraints.

In the military, planners and leaders develop crisis action plans to address a range of combat and humanitarian relief scenarios.

These pre-established plans can be quickly activated, serving as ready operational frameworks for commanders to execute when needed.

Tactical planning. Tactical plans are unit-level plans designed to support the goals, objectives, priorities, and strategies outlined in operational and strategic plans. These plans focus on short-term mission requirements, typically covering daily, weekly, monthly, and annual objectives.

Tactical planning is focused on mission execution. At this level, leaders must address critical workforce elements such as safety, production, work schedules, equipment, materials, supplies, training, staffing, inventory, budgets, travel needs, work processes, procedures, and stakeholder requirements, including those of customers and partners.

Because tactical plans directly impact an organization's cost, schedule, and performance, their short-term nature makes them subject to frequent adjustments. Successful execution depends on adequate funding to support training, equipment, staffing, and other mission-critical resources.

Building on the operational air campaign plan (O Plan) example, an Aerospace Tasking Order (ATO) is used to orchestrate daily aerospace missions that support the O Plan. Combat crews rely on ATO instructions to execute their assigned tactical air missions. These instructions detail critical elements such as aircraft call signs, take-off times, targets, airdrop locations, surveillance and reconnaissance areas, aerial refueling rendezvous points, and landing times. Each day, hundreds—often thousands—of sorties are planned, coordinated, and executed according to instructions in a classified ATO. By scheduling and directing aerospace missions, the ATO ensures that mission objectives are achieved safely and effectively.

Financial planning and budgeting. All organizations require funding to operate effectively. A key focus area is prioritizing expenditures, capital investments, staffing, and other resource requirements that support the mission. Leaders and their teams must remain actively engaged with partners, clients, customers, and stakeholders to plan, forecast, and adjust short-, mid-, and long-term fiscal needs.

Financial resources are managed through a deliberate, recurring, and collaborative budget review process involving leaders, team members, and finance partners. This systematic approach ensures resources are aligned with mission goals, objectives, and priorities.

Budgets are informed by long-range business plans and support financial decisions that reflect strategic direction. Effective financial management demands continuous planning, forecasting, and adjustment in response to evolving mission requirements—shaped by economic, political, global, customer, and market conditions.

Controlling. Sustained leadership effectiveness depends on control measures that equip leaders and team members with accurate data and actionable insights to support informed decision-making. These measures enhance situational awareness and help guide leadership decisions, communication, and actions.

Effective control involves structured processes for collecting and analyzing data related to key performance indicators (KPIs) across critical mission areas. These may include product and service safety, quality, value, delivery speed, defect rates, customer satisfaction, scheduling, hiring, training, employee development and retention, as well as financial metrics such as sales, costs, revenue, debt, and cash flow.

Together, these control measures offer a comprehensive view of cost, schedule, and performance, empowering leaders to achieve mission objectives safely and effectively over the long term.

Analyzing, assessing, and adjusting. Quantitative and qualitative metrics, key performance indicators (KPIs), and data analytics enable leaders and teams to analyze performance, assess progress, and adjust control measures as needed. Timely access to accurate and reliable data is essential for making informed decisions that drive mission success and continuous improvement.

Innovating. Effective leaders foster a work environment that promotes innovation by giving team members the time, space, and resources to think creatively and pursue new ideas. By emphasizing innovation, leaders drive improvements in the quality, performance, and value of products and services.

These improvements often emerge from innovations in processes, procedures, and policies designed to enhance safety, efficiency, and effectiveness. Leaders and their teams generate novel approaches through brainstorming and "lateral thinking," a concept introduced by Edward de Bono to describe intentionally shifting perspectives and thinking *outside the box*.[181]

Lateral thinking is fueled by active engagement, continuous learning, benchmarking, and listening to clients, customers, suppliers, partners, competitors, and other key stakeholders.

Community outreach. A leader's focus on community outreach reinforces the organization's reputation for social responsibility and should be aligned with the team's goals, objectives, and priorities. Research shows that a team's involvement in community service has a positive impact on both internal and external stakeholders. For example, a study by Cone Communications and Echo Research found that 82% of U.S. consumers consider a company's social responsibility when deciding what to buy and where to shop.[182]

Beyond its external benefits, community outreach also fosters internal team development. Participating in service projects strengthens team cohesion, enhances morale, and reinforces a shared sense of purpose—critical elements of sustained leadership and organizational excellence.

Operating Rhythm

Situational awareness regarding a team's mission is sustained through periodic reviews of actions, events, metrics, processes, changes, solutions, and progress across leadership focus areas aligned with people and mission priorities. A consistent review schedule enables leaders and teams to anticipate, plan for, and adapt to evolving needs. Establishing an organizational operating rhythm—a deliberate cycle of meetings, reviews, deadlines, and events that support informed decision-making—ensures timely adjustments to practices that drive long-term mission success.

In the profession of arms, a *battle rhythm* serves a similar function by guiding the persistent and effective prosecution of military operations. It enables combatant commanders to stay ahead of an adversary's decisions and actions. Likewise, organizational leaders can implement an operating rhythm to maintain alignment, drive performance, and ensure the successful execution of their team's mission.

Key components of an operating rhythm. An operating rhythm consists of scheduled meetings, communications, activities, and events involving both internal and external stakeholders, such as clients, customers, team members, and strategic partners. These schedules highlight recurring events on a weekly, monthly, quarterly, semiannual, and annual basis. Common elements include team and leadership meetings, budget and resource reviews, business updates and briefings, metrics and data analytics discussions, customer and partner engagements, and performance management conversations.

In addition to routine events, operating rhythms often incorporate conferences, conventions, professional development opportunities, and site visits with teams and leaders.

By maintaining a cadence, leaders gain situational awareness across the organization and with key stakeholders.

Wellness. An effective operating rhythm schedule should also prioritize wellness and work-life balance activities for leaders and their team members. Physical and mental well-being form the foundation of sustained leadership effectiveness and team performance. Leaders and team members who actively maintain their wellness are better prepared to manage stress, make sound decisions, and solve problems.

Incorporating regular exercise, sufficient rest, and stress-management practices into an operating rhythm helps sustain energy, focus, and emotional resilience. This foundation enables leaders and teams to perform at their best, whether facing high-pressure situations or managing routine daily responsibilities.

Time off. Taking time off during holidays and vacations is essential for restoring physical, mental, and emotional health. These breaks offer leaders and team members an opportunity to recharge, resulting in improved focus, creativity, and productivity. The benefits extend beyond individuals to positively impact families and the organization as a whole.

Role modeling. Leaders who prioritize wellness and work-life balance set an example for their teams. By demonstrating a commitment to physical and mental health, they inspire team members to do the same, fostering a healthier and more supportive work culture. This balance reduces burnout, boosts job satisfaction, and enhances long-term productivity. When team members see their leaders valuing both their work and personal life, they are more likely to stay engaged and perform at their best.

Operating rhythm framework. A team's operating rhythm should specify the frequency of meetings, activities, and events. The scope and scale of an operating rhythm varies and is based on the team's size, organizational level, and mission. Table 4.2 illustrates a comprehensive operating rhythm framework, which can be distilled into a concise one-page summary, as shown in in Table 4.3.

Table 4.2

Operating Rhythm Framework

Frequency	Meeting, Activity, or Event
Daily	➤ Stakeholder meetings: A variety of scheduled meetings for the current workday, including meetings with partners, clients, customers, leadership, teams, and other stakeholders. Meetings focus on information sharing, listening, providing input and feedback, collaboration, decision-making, and mission-related action items. ➤ Review email, voice mail, and direct messages: Scheduled blocks of 30 minutes to 1 hour at the start, middle, and end of work periods to review, send, and respond to messages. ➤ Coach, mentor, and recognize team members for their contributions in person, by phone, virtually, or by email.
Weekly	➤ Leadership team meetings: Scheduled meetings with leadership team members framed around a planned agenda. ➤ Team meetings: Scheduled meetings framed around a planned agenda. ➤ Special attention meetings: Nonrecurring meetings scheduled with stakeholders to address emerging mission needs.

Weekly	➢ Leadership walks, also known as *leadership by walking around*: In-person visits with team members—either at their work areas or virtually when geographically separated. Direct engagement and involvement to share information, listen to ideas and concerns, and seek input and feedback. ➢ Mission review meetings: Scheduled meetings with leadership team members, subject-matter experts, partners, and other stakeholders to review mission performance, safety, metrics, key performance indicators, and other measures of performance. ➢ Tag-up meetings: Scheduled one-on-one meetings with individual team members in person, virtually, or by phone to discuss mission needs and provide support on high-priority projects. ➢ Reports: Collect, review, consolidate, share, and up-channel weekly reports. ➢ Wellness and health-related activities.
Monthly	➢ Budget reviews: Scheduled meetings with leadership team members to review and manage financial performance, including sales, revenues, costs, product and service delivery schedules, and other mission-related funding metrics, as applicable. ➢ Talent management review meetings: For large teams, discussions with team leaders regarding staffing, hiring, diversity, education, training, professional development, assignments, promotions,

Monthly	leaves of absence, retention, and team member retirements. ➢ Awards and recognition: Review team accomplishments and solicit nominations to recognize and reward team members for exceptional performance.
Quarterly	➢ All-Team meetings: Scheduled meetings with team leaders and team members framed around a planned agenda. Meeting objectives include reviewing metrics related to operating performance, safety, budgets, financials, key performance indicators, and other key measures of performance. These meetings also seek feedback and input from team members to understand their concerns and recommendations for improving mission performance and recognizing exceptional performers. ➢ Performance management and professional development discussions: Candid, face-to-face conversations (in-person or virtually) with direct report team members to discuss performance and professional development. ➢ Off-site team visits, if applicable: Travel and visit teams, partners, and customers at regional locations. ➢ Complete recurring safety and regulatory compliance training requirements.
Semi-annually	➢ Leadership team conference: Depending on team size and scope of mission, organize and host a one-day or multi-

Semi-annually	day, face-to-face, or virtual leadership team conference framed around a planned agenda that includes guest speakers, team-building activities, and professional development events. Conferences provide leaders with the opportunity to review people and mission focus areas, adjust plans if necessary, boost morale, recognize exceptional performers, and strengthen team cohesion.
Annually	➤ Request performance self-assessment inputs from your direct reports to inform annual performance evaluations and prepare for end-of-year performance management discussions. ➤ End-of-year performance management and professional development meetings with your direct report team members: Scheduled one-on-one candid conversations to share and discuss performance and professional development accomplishments. ➤ Provide self-assessment feedback to the leader you report to—in preparation for your annual performance review. ➤ Annual performance management and professional development all-team meeting: A scheduled team meeting held before the next annual reporting period begins to review and discuss organizational goals, priorities, strategy, and expectations for the upcoming year.

Annually	The aim is to set expectations and align team members' individual performance goals and priorities with those of the organization.
	➤ Annual performance management and professional development meetings with direct reports: Scheduled one-on-one meetings at the beginning of the new annual reporting period to review, discuss, and clarify expectations regarding individual performance goals, priorities, and professional development plans for the new reporting period.
	➤ Compensation review meetings with direct reports: Scheduled one-on-one meetings to review compensation and benefits and share any available performance-based awards.
	➤ External conventions, conferences, seminars, and learning and development opportunities.
	➤ Awards and recognition: Review team accomplishments and solicit nominations from team leaders for annual awards and recognition programs.
	➤ Wellness vacations, holidays, time away from work, and other work-life balance activities.
	➤ Support community outreach programs and voluntary service projects.

Table 4.3

Example Operating Rhythm Chart

Example of Team Operating Rhythm

Daily/Weekly	Monthly	Quarterly	Semi-annually	Annually	As Required
• Scheduled meetings • Review action items • Leadership walkarounds • People to support • Reports and metrics • Special attention meetings • Wellness and health-related work-life balance	• 1st Friday: budget review • 2nd Friday: talent management review • 3rd Friday: staffing and resources deep dive • 4th Friday: awards and recognition • Reports and metrics	• All-team meeting • Performance management and professional development discussions • Off-site team visits • Recurring safety, policy, and regulatory compliance training • Review and update team engagement survey action plans • Reports and metrics	• Leadership team conference • Review team members' career development plans • Collaborate with the supervisory chain on talent management opportunities for team members	• End-of-year performance management closeout discussions with team members • Performance assessment review meetings with the supervisory chain • Compensation, benefits, and salary review discussions with team members • Annual planning meeting with the supervisory leadership team • Learning, training, and development conferences	• Awards and recognition • Hiring • Promotions • Leadership development opportunities • Wellness time off • Vacation • Holidays

The Way Ahead

Part I of this book explored the evolution of leadership theory and key leadership themes. It reviewed literature on leadership capabilities and styles and examined leadership focus areas aligned with people and mission priorities—highlighting the diverse skills, capabilities, and styles employed by effective leaders.

Part II introduces the Model for Sustained Leadership Excellence, a leadership development framework built upon the literature and best practices presented in Part I. Designed for both current and aspiring leaders across all professions, the model aims to support the development and sustainment of long-term leadership success. It offers leadership practitioners and scholars a comprehensive and integrated perspective on leadership, emphasizing that sustained excellence is driven by core values and enabling attributes that shape a leader's decisions, communication, and actions—the instruments of leadership.

Part II: A Framework for Sustained Leadership Success

> To lead people, walk beside them; as for the best leaders, the people do not notice their existence. The next best, the people honor and praise. The next, the people fear; and the next, the people hate; when the best leader's work is done the people say, 'We did it ourselves!'
> — Lao Tzu[183]

Sustained leadership excellence requires time, energy, effort, attention, and a commitment to ongoing improvement and development. As discussed in Part I, leadership demands a broad range of physical, cognitive, behavioral, and social skills—capabilities developed and enhanced through observation, study, practice, and experience. What is sustained leadership excellence? It is a leader's ability to safely and effectively achieve the correct mission results with their team over the long term. Leaders accomplish this through the instruments of leadership, their decisions, communication, and actions.

Building on this thesis, along with the literature and leadership practices explored in Part I, Part II introduces the Model for Sustained Leadership Excellence. Designed to develop and strengthen the leadership capabilities required at increasing levels of responsibility, the model empowers leaders to achieve and sustain long-term effectiveness.

The comprehensive and integrated model is constructed around three dimensions of leadership—core values, enabling attributes, and the leadership process—as illustrated in Figure II.1.

Sustained Leadership Excellence

A leader's ability to safely and effectively achieve the correct mission results with their team over the long term.

Figure II.2 depicts the model's foundation, pillars, and gabled capstone. The foundation depicts the three core values of leadership: character shaped by integrity, a service mindset, and the continuous pursuit of excellence. Three pillars symbolize the model's enabling attributes of leadership: trust, concern, and the will to lead. The gabled capstone at the top of the model illustrates the inputs, outputs, and outcomes of an interactive leadership process.

The instruments of leadership serve as inputs to this process. These inputs generate motivation, influence, and inspiration—the outputs of the process. These outputs, in turn, produce the desired outcomes: achieving the correct mission results with team members.

The leadership process is guided by a set of unifying forces that help leaders and their teams stay aligned while pursuing mission goals and objectives. The chapters ahead present an integrated framework designed to help current and aspiring leaders develop, empower, and sustain leadership success over the long term.

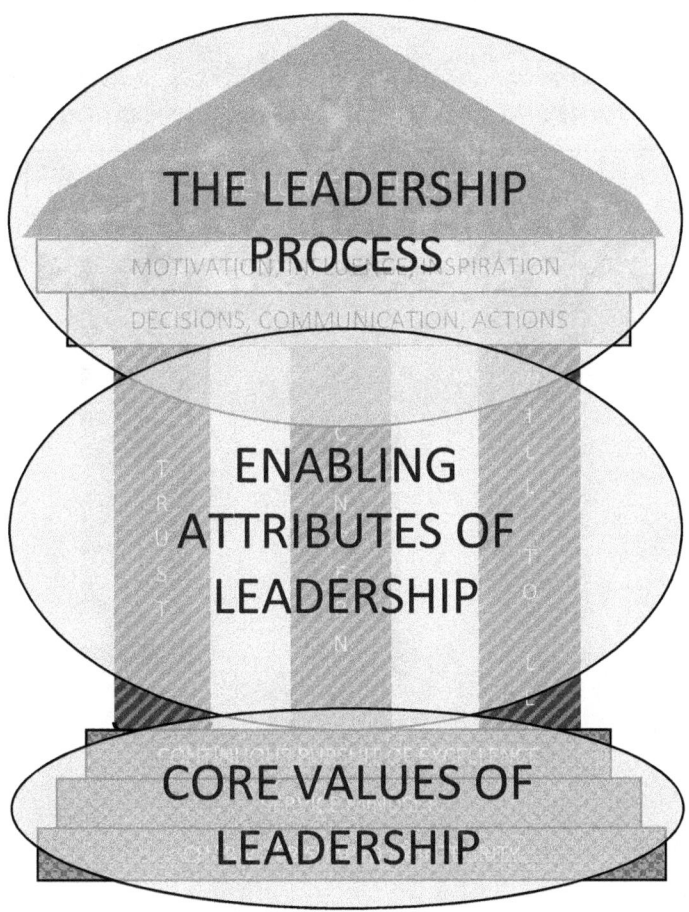

Figure II.1. Three Dimensions of the Model for Sustained Leadership Excellence

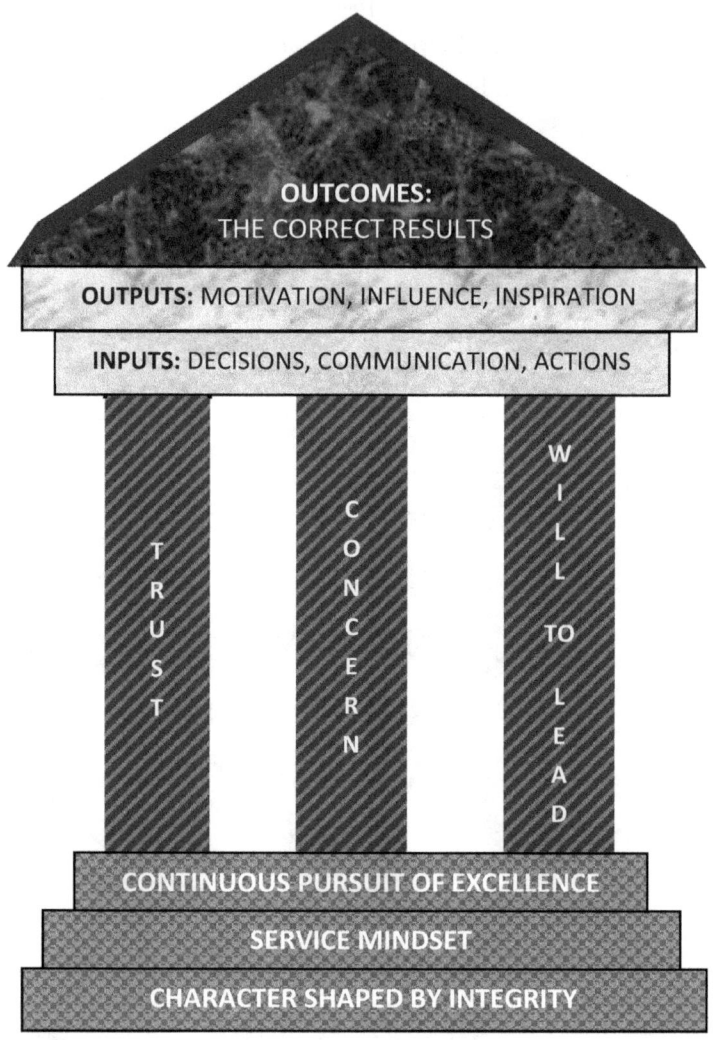

Figure II.2. Model for Sustained Leadership Excellence

The Leadership Process

> Effective leadership is not about making speeches or being liked; leadership is defined by results.
> — Peter F. Drucker[184]

In *Leadership: Theory and Practice*, Peter G. Northouse defines leadership as "a process whereby an individual influences a group of individuals to achieve a common goal."[185] Similarly, Gardner describes it as a process of persuasion or example by which an individual induces a group to pursue objectives held by the leader or shared with team members.[186] Examining leadership as a process is essential to understanding the pivotal impact a leader's decisions, communication, and actions have on motivating, influencing, and inspiring team members to consistently achieve the desired results . . . the hallmark of sustained leadership excellence.

In the Model for Sustained Leadership Excellence, the leadership process includes four key components: inputs, outputs, outcomes, and unifying forces. The following sections describe each component.

Inputs, outputs, outcomes, and unifying forces of the leadership process. As illustrated in Figure II.3, the leadership process revolves around a dynamic set of inputs, outputs, outcomes, and unifying forces. The inputs represent the instruments of leadership—decisions, communication, and actions. These instruments play a central role in motivating, influencing, and inspiring team members, which constitute the outputs of the process. When applied effectively, they yield the desired outcome of the process: achieving the intended mission results safely and effectively.

The unifying forces of the leadership process include a team's mission, vision, values, goals, objectives, priorities, and strategy. These forces align and galvanize a team's efforts toward sustained success. It is important to note that framing leadership as a process does not suggest a rigid sequence of steps. Rather, the relationship between these elements is interactive and fluid, reflecting the dynamic nature of leadership in action.

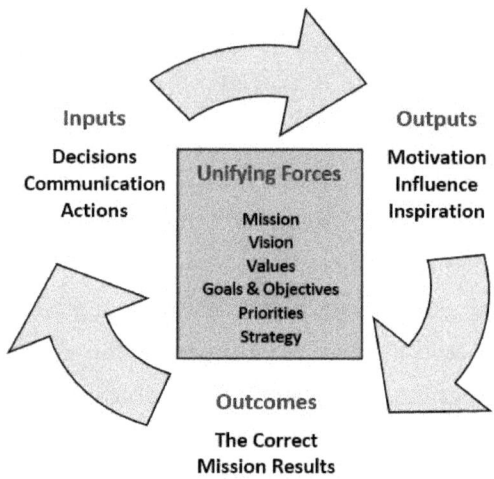

Figure II.3. The Leadership Process

Decisions, communications, and actions. The leadership process underscores the pivotal role of a leader's decisions, communication, and actions in motivating, influencing, and inspiring team members to consistently achieve desired mission results. This raises a critical question: How can leaders consistently make sound decisions, communicate effectively, and take actions that drive sustained success over the long term?

The Model for Sustained Leadership Excellence addresses this challenge by highlighting the essential role of core values and enabling attributes in shaping and informing these instruments while also fostering the development of leadership skills and capabilities.

Harnessing artificial intelligence. Artificial intelligence (AI) offers valuable insights that can enhance efficiency, productivity, quality, innovation, learning, and development—key drivers of a team's success. Leaders can harness AI to inform their decisions, communications, and actions in pursuit of their team's mission, vision, goals, objectives, priorities, and strategies.

A review of *Genesis: Artificial Intelligence, Hope, and the Human Spirit* by Kissinger, Mundie, and Schmidt provides valuable perspectives regarding AI's impact on leadership. The authors emphasize AI's immense processing power and speed in analyzing and integrating vast amounts of data: "AI . . . is able to process and generate representations of masses of information at a ferocious rate of speed. It assesses patterns across countless dimensions and fields simultaneously, creating unprecedented connectivity."[187]

Decision-making. AI enhances leadership decision-making by delivering data-driven insights that analyze vast datasets, identify trends, predict outcomes, and reveal hidden patterns. Its predictive analytics capabilities allow leaders and teams to simulate scenarios, assess risks, and weigh potential costs and benefits before making critical decisions. AI also streamlines the organization and retrieval of historical knowledge, turning lessons learned into accessible experiential intelligence. Ultimately, this increases decision-making confidence and effectiveness.

AI can also support ethical leadership by identifying and mitigating biases in decision-making, promoting fairness and integrity.

Communication. AI's large language model tools can assist leaders in tailoring communication for different audiences by analyzing tone, language, and context to ensure clarity. For multinational teams, AI eliminates language barriers, ensuring consistent and culturally appropriate communication across global teams. AI can also evaluate feedback from teams and customers to provide valuable insights into morale and satisfaction, enabling leaders to address concerns proactively.

By leveraging a team's diverse talents, ideas, and perspectives, AI can help leaders ensure that all voices, opinions, and ideas are heard and valued. Additionally, AI can assess potential personality conflicts or misunderstandings within teams through behavioral analysis, enabling proactive interventions to prevent conflicts that could negatively impact team performance.

Actions. AI can manage repetitive and administrative tasks, freeing up time for leaders to focus on team engagement, innovation, and strategy. AI systems can optimize schedules, resources, and projects to minimize cost, improve quality, and enhance overall mission performance. AI-based learning platforms can customize leadership and professional development programs by assessing areas needed for development and identifying leadership blind spots, fostering continuous performance improvements. Additionally, AI can enhance transparency and accountability by documenting decisions and actions.

AI Limitations. AI is not just a technological shift—it requires human-centered, empathetic, and trustworthy leadership to guide its implementation and build confidence in its use. According to Development Dimensions International (DDI) *Global Leadership Forecast* 2025, leaders who trust their senior leadership are 2.2 times more likely to feel excited about using AI at work.[188] The report concludes that "without this foundation of trust, organizations risk resistance to AI and a missed opportunity to maximize its impact."[189]

While AI can augment leadership decisions, communication, and actions, it cannot replace essential human qualities such as empathy, happiness, and moral judgment. As noted in DDI's report, "AI does not experience fear . . . nor does it experience shame."[190] Leaders must therefore critically evaluate AI outputs to balance data-driven insights with intuition and values. The core values in

The Model for Sustained Leadership Excellence—character shaped by integrity, a service mindset, and the continuous pursuit of excellence—serve as vital checks and balances, ensuring AI-informed decisions remain grounded in principled leadership.

Following the next section's discussion on the unifying forces of the leadership process, Chapters Five and Six explore how the model's enabling attributes and core values influence and shape leadership decisions, communication, and actions while also cultivating the leadership capabilities necessary for sustained leadership success.

Unifying forces of the leadership process

A leader's ability to consistently achieve the correct mission results with their team requires unity of effort. Vince Lombardi, the legendary championship-winning National Football League coach, described unity of effort as singleness of purpose. Lombardi believed that leaders achieved singleness of purpose with their team by:

- Embracing a set of organizational core values.
- Agreeing on a shared vision of the future.
- Defining and understanding their mission.
- Establishing short-, mid-, and long-term goals and objectives.
- Developing a strategy to achieve the right goals and objectives.[191]

As depicted in Figure II.3, the leadership process revolves around a set of unifying forces that synchronize and galvanize a team's efforts by aligning expected performance outcomes with the team's mission, vision, values, goals, objectives, priorities, and strategy. Similar to the principle of *unity of command* found in military and paramilitary operations, unity of effort emphasizes that a team's actions should be aligned, directed, and coordinated toward a common objective. Figure II.4 illustrates the Unifying Forces of the Leadership Process. The following sections examine each element.

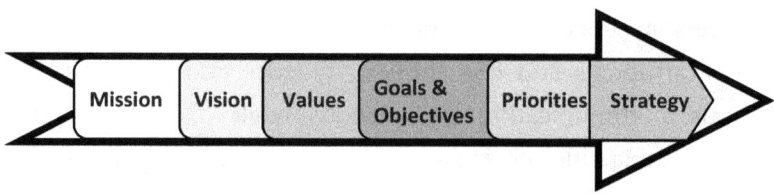

Figure II.4. Unifying Forces of the Leadership Process

Mission. Every organization and team has a mission—a clearly defined purpose that must be understood by team members, as well as internal and external customers and stakeholders. A team's mission is derived from these fundamental questions: What is our purpose? Why do we exist? The answers define and articulate the team's mission. For instance, the mission of the United States Air Force is to fly, fight, and win—providing warfighting commanders airpower anytime, anywhere.[192]

Vision. A leader's vision for their team and organization serves to communicate, inspire, and energize. It sets the direction for the team and its mission while also conveying the value the organization provides to its customers and stakeholders. Looking toward the future, a leader's vision addresses key questions, such as: What value do we offer our customers and stakeholders now and in the future? How do we foresee our mission evolving to meet their needs? How do we anticipate the scope of our mission changing?

A leader's vision clarifies the team's strategic direction and ensures alignment with customer and stakeholder expectations. This clarity is essential for inspiring long-term commitment from team members as they pursue challenging goals and objectives. A powerful organizational vision can transform work into a compelling profession, vocation, or higher calling. For example, the United States Air Force envisions itself as the world's greatest air force, powered by aerospace professionals and fueled by innovation.[193] Steve Jobs underscored the vital importance of vision to a team's success when he said, "That's what leadership is; what leadership is, is having a vision; being able to articulate that so the people around you can understand it and getting a consensus on a common vision."[194]

Values. Values are fundamental to a team's identity and culture, defining what its members collectively deem important for long-term mission success. Core values inform and guide a team's decisions and actions as they execute its mission. These values answer the question: What do we value most?

While core values may vary depending on the team's mission, they often include principles such as integrity, service, duty, honor, safety, diversity, and respect. These shared commitments provide a moral compass that shapes team behavior, fosters trust, and reinforces a cohesive organizational culture.

Goals and objectives. An organization's goals and objectives define what a team aims to achieve in both the long and short term to fulfill its mission. While closely related, they differ in time horizon and specificity: goals represent broader, long-term aspirations, while objectives are specific, measurable, and more immediate steps that support those goals.

For example, at the start of a new season, a professional basketball coach and players might set a shared goal to win the league championship. To support that goal, the team could establish objectives such as winning at least 75% of its regular-season games each month to secure a playoff spot and home-court advantage. Clear objectives guide daily efforts and help ensure steady progress toward achieving longer-term goals.

Priorities. Armed with a clear set of organizational goals and objectives, leaders and their teams must identify and focus on the highest priorities. This ensures that both labor and non-labor resources are directed toward the most critical work required to achieve desired outcomes. Prioritization typically begins with an annual flowdown of goals and objectives from the top of the organization, promoting alignment at every level. This cascading process helps ensure that each team's priorities are consistent with organizational intent and account for resource constraints.

Regular progress reviews, quarterly, for example, are essential for assessing changes in mission goals and adapting as needed. Shifts in organizational goals or strategy may require teams to start, stop, pause, or continue resource commitments across programs, projects, or initiatives. Leaders play a key role in communicating these changes promptly, providing the rationale, and working collaboratively with their teams to realign efforts and reprioritize resource commitments.

Strategy. Once an organization's goals, objectives, and priorities are established, leaders and their teams must develop a strategy to achieve them. A strategy outlines the approach the team will take to accomplish its mission safely, efficiently, and effectively. It defines *how* the team intends to achieve its goals and objectives and serves as a roadmap for action, decision-making, and performance alignment.

Continuing with the professional basketball team analogy, the team's strategy may include analyzing recent opponent performance to identify strengths and weaknesses, devising specific game plans tailored to upcoming matchups, rehearsing those plans in practice, and preparing contingency responses for various *what-if* scenarios during gameplay.

A well-crafted strategy fosters alignment across the team and provides a clear framework for consistent execution, adaptability, and continual improvement.

Key performance indicators. A leader and their team's performance is assessed using specific, time-phased quantitative and qualitative data, metrics, and analytics aligned with the team's goals, objectives, priorities, and strategy. These metrics serve as key performance indicators (KPI).

Goals, objectives, and strategies should be clear, meaningful, challenging, achievable, and measurable. They must include defined time horizons with expected completion dates and specify both quantitative and qualitative outcomes, emphasizing deliverables rather than specific actions or tasks.

Goals, Objectives, Priorities, and Strategy

Clear
Meaningful
Challenging
Achievable
Measurable

Building on the basketball team example, one key performance indicator (KPI) might track how often the team achieves its planned objectives, such as maintaining a 75% win rate each month. Another important KPI involves monitoring the individual performance of team members to reinforce accountability and identify opportunities for improvement and development.

Figure II.5 illustrates the influence of the Unifying Forces on the leadership process. Chapters Five and Six examine how this process is fueled by the model's core values and enabling leadership attributes. The final chapter presents a methodology that leaders can use to operationalize the model, along with an example of a strategic planning workshop designed to establish or revise a team's mission, vision, values, goals, objectives, priorities, and strategy.

Figure II.5. Influence of the Unifying Forces on the Leadership Process

Chapter Five: Enabling Attributes of Leadership Excellence

> It's not that I'm so smart; I just stay on the questions longer.
> — Albert Einstein[195]

As highlighted in the previous section, the instruments of leadership are pivotal to the leadership process within the Model for Sustained Leadership Excellence. These instruments—decisions, communication, and actions—work in concert to motivate, influence, and inspire team members to consistently deliver the correct mission results safely, effectively, and over the long term—the aim of sustained leadership excellence.

A leader's ability to achieve this objective is influenced by the perceptions, attitudes, and judgments team members form in response to the leader's decisions, communication, and actions. For these instruments to be effective, they must be aligned, harmonious, and mutually reinforcing. When there is discord among them, team members may experience cognitive dissonance—the perception that a leader's beliefs, words, and behaviors are in conflict—which can erode trust and negatively affect team performance.

This premise raises an important question: What leadership attributes shape and influence a leader's decisions, communication, and actions to ensure these instruments are aligned and harmonized? These attributes include a leader's trustworthiness, concern for team members, concern for the team's mission, and a willingness to lead.

Within the Model for Sustained Leadership Excellence, these attributes serve a dual purpose: they harmonize the instruments of leadership while also enabling the capabilities essential for sustaining long-term leadership effectiveness. They function as sources of reasoning, judgment, and cognition that inform a leader's decisions, communication, and actions while empowering the leadership capabilities needed to sustained leadership excellence. As such, they are recognized as the *enabling* attributes of leadership excellence.

Part I introduced key literature and best practices that highlight a wide range of competencies, behaviors, and capabilities essential to achieving and sustaining leadership success, including the ability to:

> ➢ Take risks and encourage team members to do the same.
> ➢ Delegate authority and empower others.
> ➢ Foster a culture of teamwork, professionalism, and continuous learning.
> ➢ Listen actively and with intention.
> ➢ Remain engaged and involved.
> ➢ Be accessible, available, and approachable.
> ➢ Develop and mentor team members.

- Coach and provide candid feedback.
- Take timely and appropriate corrective action.
- Drive continuous improvement in products, services, and processes.
- Lead upward and across organizational boundaries.
- Prioritize customer and partner needs.
- Demonstrate courage and take bold action.
- Show commitment and a willingness to lead.
- Exhibit persistence and resilience.
- Lead organizational change effectively.
- Think creatively and innovate consistently.

The following sections examine the model's enabling attributes, which represent the pillars of leadership depicted in Figure 5.1.

Enabling Attribute of Trust

> The ability to establish, grow, extend, and restore trust with all stakeholders—customers, suppliers, investors and employees—is the critical leadership competency in the new global economy.
> — Stephen M. R. Covey[196]

Trust, noun \ˈtrəst\
a: belief that someone or something is reliable, good, honest
b: assured reliance on the character, ability, strength, or truth of someone or something
c: one in which confidence is placed[197]

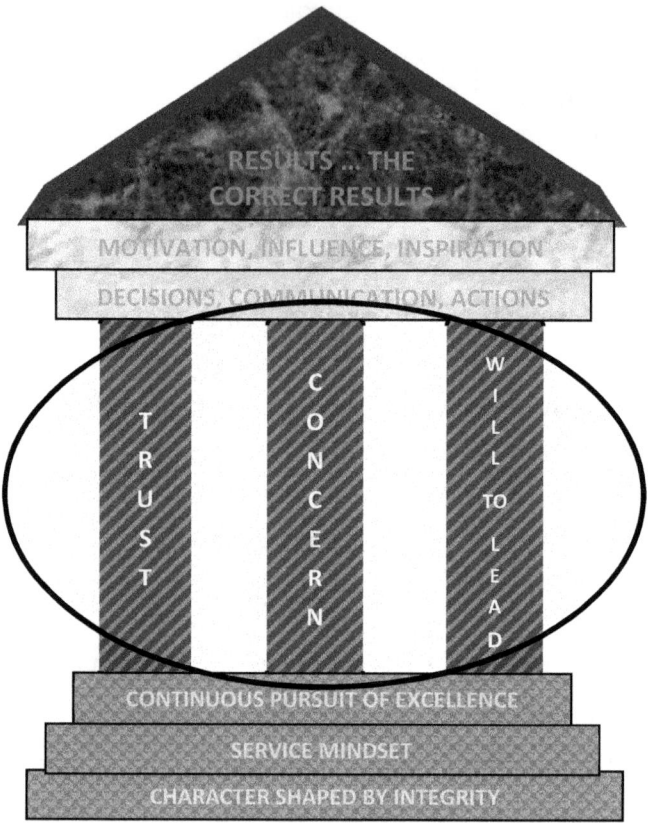

Figure 5.1. Enabling Attributes of Leadership Excellence

Leaders enable sustained leadership excellence by being both trusted and trusting. When trust informs their decisions, communication, and actions, it generates the motivation, influence, and inspiration that empower team members. Team members who trust their leaders and feel trusted willingly commit their time, energy, and attention to achieving the team's shared goals. In *The 21 Indispensable Qualities of a Leader*, Maxwell asks his readers: "What makes people want to follow a leader? Why do some people reluctantly follow one leader while passionately following another to the ends of the earth?" The answer to these questions, asserts Maxwell, lies in a leader's trustworthy character.[198]

"Trust is the currency of organizational success, yet it is rapidly deteriorating in today's volatile global landscape," stress researchers in Development Dimensions International *Global Leadership Forecast 2025*. "From 2022 to 2024, trust in immediate managers took a dramatic nosedive from 46% to 29%. This 17-point decline exposes an increasing skepticism toward managers, who are the frontline connection to the workforce and vital to team cohesion and morale," according to the study.[199]

Stephen Covey, author of the best-selling book *The Speed of Trust*, highlights one common element in every successful relationship and organization: trust. It affects every effort in which humankind is engaged, changing the quality of every outcome and altering the trajectory of future events. Trust is the foundation of the most powerful governments, the most successful businesses, and the most effective leaders.[200]

"So what is trust?" asks Covey. "Simply put, trust means confidence. The opposite of trust—distrust—is suspicion. When you trust people, you have confidence in them—in their integrity and their abilities. When you distrust people, you are suspicious of them—of their integrity, their agenda, their capabilities, or their track record. It's that simple."[201]

Trust is mutual . . . to receive trust, leaders must give trust. "Like transparency, trust is a two-way street—there is worker trust in leadership, and there is leadership trust in workers."[202] Sustained leadership excellence requires not only earning the trust of others but also placing trust in team members.

> *Trust is mutual . . . to receive trust, leaders must give trust. Sustained leadership excellence requires not only earning the trust of others but also placing trust in team members.*

Trusting team members means relying on their training, knowledge, skills, and character. It also involves giving team members the freedom to make decisions, communicate, and take action without constant oversight. Leaders who trust their teams empower them by delegating authority to carry out tasks, projects, and missions. Some leaders, however, struggle with delegation due to a reluctance to relinquish control over outcomes. Yet, with well-trained team members, along with proper supervision and support, leaders can confidently empower their teams to complete assignments safely and effectively.

Trusted and trusting leaders do not rush to conclusions. Instead, they gather and analyze data, information, and intelligence, taking time to resolve discrepancies before making final decisions. They seek to act decisively and explain even unpopular decisions with transparency. Trustworthy leaders clearly communicate the team's direction and actively invite questions and input. They remain open to alternative views and are willing to incorporate them when appropriate.

Trustworthy leaders emphasize and reinforce the importance of the team's *why* or purpose while also projecting confidence in their vision for the organization's future. They strive to be flexible, adaptable, and resilient in the face of unexpected challenges or setbacks. They also focus on building lasting working relationships—not only with team members but also with internal and external stakeholders and customers. By leveraging the talents, expertise, and capabilities of their team, they foster a collaborative environment that drives shared success.

"Without trust you cannot lead," assert James M. Kouzes and Barry Z. Posner in their investigative study on the critical role of trust in a leader's effectiveness. Their research examined how team members responded to leaders they trusted compared to leaders they did not trust. Kouzes and Posner found that when trust was lacking, team members often questioned the leader's motives. The following excerpt highlights the key outcomes of their study.

> When groups of business executives were given identical factual information about a difficult manufacturing-marketing policy decision, half of the groups were briefed to expect trusting behavior and the other half briefed to expect untrusting behavior. After thirty minutes of discussion, each team member completed a brief questionnaire, along with another set of executives who had been observing these team meetings. The responses of team members and the observers were quite consistent. The group members who had been told their peers and manager could be trusted reported their discussions and decisions to be significantly better than the low-trust group on every single factor measured. The high-trust group members in comparison to the low-trust group members were more open about feelings, experienced greater clarity about the group's basic problems and goals and searched more for alternative courses of action. The high-trust group also reported greater levels of mutual influence on outcomes, satisfaction with the meeting, motivation to implement decisions, and closeness as a management team.

Without trust, managers often take a self-protective posture. They are directive and hold tight rein over their subordinates. Likewise, subordinates of low-trust managers are likely to ignore, disguise, and distort facts, ideas, conclusions, and feelings. They are suspicious and unreceptive, perceiving their manager's actions as attempts to manipulate them.

In follow-up experiments where participants were briefed about their manager's low level of trust, attempts by the manager to be truly open and honest were ignored and rejected by subordinates. The mental set was so strong that the manager's honesty was viewed by subordinates as a clever attempt to deceive them. They were cynical and generally reacted by sabotaging the manager's efforts even further.[203]

Trust Enables Leadership Capabilities

As depicted in Figure 5.2, trust is one of three enabling attributes of leadership that frame the Model for Sustained Leadership Excellence. This attribute supports a leader's ability to consistently achieve the correct mission results with their team over the long term by guiding their decisions, communication, and actions through the lens of trust.

Part I presented research and best practices that highlight key leadership capabilities and behaviors exercised by successful leaders—such as delegation, empowerment, risk-taking, teamwork, respect, professionalism, and emotional intelligence. The following sections explore how the attribute of trust not only shapes the leadership process, but also enables, reinforces, and sustains these capabilities.

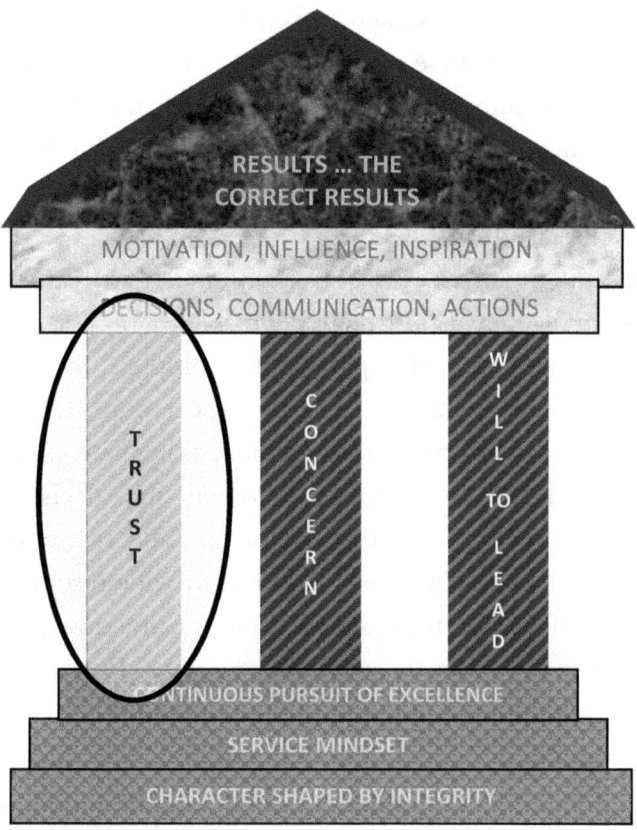

Figure 5.2. Enabling Attribute of Trust

Trust enables delegation and empowerment. Organizations grant leaders decision-making authority that aligns with their level of responsibility. Armed with this power, leaders are accountable for exercising their authority to accomplish their team's mission safely and effectively. Given time constraints and limited resources—especially when leading geographically dispersed teams, working across time zones, or managing shift operations—leaders often delegate decision-making authority to ensure mission success.

"As we look ahead into the next century, leaders will be those who empower others," stresses Microsoft co-founder Bill Gates.[204] Delegation, therefore, requires leaders to entrust and empower others with decision-making authority while retaining overall responsibility for the outcomes. This can be challenging, as it necessitates relinquishing a degree of control. Ultimately, successful delegation hinges on a leader's ability to trust others.

Delegating involves at least five key steps. First, assess competence. Ensure the team member has the necessary training, expertise, judgment, and capability to complete the assignment safely and effectively. Second, clarify expectations. Clearly define the assigned job, task, project, or mission, along with expected outcomes. Third, grant authority. Provide the decision-making authority required to fulfill the assignment, and ensure others are aware of the delegated authority. Fourth, provide resources. Equip the team member with the essential tools, information, and support needed for success. Finally, encourage learning. Foster a culture in which team members feel empowered to learn from mistakes without fear of reprisal.[205]

Delegating authority not only allows leaders to leverage their team members' talents but also fosters self-confidence and professional growth. By assigning special projects and tasks, leaders give team members the autonomy to solve problems and influence the organization's products, services, and processes. This empowerment enables individuals to lead work groups, manage projects, take calculated risks, and learn from both successes and failures.

Empowering team members demonstrates a leader's trust in their abilities, enhances job satisfaction, and prepares them for increased responsibilities and future leadership roles. As part of an ongoing learning and talent development process, leaders should provide candid feedback during and after the completion of delegated assignments. These assessments are essential for reinforcing positive behaviors, recognizing exceptional performance, and identifying areas for improvement.

Trust enables risk-taking. Sustained leadership excellence is demonstrated by leaders who encourage team members to be creative, take initiative, and take measured risks. Founded in 1902 and known for their well-branded and popular *Post-it Sticky Notes*, leaders at 3M embrace experimentation and risk-taking as part of their organizational culture. At 3M, risk-taking is a way of life. With over 100,000 patents, 3M's approach to risk-taking has led to the production of more than 60,000 diverse products, including adhesives, abrasives, laminates, passive fire protection, dental and orthodontic products, electronic materials, medical products, car-care products, electronic circuits, and optical films.[206]

Allowing team members to experiment, explore, and take risks with the organization's resources requires trust. With that trust, however, comes the responsibility to manage risks thoughtfully and responsibly.

Everyone makes mistakes—some small, others significant. Regardless of the size, team members want a second chance. What matters most is learning from those errors and using the experience to improve future performance. The following story about legendary news broadcaster Walter Cronkite illustrates the value of acknowledging mistakes, learning from them, and striving for continuous improvement.

> Early in his broadcast career, Walter Cronkite, one of America's most respected television journalists, was hired to broadcast University of Oklahoma football games. Since it was a live broadcast, he needed to identify all the players on both teams quickly. To help him with this task, he devised an electric board with the names of all the players on the opposing team. He then hired spotters from the opposing team to identify those involved in

each of the plays for him by simply pressing a button. "The broadcast was a disaster," he recalled, because the spotters made mistakes as they punched the identifying buttons on the electric board. However, "the station owners and sponsors were kinder than I deserved. They gave me another chance," said Cronkite.

Of course, he worked hard to learn from his mistake and improved his system for identifying opposing players. He recruited another station employee as a spotter. Together, they memorized the names and jersey numbers, ages, physical characteristics, and hometowns of every one of the thirty or forty members of every university team Oklahoma played. Next, the two of them spent three to four hours daily for several days testing each other's memories. "The practice worked," stated Cronkite, "and our broadcasts were highly successful from the second game on." Consider the loss to American journalism had his boss not given him that second chance.[207]

Risk management. All leaders face risks that can threaten mission success. Mission risk refers to the likelihood of an event occurring and the potential consequences associated with that event. Leaders and their teams should assess mission risks—including safety, legal, political, operational, and market risks—that could compromise the safe and effective accomplishment of the mission. Mitigating these risks requires a systematic approach to risk management.

A risk management system involves identifying risks that could jeopardize a team's mission, assessing the likelihood of high-risk events, and developing control measures to monitor those risks.

Risk management includes preplanning responses to potential risk events, formulating strategies to address their consequences, continuously monitoring the effectiveness of the risk management system, and making adjustments as new risks emerge or previously identified risks no longer pose a threat to the mission. Fundamental categories of organizational risk include:

> - *Political and economic risks*: national and international events that impact stability or operations.
> - *Health, safety, and security risks*: impacts resulting from evolving policies or conditions that affect the well-being of team members and the organization's security.
> - *Market risks*: risks stemming from economic shifts, political developments, or competitive business events.
> - *Compliance risks*: Risks tied to violations of government regulations, industry standards, or contractual obligations.
> - *Financial risks*: Risks involving revenue loss, customer non-payment, rising interest rates, or cost volatility.
> - *Operational risks*: Equipment failure, damage, theft, or process breakdowns that disrupt daily operations.
> - *Environmental risks*: natural disasters that can affect organizational assets and operations.
> - *Staffing risks*: Workforce shortages, retention challenges, or deficiencies in training and skill development.

> *Data and intellectual property risks:* Breaches or cyberattacks that compromise sensitive data or proprietary knowledge.
> *Frontline risks:* Hazards associated with military, paramilitary, or high-threat operational environments.[208]

Successful risk management systems enhance decision-making regarding strategic and operational planning, prioritizing resources, and allocating capital in anticipation of what may go wrong. Ideally, effective risk management enables an organization to innovate and capitalize on opportunities that arise from risk.

Trust enables teamwork. Trust, the belief that a person is dependable, good, and honest, builds confidence in their character, ability, and potential. Leaders and teams that consistently achieve desired mission results over the long term are distinguished by a culture of teamwork, mutual support, and camaraderie—enabled by trust. Leaders who are trusted and trust others foster group cohesion by cultivating trustworthy relationships and reinforcing the importance of trust among team members.

Leaders should not assume that trust is automatically granted by virtue of their position. For many team members, trust must be earned. Sustaining trust between leaders and their teams takes time and is built through shared experiences and consistent behavior. At its core, trust is rooted in honesty. Leaders must be straightforward and truthful, ensuring their "yes means yes and no means no."[209]

> *Leaders and teams that consistently achieve the desired mission results over the long term are distinguished by a culture of teamwork, mutual support, and camaraderie—enabled by trust.*

Trust enables respect, professionalism, and emotional intelligence. Leaders seeking to build and sustain trusting relationships must treat others professionally and respectfully, especially those over whom they hold authority, power, or influence. Scottish philosopher and historian Thomas Carlisle reminds us, "You can tell a big person by the way he treats other people."[210]

In describing poor leadership, Jack and Suzy Welch warn that this is an area where many leaders go wrong. One key reason leaders fail to gain or retain the respect of their team members is attributed to how they treat others. Leaders who are inconsiderate, bullying, or insensitive fail to recognize the negative impact they have on their teams. "Such leaders are usually protected from above because they deliver the numbers. But with their destructive personalities, they rarely win their people's trust. That's no way to run a business, which is why these types of leaders typically self-destruct. It's never as quickly as you'd hope, but unless they own the place, it does happen eventually," assert the Welches.[211]

Leadership is not a popularity contest, yet team members are motivated and inspired by leaders they trust, respect, and believe have their best interests in mind. Leaders must get to know their team members, express appreciation for their contributions to the organization's mission, and provide constructive feedback. This feedback must be communicated professionally, demonstrating the leader's commitment to the team member's development in alignment with the team's mission.

Emotional intelligence. Emotional intelligence, a term coined in 1990 by researchers John Mayer and Peter Salovey, and later popularized by psychologist Daniel Goleman, is reflected in a leader's professionalism.[212] Emotional intelligence, or EQ, refers to the ability to recognize and manage one's own emotions, as well as the emotions of others. Emotional intelligence includes the ability to identify and name emotions and harness them for tasks like reasoning and problem-solving. A leader's EQ is evident in their ability to regulate their emotions and help others do the same.

More than a decade ago, Goleman emphasized the importance of EQ in leadership, stating in the *Harvard Business Review*, "The most effective leaders are all alike in one crucial way: They all have a high degree of what has come to be known as emotional intelligence."[213]

Impact of Trust on Sustaining Leadership Excellence

Trust, one of the three enabling attributes of leadership, sustains leadership excellence by both shaping the leadership process and enabling key leadership capabilities such as delegation and empowerment, risk-taking, teamwork, respect, professionalism, and emotional intelligence. Figure 5.3 summarizes the impact of trust on developing and sustaining leadership excellence.

Trust Enables
• Delegation and empowerment
• Risk-taking
• Teamwork
• Respect, professionalism, and emotional intelligence

Figure 5.3. Impact of Trust on Leadership Excellence

Building Trust

> Trust is like the air we breathe. When it's present,
> nobody really notices. But when it's absent,
> everybody notices.
> — Warren Buffett[214]

Team members want to trust their leaders, and they also want their leaders to trust them. Trust is not established through financial incentives or benefits; it begins with fundamental honesty and fairness. "To trust a leader, it is not necessary to like him," says Drucker, "nor is it necessary to agree with him. Trust is the conviction that the leader means what he says. A leader's actions and a leader's professed beliefs must be congruent or at least compatible. Effective leadership—and again this is very old wisdom—is not based on being clever; it is based primarily on being consistent."[215]

One important way a leader builds a climate of trust is by respecting others and serving as a positive role model. Leaders demonstrate excellence by being reliable, keeping their promises, and ensuring their actions align with their words. Kouzes and Posner propose three leadership strategies to build, model, and sustain a trusting climate.

1. *Do what you say you're going to do.* A fundamental basis for being perceived as trustworthy is predictability. Predictability refers to the degree of confidence that people have in their expectations about another person's behavior or intentions. So, do what you say you are going to do. That may be as simple as getting to a meeting on time. Doing what you say you're going to do also enhances the sense of

reciprocity needed to encourage others to increase their vulnerability with the leader. Being trustworthy yourself promotes trusting behavior from other people.

2. *Reduce defensiveness.* Trust also develops when people feel safe and secure. When thoughts and ideas are shot down and ridiculed, it doesn't take long to realize the climate is neither safe nor conducive to being vulnerable, the precursor to opening up and placing trust in another person. Reduce defensive climates by providing descriptive rather than evaluative comments, expressing genuine feelings of caring and involvement, and being willing to actively seek out, listen to, understand, and utilize other people's perspectives in the projects and adventures you share.

3. *Be a risk-taker when it comes to trust.* Letting people know where you stand on important issues is a risky proposition because a leader cannot always be certain that others will appreciate the candor, agree with [their] aspirations, or interpret messages the way they were intended. But unless a leader is willing to be open, they cannot expect others to take the same risk necessary to build trust. Being open extends to acknowledging mistakes and vulnerabilities. Some people fear that by admitting mistakes they'll lose respect and power. However, experience shows that letting others know one's human side enhances credibility. People tend to distrust those who claim to be infallible.

> Revealing every fault to constituents is unnecessary, but admit when wrong, which creates approachability for enduring leadership.[216]

One of the most powerful expressions of leadership excellence is leading by example. It's through example and modeling that leaders effectively cultivate trust. In *Maximum Achievement*, Brian Tracy highlights the transformative power of leading by example.

> Alexander the Great, the king of Macedonia, was one of the most superb leaders of all time. He became king at the age of nineteen, when his father, Philip II, was assassinated. Over the next eleven years, Alexander conquered much of the known world, leading his armies against numerically superior forces. Yet, when he was at the height of his power, the master of the known world, the greatest ruler in history to that date, he would still draw his sword at the beginning of a battle and lead his men forward into the conflict. He insisted on leading by example. Alexander felt that he could not ask his men to risk their lives unless he was willing to demonstrate by his actions that he had complete confidence in the outcome. The sight of Alexander charging forward so excited and motivated his soldiers that no force on earth could stand before them.[217]

A breach of trust. Teamwork suffers when trust is weak or broken, adversely affecting the team's ability to accomplish its mission. It is imperative for a leader to restore trust to ensure the team performs safely and effectively. Repairing a breach of trust requires time and commitment. "It takes time to build trust, a second to break it, and time to build it again," stresses Zimmer.[218]

Leaders and team members interact regularly to perform their jobs, tasks, and missions as part of an organization's ongoing operating rhythm. Inevitably, unexpected challenges emerge, generating disagreement, discord, and conflict among team members. These disagreements can lead to arguments between team members or between a leader and team members. As teams confront these challenges, leaders may need to take an active role in resolving contentious disputes.

Rebuilding trusting relationships between a leader and team members, as well as among team members, is often unsuccessful because some leaders are unprepared to resolve issues, disputes, and disagreements, which are frequently rooted in personality conflicts. If not managed properly, these disputes can result in a long-term breakdown of teamwork, ultimately detrimental to team performance and mission success. Leaders need a framework to facilitate dispute resolution and rebuild trust between the leader and a team member or among team members.

Rebuilding trust. Table 5.1 presents the LEADERS Conflict Resolution Framework, a tool designed to help leaders address conflicts and disagreements constructively. Its purpose is to facilitate resolution through professional dialogue, restore or preserve trust, and achieve mutually acceptable solutions among team members.

Leaders should not delay addressing serious disagreements, as unresolved issues can often escalate into more complex disputes. When using the model, leaders should first review the framework's steps with the affected team members before discussing the specific concerns. This helps set clear expectations for professional conduct and the intended outcomes of the meeting. Depending on the nature of the conflict, it may also be appropriate to involve a colleague, deputy leader, or human resources professional.

Table 5.1

LEADERS Conflict Resolution Framework

L	**Lead, listen, and learn**: Take action as the leader to reconcile conflict. Organize and lead a meeting to address contentious issues. Explain the purpose of the meeting and outline the issue, concern, or disagreement. Many disagreements stem from assumptions and misunderstandings. Learn by listening to understand what others are trying to say—one voice at a time.
E	**Expected outcomes**: Share the expected outcomes of the meeting, emphasizing the goal of achieving a win-win solution. Discuss what a win-win outcome looks like in the context of the situation.
A	**Action**: Discuss the actions necessary to resolve the issue, dispute, or disagreement. Commit to checking progress and following up regarding the agreed-upon actions.
D	**Decide**. Determine, decide, and document the agreed-upon actions, along with timelines for progress checks.
E	**Expected meeting norms**: Emphasize the importance of professional and respectful interactions, reinforcing that it's not just what is said; it's how it's said.
R	**Respect**: Respectful dialogue. Respect the decisions made and one another. Explain the importance of not undermining the solution after the fact.
S	**Solution**: Focus on finding lasting solutions rooted in teamwork and aligned with the team's mission.

Enabling Attribute of Concern

> People will forget what you said. People will forget what you did. But people will never forget how you made them feel.
> — Maya Angelou[219]

Concern, verb \kən-ˈsərn\
a: being interested in and caring about a person or thing
b: to affect or involve (someone)[220]

Leaders enable sustained leadership excellence by showing genuine concern for their team members and the team's mission. When concern informs their decisions, communication, and actions, it generates the motivation, influence, and inspiration that empower team members. When team members feel their leader's genuine concern—and trust its sincerity—they willingly invest their time, energy, and attention in achieving the team's shared goals.

What are the characteristics of a leader who shows concern for their team members as well as the team's mission? Concerned leaders engage in thoughtful, interactive, two-way communication and demonstrate strong listening skills. They are open-minded and fair, showing empathy and respect for others' views, opinions, and time. They appreciate the diversity of people, thoughts, and ideas, recognizing that while every individual is unique, nearly everyone shares a common desire: to succeed in their work.

Concerned leaders are approachable, accessible, and make themselves available. They view failure as an opportunity to gain experience, learn, and grow. They seek and provide candid feedback, coaching, and learning opportunities to improve team member performance. When necessary, they make difficult decisions and administer progressive corrective actions, up to and including dismissal. Concerned leaders promptly address conflicts or disputes that disrupt team cohesion or interfere with the team's mission. They take action to correct breaches of policies, procedures, and ethical codes of conduct.

Chapter Three reviewed various leadership styles and how they reflect a leader's focus on mission and people priorities. Some styles were characterized by leaders who placed disproportionate emphasis on accomplishing the organization's mission, often at the expense of their team members. In contrast, other styles prioritized team members over the team's mission. These two leadership styles, characterized as Theory X and Theory Y, were found to limit a leader's ability to sustain the safe and successful accomplishment of their team's mission over the long term.

Sustained leadership excellence—one that has a lasting and positive impact on team performance—is achieved through a leader's concern for the team's mission and a commensurate concern for their team members' safety, welfare, and professional development. Team members want to know their leader cares not only about the organization's success but also about team member success.

Persistent, task-driven leadership may sometimes be necessary, especially in high-risk settings such as military, paramilitary, first-responder, security, and medical emergencies. Nevertheless, a Theory X leadership style should be bound by policies, processes, procedures, protocols, and standard operating practices to prevent unethical behaviors, such as bullying, abuse, or harassment. When persistent, aggressive, task-centered leadership is applied over the long term, it can negatively affect team members' safety, morale, and welfare, ultimately limiting the team's long-term mission success.

In a review of over 400 studies across 36 countries with nearly 150,000 people, researchers found that team members are less productive, less collaborative, and more inclined to shirk their responsibilities in the face of workplace aggression from leaders. Abusive bosses break confidence and breed resentment, according to the study.[221] Adam Grant, an organizational psychologist at the University of Pennsylvania and author of *Think Again*, affirms that, "denigrating people is not a path to accomplishing meaningful goals. It reflects a lack of self-control and a shortage of emotional intelligence."

Instead, a leader's decisions, communication, and actions should strike a balance, demonstrating concern for both team members and the mission rather than focusing disproportionately on one at the expense of the other.

Concern Enables Leadership Capabilities

Figure 5.4 illustrates the leadership attribute of concern, the second of three enabling attributes framing the Model for Sustained Leadership Excellence. This attribute supports a leader's goal of consistently achieving the correct mission results with their team over the long term by informing their decisions, communication, and actions through the lens of concern.

Part I presented research and best practices showcasing key leadership capabilities and behaviors exercised by successful leaders, such as selflessness, interactive listening, engagement, involvement, approachability, availability, visibility, and hiring. Additional capabilities include developing team members, recognition, appreciation, coaching, candid feedback, corrective actions, mentoring, continuous product, service, and process improvements, leading up, and focusing on customer and partner needs. The following sections examine how the attribute of concern not only shapes the leadership process, but also enables, reinforces, and sustains these capabilities.

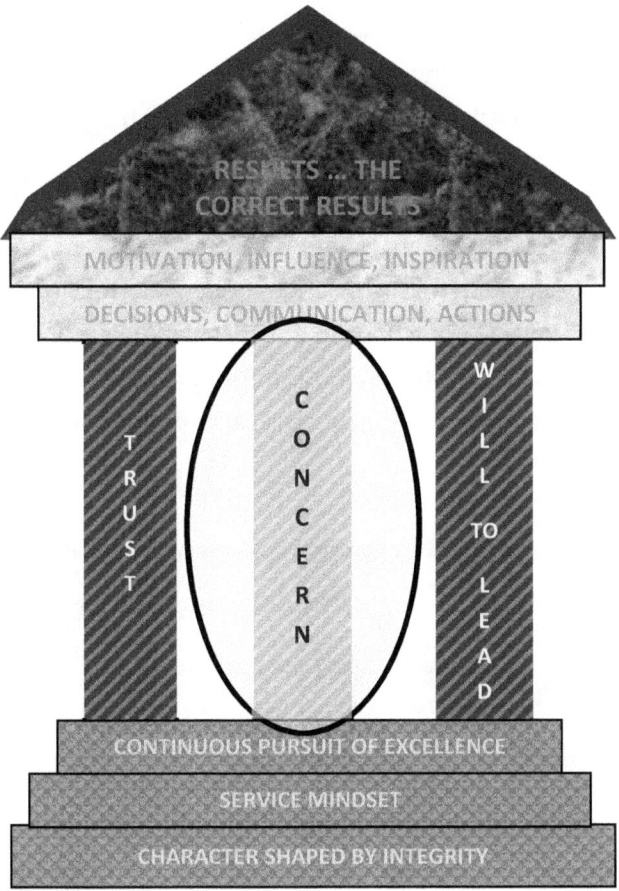

Figure 5.4. Enabling Attribute of Concern

Concern enables selflessness. Selflessness stems from an attitude of service before self. It guides a leader's decisions, communication, and actions in ways that support their team's mission and the development of its members. A leader's selflessness manifests itself through humility and empathy and is demonstrated by doing the right thing and acting ethically, even when no one is watching. Selflessness cultivates an environment of teamwork and professionalism grounded in mutual respect. The path to sustained leadership excellence is paved by consistently putting the best interests of the team first.

Concern enables interactive listening. Interactive listening promotes open communication, generates ideas and solutions, encourages innovative thinking, conveys interest and concern, and affirms a leader's approachability. Active listeners hear and comprehend what others say by using their eyes, ears, facial expressions, and body language. They engage others with verbal and nonverbal feedback, such as questions and paraphrasing, to convey that the other person's ideas and opinions are understood, important, respected, and valued.

Interactive Listening

Promotes open communication
Generates ideas and solutions
Encourages innovative thinking
Conveys interest and concern
Affirms a leader's approachability

Peter Nulty, a former member of the board of editors at *Fortune* magazine, maintains that "of all the skills of leadership, listening is one of the most valuable—and one of the least understood."[222] Most leaders listen only sometimes and remain ordinary leaders, but a few, the great ones, never stop listening, according to Nulty. "They are 'hearaholics'—ever alert, bending their ears while they work and while they play, while they eat and while they sleep. They listen to advisers, to customers, to inner voices, to enemies, to the wind. That's how they get word before anyone else of unseen problems and opportunities."[223] However, some leaders listen only to form and reinforce their response rather than truly understand.

Emphasizing the importance of listening, Jack and Suzy Welch point out that many leaders fall short in this area, asserting that one of the most frustrating ways leaders fail is by acting like know-it-alls, stating:

> Know-it-alls can tell you how the world works, what corporate is thinking, how it will backfire if you try this or that, and why you can't change the product one iota. They even know what kind of car you should be driving. Sometimes these blowhards get their swagger from a few positive experiences. But usually they're just victims of their own bad personalities. And you and your company are victims, too. Because know-it-alls aren't just insufferable, they're dangerous. They don't listen, and that 'deafness' makes it very hard for new ideas to get heard, debated, expanded, or improved. No single person, no matter how smart, can take a business to its apex. For that, you need every voice heard. And know-it-all leadership creates a deadly silence.[224]

Advanced communication systems, networking, and transportation systems are creating a world that is increasingly less defined by borders and nationalities. In this sense, the world is getting smaller. The shift toward economic and political globalization makes it imperative for leaders to listen, learn, and understand the various norms, customs, and courtesies of international team members, business partners, clients, and customers. By doing so, leaders can avoid confusion, misunderstandings, or unintentional offense when collaborating across cultures.

Concern enables engagement and involvement. A leader's concern for team members and the team's mission drives their engagement and involvement with the team, business partners, clients, customers, and other stakeholders. This engagement and involvement foster supportive and lasting working relationships, hallmarks of sustained leadership excellence.

Leadership engagement and involvement enhance a leader's situational awareness, increase productivity, build strong working relationships, and provide valuable feedback that might otherwise be overlooked. The information and intelligence gathered through engagement and involvement enable a leader to address concerns, assess mission performance, and adjust priorities and strategies in a timely manner. Further, engagement and involvement enable leaders to learn more about their team members, both professionally and personally, contributing to strong, respectful, and lasting working relationships.

"If know-it-alls are too in-your-face," say Jack and Suzy Welch, "a second kind of lousy leader is too remote. These emotionally distant bosses are more comfortable behind closed doors than mucking it out with the team. Sure, they attend meetings and other requisite functions, but they'd rather be staring at their computers. If possible, all the messy, sweaty people stuff would be delegated to HR managers on another floor. Like know-it-alls, this breed of leader is dangerous, but for a different reason. They don't engage, which means they can't inspire. That's a big problem. Leaders, after all, need followers to get anything done. And followers need passion for their fuel."[225]

> ### *Engagement and Involvement*
>
> *Enhances situational awareness*
> *Increases productivity*
> *Builds strong working relationships*
> *Provides valuable feedback*

Concern enables approachability, availability, and visibility. When leaders genuinely care about their team members and the mission, they naturally become more present and engaged. Whether in the office or on the front lines, leaders should strive to be approachable and available. Spending time in work areas and operational environments—often referred to as *leadership by walking around*—further enhances their visibility and connection to the team. Interactions on the shop floor, in offices, during training, or with clients, customers, regulators, and auditors help leaders stay attuned to emerging challenges and opportunities. These real-time engagements build trust, uncover insights, and enable timely solutions that support team success.

Concern enables hiring the best team and talent. Hiring isn't just a transactional process; it's a strategic decision that reflects a leader's priorities and commitment to building a high-performing, values-aligned team. Concern for mission success and team cohesion compels leaders to seek not just skilled individuals, but the right individuals—those whose character, capabilities, and potential align with the team's purpose and culture. This philosophy is echoed in the work of leadership expert Jim Collins.

Collins asserts, "First who ... then what." He hypothesized that most leaders, after joining a new team, begin by setting a new vision and strategy for the organization. His research, however, revealed a different approach to successful leadership. "We found they *first* got the right people on the bus, the wrong people off the bus, and the right people in the right seats—and *then* they figured out where to drive it. The adage that 'people are your most important asset' turns out to be wrong," claims Collins, arguing instead that "People are not your most important asset. The *right* people are."[226]

Concern enables developing team members. Concerned leaders invest in development programs for team members to support their professional growth and enhance their knowledge, skills, and abilities to broaden and deepen their technical, professional, and leadership capabilities beyond their current roles. These development opportunities encompass internal and external learning and training programs, job rotation programs, and temporary leadership assignments that involve increased levels of responsibility. Development Dimensions International *Global Leadership Forecast 2025* found that leaders who actively support their team members' development are eleven times more likely to be trusted by their team members.[227]

Succession planning is closely tied to developing team members and preparing aspiring leaders to take on future leadership roles. In a comparative study of 28 Fortune 500 companies over 15 years, researchers discovered that leaders who prioritized succession planning led the most successful organizations. These leaders invested in developing their team members, ensuring they were well-prepared to move into a departing leader's position when the time came.[228]

Enduring leaders apply a systematic approach to leadership development that integrates performance evaluations, career counseling, mentoring, and succession planning into a robust learning culture. This systems approach recognizes that leadership development, like product and service development, is a strategic imperative vital to the organization's long-term success.

Concern enables recognition and appreciation. A leader's concern for team members drives them to invest time and effort in recognizing team member contributions and exceptional performance. Appreciation is a fundamental human need expressed through various forms of communication and actions, ranging from a sincere thank you to formal awards and recognition ceremonies. Team members respond positively to appreciation and recognition because it affirms that their work and contributions are valued. When individual or group performance is recognized and appreciated, team members are inspired to excel, resulting in greater job satisfaction and increased productivity.

Warren Buffett, the highly successful chairman of Berkshire Hathaway, views showing appreciation as a cornerstone of his success. Renowned for generously acknowledging employees' contributions, large and small, he is celebrated in *Warren Buffett's Management Secrets* for his consistent, thoughtful recognition of team members. As the team's biggest advocate and consummate cheerleader, Buffett seizes every opportunity—whether at Berkshire's annual meetings or in its reports—to celebrate their achievements. His praise for even the smallest efforts inspires team members to strive for even greater accomplishments.[229]

Despite the importance of recognition and appreciation, a 10-year survey by Sirota Consulting, which involved 2.5 million employees across 237 private, public, and not-for-profit organizations in 89 countries, found that only 51% of workers were satisfied with the recognition they received for doing their jobs well.[230]

One reason leaders may hesitate to recognize team members is the significant time and effort involved. Awards and recognition programs often require detailed narrative submissions, which demand research, writing, editing, and coordination of approvals. For competitive awards, nomination packages may undergo rigorous review and selection across multiple organizational levels. Given the high level of competition, many deserving nominees are not selected, which can discourage leaders from investing time and resources in future nominations. However, this reluctance overlooks the substantial benefits of the recognition process itself—boosting morale, strengthening motivation, and enhancing mission performance.

Concern enables coaching and candid feedback. Coaching and feedback aim to improve mission performance through the development of team members. Candid feedback, delivered through coaching and performance evaluations, is a crucial component of the learning and development process. According to DDI's *Global Leadership Forecast 2025*, team members with leaders who are effective coaches are nine times more likely to trust their leader.[231] Coaching and feedback should be interactive, not one-sided.

Providing constructive feedback is essential for improving team member performance and fostering both individual and team success. When offering coaching and feedback, team members should have the opportunity to ask questions, clarify what is being communicated, and understand the expected changes in behavior or performance.

Concern enables corrective action. A leader's concern for team members and the mission empowers them to take corrective actions when necessary. This includes enforcing the organization's policies, code of conduct, ethical and safety standards, and governing regulations. The severity of any breach must be carefully evaluated, and consequences must be administered fairly and consistently across the organization.

Serious infractions should be examined and addressed by a panel of experienced leaders, human resource professionals, and when warranted, legal counsel. The most egregious violations will result in dismissal from the organization.

Concern enables mentoring. Mentoring is an influential tool for development and empowerment, helping others advance in their professional careers through the advice, counsel, and networking that mentors provide. Built on mutual trust and respect, mentoring forms a partnership between a leader and those aspiring to grow and develop professionally.

The most impactful leaders mentor protégés inside and outside their organization while prioritizing mentorship for their team members. Often, mentees initiate the mentoring relationship with a mentor, demonstrating their initiative to shape their professional development. Leaders also initiate mentoring relationships, recognizing talent and potential in others. Mentors unlock a protégé's potential by offering them challenging assignments and projects.

Concern enables continuous product, service, and process improvements. Initiatives and innovations aimed at improving the quality and value of an organization's products, services, and processes are crucial for a team's long-term success. Before the latter half of the twentieth century, such improvements typically followed cycles limited by slow communication systems, contributing to time-consuming decision-making. The paradigm has shifted, however, toward continuous innovation, requiring quick, accurate, and efficient adaptation.

With advancements in high-speed computing, artificial intelligence, automation, robotics, predictive analytics, and high-capacity information management systems, forward-thinking leaders embrace new technologies to drive rapid, continuous improvements in products, services, and processes. Effective leaders maintain situational awareness of the strategic operating environment to uncover opportunities for continuous improvement, seeking input from all organizational levels and listening to customer, partner, and stakeholder concerns and suggestions.

Concern enables leading up. While much of a leader's focus is centered on their team members and customers, it is equally important for leaders to understand and fulfill the expectations of the leader they report to, as well as those of higher-level leaders within the organization. Sustained leadership excellence is enabled by *leading up*. Leaders who *lead up* focus on supporting their immediate supervisor and the leadership team above them. This entails understanding their supervisor's leadership style, knowing their priorities, and aligning the team's goals, objectives, and strategy with those imperatives. It also means anticipating their questions and proactively seeking solutions to potential problems. In essence, *leading up* is about establishing a productive relationship with your immediate supervisor. It calls for leaders to support their organizational goals, objectives, priorities, and operating rhythm, thereby contributing to success at higher levels within the organization.

Concern enables a focus on customer and partner needs. Sustained leadership excellence is enabled by a leader's concern for their customers and partners. A team's ability to create products and services that meet and anticipate internal and external customer and partner needs is vital for an organization's long-term success. How do enduring leaders focus their team members' attention on these needs? They encourage team members to ask: What value can we provide our customers and partners? How can we help them be successful?

Impact of Concern on Sustaining Leadership Excellence

Concern for team members and the mission—combined with trust and the will to lead—sustains leadership excellence by shaping the leadership process and enabling key leadership capabilities such as selflessness, interactive listening, engagement, and involvement. It fosters approachability, availability, and visibility; influences hiring decisions; promotes team-member development, recognition, and appreciation; drives coaching and candid feedback; reinforces accountability and corrective actions; supports mentoring; and encourages continuous improvement in products, services, and processes. Concern also enables leaders to effectively support the leadership team above them and respond to the evolving needs of customers and partners. Figure 5.5 summarizes the impact of concern on developing and sustaining leadership excellence.

Concern Enables
• Selflessness
• Interactive listening
• Engagement and involvement
• Approachability, availability, and visibility
• Hiring the best team and talent
• Developing team members
• Recognition and appreciation
• Coaching, candid feedback, and corrective action
• Mentoring
• Product, service, and process improvements
• Leading up
• Focus on customer and partner needs

Figure 5.5. Impact of Concern on Leadership Excellence

Exercising Concern

> To be able to use the power of other people, it is necessary to win people's hearts.
> — Huainanzi[232]

How do enduring leaders show concern for their team members and the mission? Leaders demonstrate concern by dedicating time, energy, effort, resources, and attention to their team members and the mission, ensuring outcomes are achieved safely, effectively, and in alignment with the organization's goals, objectives, and priorities. The following tenets of concern offer practical guidance for leaders as they strive to support their team members, accomplish the mission, and sustain their leadership excellence.

1. *Be a problem solver.* Help your clients, customers, stakeholders, the team, and the leader you report to solve their problems. Anticipate their needs, listen actively, and work to solve issues collaboratively.
2. *Grow leaders.* Invest in the team's next generation of leaders. Provide education, development, and mentoring opportunities to enhance technical, professional, and leadership capabilities.
3. *Reward performance.* Recognize exceptional contributors. Celebrate significant achievements and contributions from team members and partners who advance the mission.
4. *Give and seek feedback.* Offer candid, constructive feedback—and invite it in return—to strengthen individual and team performance.
5. *Be there.* Be approachable, accessible, present, and available.

Enabling Attribute of the Will to Lead

> Becoming the kind of person who is a leader is
> the ultimate act of free will.
> — Warren Bennis[233]

Will noun \ ˈwil\
a: a strong desire or determination to do something
b: used to express determination, insistence, or persistence[234]

Leaders enable sustained leadership excellence by embodying a genuine will to lead. This willingness shapes and informs their decisions, communication, and actions, which generate the motivation, influence, and inspiration that empower team members. When team members trust their leader's commitment to the responsibilities of leadership, they willingly invest their time, energy, and attention in pursuing the team's shared goals.

While many aspire to be in charge, relatively few sustain the will to endure its long-term challenges, responsibilities, and demands. "Leadership requires major expenditures of effort and energy—more than most people care to make," according to Gardner.[235] Peter Koestenbaum, a classically trained philosopher and Fortune 500 consultant, poses a compelling question in the title of his book, *Do You Have the Will to Lead?*[236]

For many leaders, one of the most challenging and discouraging aspects of their role is addressing and resolving personality conflicts among team members. Research from the National Bureau of Economics revealed that the typical leader spends seven hours per week addressing personality conflicts.[237] This time-consuming responsibility can make leadership less appealing, a sentiment echoed by a Berrett-Koehler survey in which 68% of leaders admitted they did not enjoy their leader role.[238]

What does it mean to be a willing leader? Sustained leadership excellence requires time, energy, courage, persistence, resilience, and mental flexibility to overcome setbacks, learn from failures, and celebrate successes. The will to lead reflects a leader's readiness to embrace these responsibilities and remain accountable for their team's performance. As Lussier and Achua assert, "To reach full leadership potential, a person must want to be a leader."[239]

What are the characteristics of willing leaders? Willing leaders accept responsibility and accountability for their decisions and actions. They own the team's failures and give credit to others for the team's successes. They are proactive problem identifiers, anticipators, and solvers. They confront challenges and collaborate with others to implement solutions. Willing leaders see their team members' problems as their problems.

The Will to Lead Enables Leadership Capabilities

Illustrated in Figure 5.6, the will to lead is the third enabling attribute of leadership framing the Model for Sustained Leadership Excellence. Alongside the pillars of trust and concern, the will to lead strengthens a leader's ability to consistently achieve the correct mission results with their team over the long term by informing their decisions, communication, and actions through the lens of a willing-to-lead perspective.

LEADERSHIP EXCELLENCE | 177

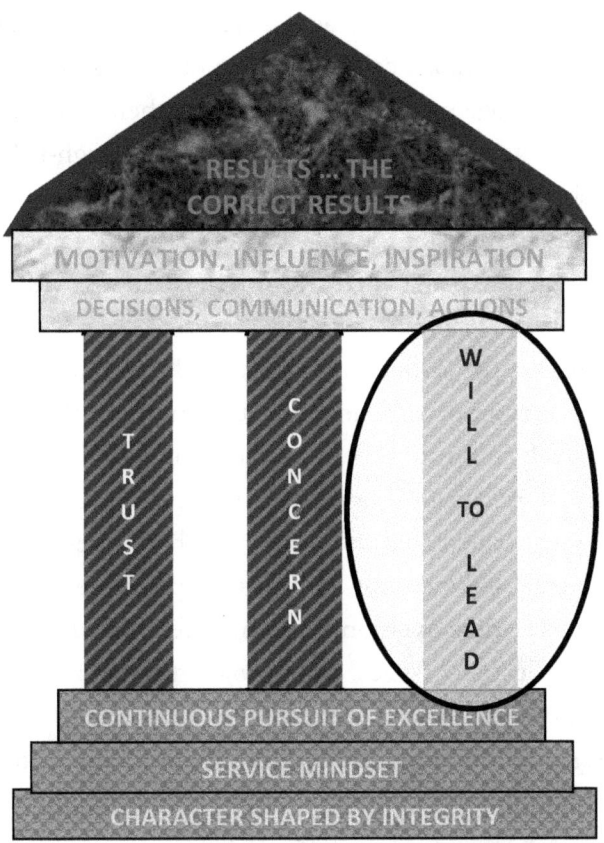

Figure 5.6. Enabling Attribute of the Will to Lead

Part I of the book presented research and best practices highlighting key leadership capabilities and behaviors demonstrated by successful leaders, including courage, confidence, bold action, commitment, passion, energy, learning, development, expertise, competence, persistence, grit, leading change, resilience, flexibility, creativity, and innovation. The following sections explore how the will to lead not only shapes the leadership process, but also enables, builds, and sustains these capabilities.

The will to lead enables courage, confidence, and bold action. Courage, confidence, and bold action are indispensable characteristics of sustained leadership excellence. These behaviors are fueled by the will to lead. Courage motivates and inspires others to excel, especially in the face of adversity, uncertainty, change, or high-risk operating environments. Emphasizing its importance, Sir Winston Churchill, Britain's Prime Minister during World War II, famously stated, "Courage is rightly considered the foremost of the virtues because upon it, all others depend."[240]

Courage helps leaders confront and overcome challenges, building a reservoir of experience that strengthens their confidence to act decisively in future situations. This combination enables bold, consequential decisions—especially in time-critical scenarios. It also encourages calculated risk-taking, such as investing in innovative products, services, or process improvements. Moreover, courage helps leaders overcome common fears like public speaking, delivering difficult messages, and navigating high-stakes situations with resilience and resolve.

Courage in the face of failure. An impediment to sustained leadership excellence is the fear of failure. Leaders need courage and confidence to persevere in the face of failure, enabled by the will to lead. Failure can be transformed into a motivator. J.K. Rowling, novelist, screenwriter, film producer, and author of the highly successful *Harry Potter* fantasy series, explained how failure often leads to success. In an interview with Oprah Winfrey, Rowling stated, "Failure ... failure doesn't get spoken about enough. We speak about success all the time, but ... it's the ability to resist failure, in many ways, or use failure that often leads to the greatest success."[241]

The will to lead enables commitment, passion, and energy. A leader's genuine commitment and passion for the team's mission and the welfare of its members set the tone for the organization. Commitment and passion are energizing; they motivate, influence, and inspire team members to persist in accomplishing the team's goals and objectives. A leader's commitment, passion, and energy—enabled by the will to lead—convey the importance and urgency of the team's mission to internal and external stakeholders, helping keep team members focused on mission priorities.

When a team operates under a sense of urgency, safety systems and quality control measures become crucial to maintaining safe operations and delivering high-quality products and services.

The will to lead enables learning and development. All leaders are learners . . . constantly observing, assessing, studying, and identifying ways to enhance their leadership capabilities. Sustained leadership excellence requires ongoing learning and development. A leader's professional development is marked by formal, informal, and experiential learning.

Organizations must invest in systematic training and development for aspiring leaders to cultivate and sustain their leadership pipeline. As Noel Tichy proposes in *The Leadership Engine*, successful organizations recruit and grow leaders, a leadership development methodology he describes as a "leadership engine."[242] Tichy uses the term to illustrate the process of identifying, educating, training, and producing leaders who progress along a phased development track. The aim for current and aspiring leaders is to get—and remain—on this learning and development track.

An illustrative example of systematic leadership development can be found in the U.S. military's approach to developing commissioned and noncommissioned officers. The U.S. military employs a comprehensive, systematic approach to leadership development for both career officers and non-commissioned officers, integrating education, training, mentorship, and practical experience across all stages of professional growth. For officers, this progression typically includes commissioning through service academies, reserve officer training corps, or officer candidate school, followed by structured professional military education (PME) at key career milestones, such as the Basic Officer Leader Course, Captains Career Course, Command and General Staff College, and Senior Service Colleges. Similarly, NCOs advance through a series of leadership schools—ranging from the Basic Leader Course to the Sergeants Major Academy—designed to build tactical expertise, operational competence, and strategic insight. Both tracks emphasize ethical leadership, joint operations, mission command, and continuous self-development, ensuring that leaders are prepared to meet evolving challenges at the tactical, operational, and strategic levels.

The will to lead enables expertise and competence. A key element of sustained leadership excellence is credibility, which stems from expertise, competence, and reputation, along with a thorough understanding of the organization's products, services, and operations. The more team members, fellow leaders, and stakeholders perceive the leader as knowledgeable about the organization's mission, the more they value that leader's credibility. High-value leaders are recognized as competent experts in their field, earning a reputation for building winning teams. A leader's credibility is imperative for motivating, influencing, and inspiring team members to consistently achieve the correct results safely and effectively over the long term.

Building credibility demands time, energy, effort, and focus. It requires a willingness to make personal sacrifices and a commitment to honing expertise. Credibility is rooted in competence and reinforced by consistently delivering successful results. A leader's desire to be a credible expert fuels their ability to overcome inevitable challenges, failures, and setbacks along the journey while leveraging lessons learned from those experiences.

A leader's position within the organizational hierarchy typically determines the technical expertise required. In addition to leadership responsibilities, entry-level leaders should possess expertise in one or more functional areas, such as finance, engineering, operations, information technology, sales and marketing, or supply chain management. They must also have a solid understanding of their team's products, services, and operating processes.

Building on their experience as entry-level leaders, middle-level leaders typically navigate more complex aspects of an organization's operations, including budgeting, purchasing, sales, marketing, supply chain management, and strategic and operational planning at local, regional, national, or international levels, when applicable. Most mid-level leaders oversee entry-level leaders, expanding their scope of responsibility, accountability, and oversight.

At the highest levels of an organization, senior leaders hold the greatest responsibility and are ultimately accountable for the safe and effective accomplishment of the organization's mission. These leaders must build strong leadership teams that provide expertise across all operational and functional domains, offering the knowledge, intelligence, and situational awareness needed to run the organization successfully.[243] Additionally, senior leaders are responsible for establishing and cascading strategic and operational guidance by clearly and regularly communicating the organization's mission, vision, values, goals, objectives, priorities, and strategy. Mid- and entry-level leaders must align their team's goals, objectives, priorities, and strategies to support these aspirations.

The will to lead enables persistence and grit. Persistence and grit are essential to sustaining leadership excellence. Enduring leaders remain committed and steadfast in the face of challenges and adversity. They demonstrate grit—the ability to persevere and lead without complaining or criticizing. As Richard DeVos, co-founder of Amway, said, "If I had to select one quality, one personal characteristic that I regard as being most highly correlated with success, whatever the field, I would pick the trait of persistence. The will to endure to the end, to get knocked down seventy times and get up off the floor saying, 'Here comes number seventy-one.'"[244]

The will to lead enables the capability to persevere through setbacks and failures. In *Good to Great, Why Some Companies Make the Leap . . . and Others Don't*, Jim Collins emphasizes that great leaders are "infected with an incurable need to produce sustained results. They are resolved to do whatever it takes to make their companies great, no matter how big or hard the decisions."[245]

Brian Tracy reinforces this view, affirming that while it is easy to develop a grand vision for yourself and the person you want to be, it takes incredible persistence and grit to follow through on your vision and commitments. "As soon as you set a high goal or standard for yourself," Tracy explains, "you will run into all kinds of difficulties and setbacks. You will be surrounded by temptations to compromise your values and your vision. You will feel an almost irresistible urge to 'get along by going along.' Your desire to earn the respect and cooperation of others can easily lead to the abandonment of your principles. Persistence is the ability to stick to principles, to stand for what you believe in and to refuse to budge unless you feel right about the alternative."[246]

The will to lead enables leading change. One of the most challenging and important leadership responsibilities is guiding a team through change—whether those changes are to a team's mission, operating procedures, processes, policies, organizational restructuring, or staffing levels.[247] While some people welcome change as an opportunity, most are uncomfortable with significant transitions. Change often triggers resistance, skepticism, distrust, fear, or resentment due to uncertainty. Team members may perceive change as a threat to job security, raising concerns about their future after the change is implemented. Leaders must provide clarity and explain the intended purpose of the change , along with expected outcomes.

Leaders can employ various people-focused and mission-focused strategies to ensure the effective implementation of change.

People-focused actions include keeping team members informed throughout the change process and providing one-on-one support to help them navigate the transition. Leaders can also form sub-teams to guide the group, solicit active support from informal influencers, and gather feedback from team leaders and members throughout the change process. A key objective is to address rumors and innuendos, ensuring clarity and transparency.

Mission-focused actions may include restructuring teams to help facilitate the change, offering training for new job requirements, building a coalition of team members to support the change, creating a sense of urgency, and demonstrating commitment to the change.

Leaders must recognize that adapting to change involves progressing through various phases. In *Managing Transitions: Making the Most of Change*, William Bridges highlights the psychological transitions that individuals and organizations experience. Bridges describes these phases as awareness, assessment, implementation, and stabilization.[248] Rushing through these phases can produce anxiety and jeopardize the success of a change effort. Although emotions can complicate the change process, they also provide valuable feedback that leaders should not overlook.

Engaging team members and helping to guide them through the process is important. Leaders can reduce apprehension and ease the transition by actively listening and encouraging them to share their views, concerns, and ideas during one-on-one discussions and team meetings. The following sections summarize each phase of the change management process, according to Bridges.[249] These transitional phases should be adapted to the organization's size and geographical scope of operations.

> ### Phases of Change
>
> *Awareness*
> *Assessment*
> *Implementation*
> *Stabilization*

Awareness. The awareness phase marks the point when team members are first informed of a pending change. Generally, the sooner this happens, the better—though the timing and method of communication are equally important. Depending on the size of the team and the scope of the change, leaders should first discuss the planned changes with their leadership team, followed by a meeting with all team members.

For organizations operating virtually, across multiple shifts, or in different time zones, archived video presentations or audio messages should be available for those unable to attend key meetings announcing changes. In addition, town-hall-style sessions can support two-way communication, providing opportunities to address concerns and answer questions.

Regular team meetings at all levels help ensure consistent communication, alignment among leaders, and clarity in messaging. Communication with external stakeholders may also be required, using channels such as emails, newsletters, intranet and internet updates, or, when appropriate, mailed correspondence.

This awareness phase lays the foundation for the next step in the change management process: assessment.

Assessment. In the assessment phase, team members and stakeholders evaluate the personal and collective impact of the planned change. Emotional reactions—both positive and negative—are common and must be acknowledged. During this stage, leaders play a pivotal role in providing meaning, clarity, and reassurance while addressing concerns. Their decisions, communication, and actions are critical to maintaining momentum and trust. The will to lead is especially important here, as it sustains the character and integrity needed to guide teams toward the implementation phase of the change management process.

Implementation. The implementation phase is often the most challenging, as team members begin to experience the direct impact of the change on their work, schedules, locations, and personal lives. This stage can be chaotic, unpredictable, and emotionally taxing. Common reactions include apprehension, anxiety, anger, and fear—though some may welcome the change, feeling reassured, optimistic, or secure. Team performance may temporarily decline as members reset, adjust, learn, and work toward accepting the changes—all while maintaining the team's ongoing responsibilities and mission.

Stabilization. The stabilization phase marks the desired end state of the change management process. During this stage, team members begin to settle into new roles and responsibilities brought on by the change. Ideally, the result is improved team performance through greater efficiency, effectiveness, and enhanced value delivered to both internal and external customers.

Not all changes produce the intended outcomes. Leaders must assess the impact of the change and determine whether further actions are necessary to reinforce stability and optimize performance.[250]

The will to lead enables resilience and flexibility. Sustained leadership excellence requires resilience and flexibility, especially in the face of adversity, setbacks, and failure. The will to lead enables this capability by helping leaders overcome the fear of failure and view challenges as opportunities for growth and learning. Adopting a long-term perspective, rather than being consumed by short-term obstacles, further strengthens a leader's ability to remain resilient and flexible.

Moreover, a leader's resilience and flexibility enable a measured approach to decision-making, communication, and action, which in turn motivates, influences, and inspires team members to persevere through difficult times.

Research suggests that 70% of the decisions people make turn out to be incorrect.[251] Over time, people, situations, and conditions change, making mistakes inevitable. Long-term success depends on a leader's ability to recognize, acknowledge, and accept those mistakes. Effective leaders learn from their errors, reassess the situation, minimize losses, and chart a better path forward. The most damaging mistakes are often not the ones made, but the ones denied—when leaders refuse to admit their own or their team's missteps.

Flexibility is sometimes misperceived as a weakness because it can reveal vulnerability. Yet, sustained leadership success demands honesty about one's weaknesses, mistakes, and the need for support. Vulnerability, rather than undermining authority, fosters trust and deepens connection. Patrick Lencioni, management consultant and best-selling author reinforces this perspective: "Nothing inspires trust in another human being like vulnerability—there is just something immensely attractive and inspiring about humility and graciousness."[252] His influential works, including *The Advantage: Why Organizational Health Trumps Everything Else in Business* and *The Five Dysfunctions of a Team*, underscore the critical role vulnerability plays in effective leadership.[253]

The will to lead enables creativity and innovation. Excellence in leadership demands creativity and bold action to uncover, develop, and implement innovative solutions that enhance an organization's value. The will to lead fuels this process, driving leaders to challenge the status quo and inspire breakthrough thinking. Innovation is essential to keeping products, services, and processes relevant and compelling for customers and stakeholders.

To foster a culture of innovation, leaders must empower their teams to take risks, experiment, and boldly pursue transformative ideas. The freedom to explore innovative solutions reflects an organization's culture. Creating space for new ideas signals a leader's commitment to investing in the future and fostering transformation while still executing the team's current mission. Providing this space, however, often competes with limited resources such as time, funding, and attention. Effective leaders navigate these constraints by balancing immediate mission demands with mid- and long-term goals, ensuring that innovation and execution move forward together.

Impact of The Will to Lead on Sustaining Leadership Excellence

The will to lead, along with the enabling attributes of trust and concern, sustains leadership excellence by both shaping the leadership process and enabling key leadership capabilities—including courage, confidence, and bold action; commitment, passion, and energy; learning and development; expertise and competence; persistence and grit; leading change; resilience and flexibility; and creativity and innovation. Figure 5.7 summarizes the impact of the will to lead on developing and sustaining leadership excellence.

The Will to Lead Enables
• Courage, confidence, and bold action
• Commitment, passion, and energy
• Learning and development
• Expertise and competence
• Persistence and grit
• Leading change
• Resilience and flexibility
• Creativity and innovation

Figure 5.7. Impact of the Will to Lead on Leadership Excellence

A Willingness to Lead

> The difference between a successful person and others is not a lack of strength, not a lack of knowledge, but a lack of will.
> — Vince Lombardi[254]

Willing leaders are characterized by their readiness to take responsibility for their team's mission and their commitment to being held accountable for the performance of others. As a leader, how do you act when risks seem overwhelming? Are you willing to accept the solitude of leadership and the loneliness of tough decisions? Are you willing to make yourself vulnerable to the risk of failing as a leader or the uncertainty of success? These questions, posed by Marvin Bower, former chief executive officer of McKinsey & Company, in *The Will to Lead: Running a Business with a Network of Leaders*, underscore significant leadership challenges—demands that can adversely impact a leader's willingness to lead over the long term.[255]

Few leadership challenges are more testing than being held responsible and accountable for the performance of others, particularly when a leader may be reluctant to handle that responsibility. Even willing leaders can find themselves in situations where they are given the reins of leadership, only to subsequently lose their desire to lead due to the demands and challenges of leadership. A leader's indifference to their role is a recipe for poor performance.

Lencioni emphasizes that the single most important factor determining whether an organization will be healthy and prosper is the genuine commitment and active involvement of its leader.[256] When a leader's commitment comes into question, it's essential to address those concerns directly, ideally through a candid discussion with their supervisor. This conversation can explore options such as additional leadership development or a potential transition to an individual contributor role that better aligns with their strengths and aspirations. The will to lead can be eroded by risk, uncertainty, vulnerability, and other personal challenges, but recognizing and addressing these issues is vital to sustaining effective leadership.

Strengthening the will to lead. To strengthen the will to lead, it is essential to embrace the vulnerability that comes with the possibility of failure and to develop a resilient mindset that views setbacks as opportunities for growth. As Tracy explains, leaders can take specific, actionable steps to reinforce their determination and effectiveness, even in the face of adversity.

> First, imagine that your biggest problem or challenge in life has been sent to you at this moment to help you, to teach you something valuable. Second, be willing to cut your losses and walk away if you have made a mistake or a bad choice. Accept that you are not perfect, you can't be right all the time and then get on with your [job]. Third, learn

from every mistake you make. Write down every lesson it contains. Use your mistakes in the present as stepping stones to great success in the future.[257]

Figure 5.8 summarizes how the attributes of trust, concern, and the will to lead enable leadership excellence by shaping a leader's decisions, communication, and actions.

Enabling Sustained Leadership Excellence
Trust, concern, and the will to lead enable leadership excellence by building and sustaining key leadership capabilities while informing a leader's decisions, communication, and actions—instruments of leadership responsible for motivating, influencing, and inspiring team members to consistently achieve the correct mission results over the long term.

Figure 5.8. Trust, Concern, and the Will to Lead Enable Leadership Excellence

Having examined how the enabling attributes of trust, concern, and the will to lead inform and shape a leader's decisions, communication, and actions, Chapter Six explores the Core Values of Leadership Excellence. These foundational values—character shaped by integrity, a service mindset, and the continuous pursuit of excellence—provide the cognitive fuel that powers the model's enabling attributes and drives the leadership process.

Chapter Six: Core Values of Leadership Excellence

> Try not to become a man of success, but rather
> try to become a man of value.
> — Albert Einstein[258]

As illustrated in the Model for Sustained Leadership Excellence, the aim of leadership is to consistently achieve the correct mission results. Leaders accomplish this by motivating, influencing, and inspiring team members through their decisions, communication, and actions. These instruments of leadership generate the motivation, influence, and inspiration essential to achieving mission success and sustaining leadership excellence over the long term. The model emphasizes how trust, concern, and the will to lead enable and harmonize these instruments, working together to sustain leadership excellence. This chapter turns to an exploration of the model's three Core Values of Leadership Excellence: Character

Shaped by Integrity, a Service Mindset, and the Continuous Pursuit of Excellence.

Core values are deeply held beliefs that remain constant over time, providing leaders with a clear sense of identity and purpose. As symbolized in Figure 6.1, these values form the model's foundation, serving as cognitive fuel that energizes the enabling attributes and, in turn, powers the leadership process. The model's core values are inspired by the United States Air Force profession of arms doctrine.[259]

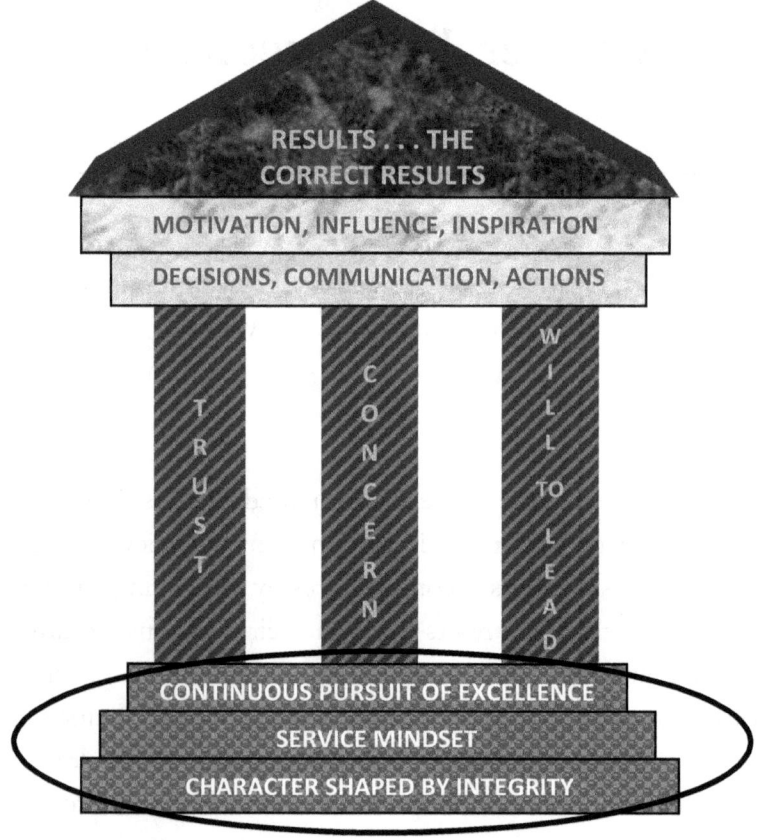

Figure 6.1. Core Values of Leadership Excellence

These values are essential to developing and sustaining long-term leadership excellence. The following sections explore the core values and their role in powering the Model for Sustained Leadership Excellence.

Character Shaped by Integrity

> Nearly all men can stand adversity, but if you want to test a man's character, give him power.
> — Abraham Lincoln[260]

There is near-unanimous agreement among leadership scholars and practitioners that, of all values, an honorable character is a vital trait for leaders. As Bennis asserts, "Timeless leadership is always about character."[261] In an extensive study spanning 35 years, Edgar F. Puryear analyzed the leadership characteristics of four prominent American generals: George S. Patton, Jr., Douglas MacArthur, Dwight D. Eisenhower, and George C. Marshall. Despite divergent personalities and leadership styles, Puryear's research aimed to identify the key characteristics that define successful leaders. His study concluded that "leadership is really the unconscious expression of the character of the leader."[262]

Integrity lies at the core of character. It refers to honest and ethical behavior, making a person trustworthy. Integrity stands in direct opposition to self-interest; it is about being truthful—no lying, cheating, or stealing.[263] To be seen as a person of integrity, a leader must be honest, support their team members, and honor the confidence their team members place in them. If team members and other stakeholders believe a leader has been dishonest or manipulated others for personal gain, the leader will lose their trust.[264]

As shown in Figure 6.2, Character Shaped by Integrity is one of three foundational core values underpinning the Model for Sustained Leadership Excellence. A leader's character, along with a

Service Mindset and the Continuous Pursuit of Excellence, fuels their trustworthiness, concern, and will to lead; values that, in turn, shape the instruments of leadership. These instruments drive the leadership process by motivating, influencing, and inspiring team members to consistently achieve the correct mission results over the long term. The following sections explore how Character shaped by integrity builds and sustains leadership excellence.

Figure 6.2. Character Shaped by Integrity

Character development. We have little control over many aspects of life. We do not choose our parents or the environment we are raised in, nor do we select our special skills and talents. However, as we reach the age of reason, we gain control over our character development. Our decisions, communication, and actions become expressions of that character. Zenger and Folkman contend that character is "the center pole of the leadership tent," asserting that character is the most important factor in a leader's long-term success.[265]

In their comprehensive empirical study for *The Extraordinary Leader: Turning Good Managers into Great Leaders*, Zenger and Folkman analyzed over 200,000 professionals, ultimately narrowing their focus to more than 25,000 leaders to identify the key factors associated with effective leadership. Their analysis concluded that a leader's effectiveness is significantly diminished when their character is called into question. Often described as doing the right thing, Zenger and Folkman observed, "If a person is not honorable, does not keep promises, does not tell the truth, or places personal gain above the needs of the organization, then this flaw will cause the person to be ineffective."[266]

A leader's actions are a true measure of character. Character and action are inseparable; what a leader chooses to do reflects who they truly are. When actions align with decisions and communication, character becomes both transparent and credible, earning the trust and respect of others. Leaders of high character demonstrate the courage to do what's right, even when no one is watching. As Maxwell asserts, "Being bigger on the inside than on the outside, now that's real character."[267]

The importance of character has been emphasized in philosophical writings since antiquity. In *Master Strategies for Higher Achievement*, Brian Tracy underscores this timeless virtue by highlighting its significance to the ancient Greeks in the following passage.[268]

From the earliest civilizations and throughout the ages all education has been based on teaching values to young people. When young people grow up with clear values to which they're committed they grow up as productive members of society with a strong sense of character capable of achieving great things with their lives. A person was considered educated by the ancient Greeks when he or she was brought up to have a noble character expressing self-esteem, self-respect, and personal pride. An uneducated person was one who had not been brought up with clear, strong values and whose behavior, therefore, was unpredictable and unreliable.

Throughout all of history, men and women of character have always risen to the top of most of the great institutions. Throughout all of American history, up until the twentieth century, values were taught and reinforced at every grade level and in every subject. It was always understood that a good country required good citizens and good citizens were those who had good values. We know today that high-achieving men and women are very clear about their values and refuse to compromise them for any reason. One of the most important things you will do in life is to develop clear, positive values and to organize your life around them.

At the beginning of Western thought, three major philosophers stand out above all others; they are Socrates, Plato, and Aristotle. Socrates taught the importance of goodness and wisdom. He first articulated what came to be called the Socratic law of causality, which we refer to as the law of cause and effect. He said for every effect there's a cause and the effects that take place in human life are primarily caused by the character and values of the people themselves. Socrates inherently knew that if young people grew up with true values and character, they would have good lives. Plato was a student of Socrates. Plato wondered how society could be best organized to assure the greatest good for the greatest number.

Aristotle, the third of the three great philosophers, was a student of Plato. Aristotle studied under Plato for many years and then formed his own school of philosophy. Aristotle was so highly respected in his day that King Phillip of Macedon hired Aristotle to be the personal tutor to his son, Alexander, who became the master of the known world during his lifetime.

Aristotle is often considered the greatest philosopher who has ever lived. His key question, which was developed in his Nicomachean Ethics, was, "How shall we live in order to be happy?" Aristotle's answer to his own question was that only the good can be truly happy, and only the virtuous can be good. His conclusion, which is relevant to us today, was that if you wanted to be happy and fulfilled, you must become virtuous and good in your inner life. Aristotle then went on to describe the values and virtues that a truly good and happy person would have to develop in order to enjoy an exceptional life. As a result of this incredible insight, someone once wrote that all philosophy for 2,000 years was merely a footnote to Aristotle.

You develop the values that lead to an extraordinary, happy, fulfilling life very much the same way you learn a subject or physical ability. First, you decide the value that you wish to internalize and make a part of your character. What are the values that might be the best to have and hold most dearly? You really only need three to five key values to serve as the organizing principles of your life.

The first of the values is integrity or honesty. Integrity is perhaps the most respected value of a human being. Virtually all of your success in life will be determined by the quality of your relationships. By the people who know you, believe in you and trust you. Trust, therefore, is the basis of all long-lasting relationships and integrity is the basis of trust. In fact, a person has true character by the degree by which they have true integrity. A person who is honest only 80% of the time is a person who lacks integrity and who cannot be trusted. Integrity means simply that you keep your word. That you do what you say you will do. Integrity means that people can rely on you to do what is right and good and necessary under all circumstances. They can trust you.

Our greatest leaders have been men and women of integrity. One of your chief aims in life is to become known as a man or woman of honor, which stems from trust and integrity. And this reputation will come naturally when you make a habit of always doing what you say you will do under all circumstances.

A leader's power to motivate others is directly correlated to the followers' belief in the leader's integrity. Followers must believe the leader will abide by the highest ethical standards of fairness and justice. Integrity appears over and over as the most important leadership quality. People can only put their whole hearts into their work when they feel secure and they can only feel secure when they can trust you completely.

The most effective leaders are men and women of integrity. It was said that it was the integrity of George Washington, above all else, that made the formation of the United States possible. The power of his character and integrity was so strong that although he didn't take part in the constitutional debates, in the end, they all turned to him and asked him to be the first president of the United States of America.[269]

As the Greek philosophers taught, character is the foundation of leadership, with integrity as the driving force behind building and sustaining it. Stephen Covey underscores this principle: "In the last analysis, what we *are* communicates far more eloquently than anything we say or do. We all know it. There are people we trust absolutely because we know their character. Whether they're eloquent or not, whether they have the human relations techniques or not, we trust them, and we work successfully with them."[270]

To further emphasize the enduring value of character, Covey cites William George Jordan, a renowned nineteenth-century American editor and essayist, who wrote, "Into the hands of every individual is given a marvelous power for good or evil—the silent, unconscious, unseen influence of [their] life. This is simply the constant radiation of what [a man or woman] really is, not what [they] pretend to be."[271] A leader's character, therefore, is seen as a true reflection of their authentic self.

In his article, "The Seven Keys to Lasting Leadership," international leadership speaker Alan Zimmerman affirms that character is essential to building a reputation for leadership excellence. "When you focus solely on what you can DO," he asserts, "without first deciding what kind of person you should BE, you're making a mistake. Your talent will make your name known, but your character will determine what people associate with your name. Your talent will dictate your potential, but your character will determine your legacy."[272]

Emotional intelligence. Emotional intelligence (EQ) is a reflection of a leader's character. Research by TalentSmart suggests that leaders with high EQ are more likely to remain calm under pressure, resolve conflict effectively, and respond to others with empathy.[273] Lauren Landry, Director of Marketing and Communications for Harvard Business School Online, reports that emotional intelligence comprises four core competencies: self-awareness, self-management, social awareness, and relationship management.

Self-awareness describes a leader's ability to understand their strengths and weaknesses while recognizing the impact of their emotions on their team's performance. Self-management refers to a leader's ability to manage their emotions, particularly in stressful situations, while maintaining a positive outlook despite setbacks. While it is essential for leaders to manage their own emotions, social awareness focuses on their ability to recognize others' emotions and understand the perspectives of colleagues and team members. According to Landry, relationship management involves a leader's ability to influence, coach, and mentor others while effectively resolving conflicts.[274]

Leaders set the tone for their organization. A lack of emotional intelligence can erode a positive work environment, resulting in lower team engagement, reduced performance, and increased turnover. Even when leaders possess strong technical skills, an inability to manage their emotions can diminish their effectiveness and overshadow their professional competence.

A Service Mindset

> Leaders Eat Last.
> — Simon Sinek[275]

In addition to character, a service mindset is essential to sustaining long-term leadership success. Effective leaders prioritize the needs of others—team members, partners, clients, customers, and stakeholders. This mindset stems from the belief that a leader's decisions, communication, and actions should create value and deliver meaningful benefits to those they serve. A commitment to serving both internal and external stakeholders is a driving force behind sustained leadership excellence.

A service-oriented mindset shifts a leader's focus from exerting control to supporting and empowering others. This approach stands in contrast to traditional leadership models, such as the Great Man Theory, which portray leaders as heroic figures and emphasize authority and charisma as central to leadership.[276] Instead, the service-minded leader champions the interests of others, offers meaningful support, and advocates on their behalf. This shift reflects a deeper sense of duty, purpose, and responsibility—one that transcends positional power and embraces a genuine commitment to those they lead.

As depicted in Figure 6.3, a service mindset is one of the foundational core values underpinning the Model for Sustained Leadership Excellence. Alongside Character Shaped by Integrity and the Continuous Pursuit of Excellence, a leader's Service Mindset fuels their trustworthiness, concern, and will to lead. These attributes, in turn, shape leadership decisions, communication, and actions, which drive the leadership process. Through these instruments, leaders motivate, influence, and inspire team members to consistently achieve the correct mission results over the long term. The following sections explore how a service mindset contributes to building and sustaining leadership excellence.

Figure 6.3. A Service Mindset

Service leadership. An appreciable body of contemporary leadership literature highlights service leadership as a key component of leadership excellence. These theories emphasize that effective leaders prioritize the growth and well-being of their team members, organizations, and communities—placing service above the pursuit and exercise of power at the top of an organization. In *Leaders Eat Last: Why Some Teams Pull Together and Others Don't*, Simon Sinek underscores service as a core value of successful leadership. He asserts that effective leaders prioritize the welfare of their teams and lead by placing the needs of others before their own.[277]

Leaders who embrace a service mindset spend time engaged and involved with their team members. They demonstrate *leadership by walking around*. Research conducted by McKinsey & Company, referenced in the best-selling book *In Search of Excellence* by Thomas Peters and Robert Waterman, found that unassuming leaders frequently walk around and interact with their teams, rather than remaining isolated in meetings or behind office doors.[278]

In *The Will to Lead*, Marvin Bower urges leaders to invert the traditional command-and-control approach to leadership, advocating instead for a service-oriented mindset that motivates, influences, and inspires others. Drawing on research, Bower provides examples of leaders who embody this attitude, including a notable instance from the United States-led liberation of Kuwait during Operation Desert Storm in 1991. Bower recounts how U.S. Army General Norman Schwarzkopf, the international coalition commander, was offered a luxurious villa by the Saudi government for his living quarters but chose instead to stay with his campaign staff in a small room tucked away behind his office. General Schwarzkopf understood the importance of being present with and serving alongside his troops during the critical phases of the military campaign.

In the military, a key tenet of service leadership is that when leaders take care of their people, their people will take care of the mission—*take care of your people and they will take care of the mission*. Achieving the team's mission safely and effectively, while ensuring the well-being of those executing it, embodies the essence of a service mindset.

James Kouzes and Barry Posner have conducted extensive research on leadership over the decades. In *Credibility: How Leaders Gain and Lose It, Why People Demand It*, they summarize the impact of a leader's service-oriented mindset, stating "Leaders we admire do not place themselves at the center; they place others there. They do not seek the attention of people; they give it to others. They do not focus on satisfying their own aims and desires; they look for ways to respond to the needs and interests of their constituents. They are not self-centered; they concentrate on the constituent."[279]

Servant leadership. The concept of servant leadership is rooted in the principle of selfless service. "Servant leadership has a strong moral dimension. It makes altruism the central component of the leadership process and frames leadership around the principle of caring for others," asserts Peter Northouse.[280]

In *Servant Leadership*, Robert Greenleaf, former director of management research, development, and education at American Telephone and Telegraph Company, describes servant leaders as those who prioritize serving others first.[281] This approach contrasts sharply with leaders who pursue leadership roles primarily for personal ambition. Between these two types of leaders, "there are shadings and blends that are part of the infinite variety of human nature. The difference manifests itself in the care taken by the servant-first leader to make sure that other people's highest priority needs are being served," Greenleaf explains.[282]

According to Greenleaf, the best—and most challenging—test for servant leaders is to ask: "Do those served grow as persons? Do they, while being served, become healthier, wiser, freer, more autonomous, more likely themselves to become servants? Does the leader bring value to their followers' lives?"[283] Servant leaders share power, put others' needs first, and help others develop and reach their maximum potential and performance.[284]

In his essay "The Servant as Leader," first published in 1970, Greenleaf derived the idea of the servant as leader from his reading of Hermann Hesse's *Journey to the East*. Greenleaf recounts a story from Hesse's novel in which a group of important men embark on a long journey into the wilderness, accompanied by a servant. The servant performs menial chores and sustains the group with his spirit and song.[285] When the group loses its way, the servant becomes particularly helpful in leading them to their destination. His masters came to trust him because his leadership helps them navigate their challenges. In the end, as a servant, he becomes their leader, and they, in turn, became his constituents.[286]

Serving customers and partners. Quality Management Systems (QMS) are designed to refine work processes, enhance organizational efficiency, optimize resource allocation, and elevate overall performance, all with the goal of improving the quality of products and services delivered to customers. While QMS primarily focuses on external customers, it also recognizes internal partners as both customers and suppliers. This internal, service-oriented perspective encourages leaders and their teams to continuously improve products, services, and processes—not only for external stakeholders but also for internal partners.

Paradox of ambition and humility. Humility is a hallmark of a service-oriented mindset. In reviewing *Good to Great: Why Some Companies Make the Leap . . . and Others Don't*, Chade-Meng Tan, co-founder of the Search Inside Yourself Leadership Institute and known informally as Meng from his days at Google, highlights one of author Jim Collins' key findings: humility is essential to leadership excellence. Collins and his research team sought to discover what enabled certain companies to make the leap from good to great. They began by analyzing every company that appeared on the Fortune 500 list between 1965 and 1995. From this, they identified the companies that outperformed the general market by at least a factor of three for fifteen consecutive years, eliminating one-hit wonders and companies that benefited from luck alone. Ultimately, Collins identified eleven companies that made the sustained leap and compared them to a set of peers that did not. One striking difference was leadership.[287] Collins discovered that two-thirds of the struggling companies "had leaders with gargantuan personal egos that contributed to the demise or continued mediocrity of the company."[288]

Another important insight by Meng is the role of selfless leadership in helping companies move from good to great. Collins describes these individuals as *Level 5 leaders*, those who, beyond being highly capable, exhibit a paradoxical mix of two important, yet conflicting qualities: great ambition and personal humility. While deeply ambitious, their ambition is not self-serving. Instead, they channel it toward the success of the organization. As Collins notes, "ambitious, first and foremost for the company, not themselves."[289] Because their attention is directed toward the greater good, they feel no need to inflate their egos, which makes them highly effective and inspiring.[290]

Level 5 leaders, Collins emphasizes, display a compelling modesty; they are self-effacing and understated. "The great irony is that the animus and personal ambition that often drive people to positions of power stand at odds with the humility required for Level 5 leadership. When you combine that irony with the fact that boards of directors frequently operate under the false belief that they need to hire a larger-than-life, egocentric leader to make an organization great, you can quickly see why Level 5 leaders rarely appear at the top of our institutions."[291]

A leader's service-oriented mindset fosters a spirit of humility, empowering them to take responsibility for their team's setbacks and failures while giving credit to others for the team's accomplishments and successes.

Character Shaped by Integrity and a Service Mindset represent two of the model's three core values of leadership excellence. The final section of this chapter examines the importance of continually striving for excellence to sustain leadership success.

The Continuous Pursuit of Excellence

> All labor that uplifts humanity has dignity and importance and should be undertaken with painstaking excellence.
> — Martin Luther King, Jr.[292]

In addition to a leader's character and service-oriented mindset, the Continuous Pursuit of Excellence, depicted in Figure 6.4, is the third core value fueling the Model for Sustained Leadership Excellence. This value emphasizes the imperative for leaders to continuously strive to enhance their leadership acumen and elevate their team's mission success. Pursuing excellence requires ongoing learning, development, observation, study, and professional growth shaped by lessons learned through leadership experiences.

A leader's commitment to ongoing improvement strengthens the quality and value of products and services delivered to customers, partners, and stakeholders. Leaders who prioritize excellence adopt a long-term perspective, making decisions that benefit the organization's future while fostering team member growth.

Excellence is not a fixed destination but a continuous journey, where even small gains can lead to significant progress over time. This forward-looking approach enables the organization to thrive beyond the leader's tenure while also enhancing the leader's readiness to assume greater responsibilities.

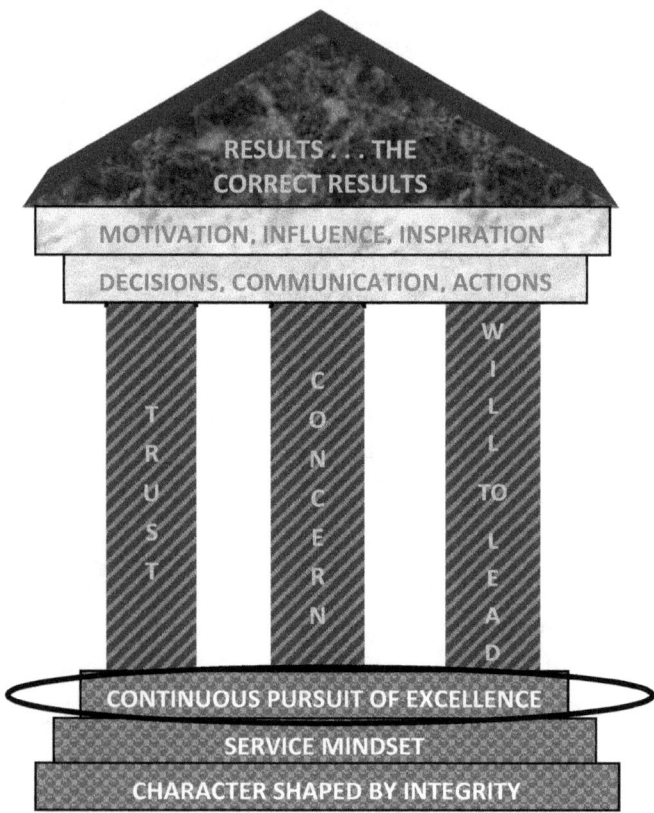

Figure 6.4. The Continuous Pursuit of Excellence

Alongside character shaped by integrity and a service mindset, the continuous pursuit of excellence fuels a leader's trustworthiness, concern, and will to lead. These enabling attributes shape a leader's decisions, communication, and actions—powering the leadership process by motivating, influencing, and inspiring team members to consistently achieve the correct mission results over the long term.

The sections ahead explore how a leader's continuous pursuit of excellence is empowered by lifelong learning, development, and an ongoing focus on improving products, services, and processes.

Learning and development. Driven by curiosity, learning and development are vital to the continuous pursuit of excellence. Curiosity sparks questions—the foundation of learning—and is essential to expanding leadership capability. Curious leaders are lifelong learners who actively seek opportunities to grow their knowledge and skills. Continuous learning and development help leaders remain at the forefront of their fields, strengthening their expertise and enhancing their credibility. This commitment equips them to adapt to evolving challenges and seize emerging opportunities.

Leaders who prioritize lifelong learning cultivate dynamic, resilient organizations that thrive in a rapidly changing world. By modeling a dedication to learning and development, they also foster a team culture of continuous improvement. In such environments, team members are motivated to build their skills and contribute meaningfully to organizational success.

The following subsections—drawing from Peter Senge's *The Fifth Discipline: The Art and Practice of the Learning Organization*,[293] and Zenger and Folkman's "Continuous Learning: A Key Leadership Capability"[294]—highlight the value of learning and development in advancing the continuous pursuit of excellence across eight key areas: decision-making, communication, team-member development, resilience, adaptability and flexibility, innovation and creativity, ethical leadership, and performance feedback.

Decision-making. Continuous learning sharpens critical thinking skills, enabling leaders to evaluate information objectively, recognize assumptions, and make sound decisions. This analytical ability improves both strategic and operational outcomes while reducing the risk of error. Curious leaders seek diverse perspectives and timely, relevant data before acting, resulting in well-informed decisions that consider a broad range of factors and potential consequences. They ask probing questions and examine complex issues from multiple angles, helping to identify root causes, uncover hidden opportunities, and generate creative solutions to difficult challenges.

As discussed in Chapter One, artificial intelligence (AI) systems can serve as a valuable resource in supporting informed decision making. AI enhances the speed, accuracy, and depth of analysis available to leaders, helping them make better choices. Importantly, AI augments human judgment—it does not replace it. When guided by core values such as character shaped by integrity, a service mindset, and the continuous pursuit of excellence, leaders can use AI to support ethical, forward-looking decisions that contribute to sustained leadership success. Here's how:

Data-driven insights. AI can process vast amounts of structured and unstructured data to uncover trends, patterns, and anomalies that might otherwise go unnoticed. This enables leaders to make evidence-based decisions grounded in real-time information rather than intuition alone.

Predictive analytics. AI tools can forecast future scenarios by analyzing historical data. This helps leaders anticipate outcomes, evaluate risks, and make proactive decisions rather than reactive ones.

Bias reduction. Properly designed and monitored AI algorithms can help mitigate human cognitive biases by offering objective recommendations and flagging inconsistencies in decision-making.

Scenario planning and simulation. AI can simulate various *what-if* scenarios, enabling leaders to evaluate potential strategies, assess trade-offs, and plan for contingencies more effectively.

Enhanced personalization. For decisions involving customers, stakeholders, or team members, AI can tailor recommendations based on individual preferences, behaviors, and needs—improving team engagement and satisfaction.

Real-time monitoring. Leaders can leverage AI to continuously monitor operational performance and environmental conditions, allowing for more agile and informed responses to emerging challenges.

Natural language processing (NLP). AI tools with NLP capabilities can analyze sentiment from customer feedback, social media, or team member surveys, giving leaders deeper insight into morale, brand perception, and stakeholder concerns.

Team-member development. Learning-oriented leaders inspire their teams to pursue excellence by modeling a passion for learning and exploration. By prioritizing learning, these leaders create a culture that empowers team members to continuously improve their skills and capabilities. They foster an environment where growth is encouraged, supported, and celebrated.

In addition to leading by example, learning-oriented leaders serve as mentors and coaches, guiding team members through their development journeys. This approach not only helps individual team members grow but also strengthens the organization as a whole.

Communication. Learning and development play a vital role in strengthening a leader's communication skills. As leaders grow in knowledge, self-awareness, and emotional intelligence, they become better equipped to express ideas clearly, listen actively, and adapt their communication style to different audiences and situations.

Continuous development enhances a leader's ability to provide constructive feedback, build trust, and engage others with authenticity and empathy. It also supports confident, persuasive communication that inspires action, fosters collaboration, and aligns teams around shared goals.

Resilience. Learning and development are essential to building a leader's resilience. Through continuous learning, leaders gain new perspectives, problem-solving skills, and adaptive thinking that help them navigate uncertainty and recover from setbacks. Development experiences—facing challenges, reflecting on outcomes, and applying lessons learned—strengthen mental toughness and emotional agility. Over time, these experiences build the confidence and composure needed to lead through adversity. Resilient leaders model perseverance, instill confidence in their teams, and maintain focus on long-term goals even under pressure.

Adaptability and flexibility. Adaptability is a leader's capacity to adjust effectively to new conditions, changes, or unexpected circumstances. It's about being open to change and willing to modify strategies, behavior, or plans in response to evolving environments. Flexibility refers to a leader's willingness and ability to shift perspectives or approaches when needed, without becoming rigid or stuck in one way of thinking. It supports collaboration, innovation, and problem-solving in the continuous pursuit of excellence.

Adaptability and flexibility are vital leadership qualities in today's fast-changing environment. Continuous learning and development play a key role in strengthening these capabilities. Leaders who actively seek new knowledge and experiences are better prepared to understand emerging trends, explore alternative strategies, and respond to evolving circumstances with confidence.

Through development activities such as training, mentorship, and cross-functional experiences, leaders gain new insights to reassess plans, shift priorities, and embrace innovation. Learning fosters the curiosity, humility, and growth mindset that help leaders remain open to change and resilient in the face of disruption. By modeling adaptability and flexibility, learning-oriented leaders encourage their teams to stay agile, responsive, and aligned with organizational goals—no matter how conditions evolve.

Innovation and creativity. Continuous learning exposes leaders to new ideas, concepts, and methodologies that ignite innovation and creativity. Curious leaders actively seek fresh perspectives and unconventional approaches, fostering a mindset open to experimentation and discovery. Their willingness to challenge assumptions and think beyond traditional boundaries encourages creative problem-solving and cultivates a culture of innovation. By embracing ongoing learning, leaders become more comfortable with ambiguity and risk-taking, enabling them to explore uncharted territory with confidence. This inquisitive, growth-oriented mindset helps create an environment where innovation can flourish across the organization.

Ethical leadership. Continuous learning ensures that ethical principles and practices remain at the forefront of a leader's mind and are thoughtfully applied in decision-making and daily practice. Leaders who demonstrate integrity, transparency, accountability, empathy, and fairness actively model and sustain a positive ethical culture. By consistently upholding high ethical standards and modeling principled behavior, leaders earn trust and credibility with their teams, customers, and stakeholders, creating an environment grounded in respect, responsibility, and sustained excellence.

Performance feedback. Performance feedback is a vital component of learning and development and plays a central role in sustaining success. By embracing 360-degree feedback from supervisors, peers, team members, partners, clients, and customers, leaders can identify their strengths and areas for growth. Constructive feedback provides valuable insights into how a leader's behavior and decisions impact others, promoting greater self-awareness and understanding of their leadership style. This reflection helps leaders hone specific skills and competencies, guiding their professional development.

Leaders who seek and respond to candid feedback demonstrate openness and vulnerability, building trust and credibility. They use feedback not only to enhance their leadership effectiveness but also to align their actions with organizational goals, strategies, and values, ensuring their leadership contributes to long-term success.

Receiving input from multiple sources also uncovers blind spots, helping leaders address issues they may not have been aware of. By actively embracing and acting on feedback, leaders set a positive example for their teams, promoting a culture of continuous learning and growth.

The following key points outline a framework for leaders to apply when soliciting feedback, drawn from Douglas Stone and Sheila Heen's *Thanks for the Feedback: The Science and Art of Receiving Feedback Well*,[295] Kim Scott's *Radical Candor: Be a Kick-Ass Boss Without Losing Your Humanity*,[296] and Marcus Buckingham and Ashley Goodall's *The Feedback Fallacy*.[297]

- *Solicit feedback regularly*: Actively seek feedback from various sources, including peers, subordinates, and supervisors, to ensure a well-rounded perspective.
- *Create a safe environment*: Foster an atmosphere of honesty and openness where individuals feel comfortable providing feedback.
- *Listen actively*: Show genuine interest and understanding by paying close attention to feedback. Ask clarifying questions when necessary.
- *Act on feedback*: Demonstrate a commitment to personal growth by implementing meaningful changes based on the feedback received.
- *Follow up*: Regularly check in with feedback providers to assess progress and demonstrate ongoing commitment to improvement.

Continuous product, service, and process improvements. Continuous improvement in the quality of products, services, and processes strengthens and expands a team's mission capability. Just as curiosity drives learning and development, it also sparks continuous product, service, and process improvements. Curiosity prompts questions. These questions serve as the foundation for identifying opportunities to enhance mission effectiveness and operational performance.

Curious leaders and team members challenge assumptions, question the status quo, and pursue objective, data-driven, and evidence-based solutions. This critical thinking approach leads to innovative, sustainable improvements grounded in analysis and insight. Leaders play a vital role by modeling a commitment to improvement, setting high expectations, and creating a culture where continuous learning and innovation are encouraged and rewarded.

By embracing continuous improvement, teams become more adaptable and responsive to emerging challenges and evolving stakeholder needs—key factors for long-term organizational success. Improvements must also align with ethical standards and organizational values, ensuring that innovation is both responsible and sustainable.

Moreover, measuring progress through key performance indicators, benchmarking, and structured feedback loops helps leaders assess effectiveness and guide future improvements. These practices reinforce accountability and ensure that efforts to improve are purposeful, strategic, and results-oriented.

The following subsections summarize the importance and value of continuous product, service, and process improvements for achieving and sustaining leadership excellence. The insights are derived from Clayton Christensen's *The Innovator's Dilemma: When New Technologies Cause Great Firms to Fail*,[298] Robert Camp's *Benchmarking: A Signpost to Excellence in Quality and Productivity*,[299] Charles Rarick's *Best Practices: The Ultimate Guide to Improving Your Company's Performance*,[300] and Bruce Weinstein's *Ethical Leadership: Creating and Sustaining an Ethical Business Culture*.[301]

Innovation and creativity. Leaders committed to excellence consistently seek innovative and creative solutions with their teams to improve products, services, and processes. This focus on innovation and creativity drives the development of effective strategies and operational efficiencies. These efforts are future-focused, prompting leaders to anticipate opportunities and proactively address challenges.

By continuously seeking new information, insights, and perspectives, leaders can mitigate risks and capitalize on emerging trends. A commitment to excellence means remaining open to new ideas and approaches—an essential mindset for fostering continuous improvement. Charles Schwab, founder of Charles Schwab & Company, underscores the value of innovation as a catalyst for long-term success, emphasizing, "The innovation that goes on [at Schwab] is profoundly important—it continues to be the engine that drives our future. If you're not innovating, you're going to go out of business fairly quickly. In this fast-paced world, you've got to stay nimble and inventive if you want to survive."[302]

Benchmarking. Benchmarking is a strategic approach for identifying opportunities to improve products, services, and processes by comparing an organization's performance against leading organizations—internal and external—or industry standards. This practice allows leaders and their teams to learn from the best by identifying performance gaps and areas for growth.

Benchmarking involves selecting areas to benchmark, choosing benchmarking partners, collecting and analyzing data, identifying gaps, and implementing changes while monitoring progress. For example, an organization might compare its customer service response time to industry leaders, pinpoint performance gaps, and develop strategies to meet or exceed those benchmarks. By using benchmarking, leaders drive continuous improvement and ensure their teams sustain high levels of performance.

Best practices. Best practices are proven methods, processes, procedures, and techniques widely recognized as superior because they consistently yield better results across an industry or professional field. Organizations adopt best practices to leverage safe, high-performing methods that ensure consistent, optimal performance and improve efficiency. For instance, an organization might adopt proven infection control procedures from leading healthcare institutions. Leaders and teams identify these practices through research and analysis, adapting them to align with their organization's mission. They also monitor and assess effectiveness after implementation. Best practices often include strategies for crisis management, safety, and recovery, helping leaders and teams maintain stability and perform effectively under time or financial pressures.

Figure 6.5 summarizes how the foundational Core Values of Leadership Excellence fuel and sustain leadership excellence within the Model for Sustained Leadership Excellence.

Core Values of Leadership Excellence
Character Shaped by Integrity, a Service Mindset, and the Continuous Pursuit of Excellence represent the core values of leadership excellence. These values form the foundation of the Model for Sustained Leadership Excellence and fuel the model's enabling attributes of trust, concern, and the will to lead. These attributes, in turn, enable the leadership process by shaping a leader's decisions, communication, and actions—the instruments of leadership—to motivate, influence, and inspire team members to consistently achieve the correct mission results over the long term.

Figure 6.5. Sustaining Leadership Excellence from a Foundation of Character, Service, and Excellence

Operationalizing the model. Rooted in the literature and leadership best practices explored in Part I, Part II introduced the Model for Sustained Leadership Excellence—a framework designed to develop, empower, and sustain long-term leadership success. The model supports current and aspiring leaders across all professions in achieving enduring effectiveness in their roles. This final chapter recaps the model's integrated components and offers strategies to transform its principles into actionable leadership practices.

Chapter Seven: Empower Your Leadership—Turn Principles Into Sustained Performance

> Nothing in the world can take the place of persistence. Talent will not; nothing is more common than unsuccessful men [and women] with talent. Genius will not; unrewarded genius is almost a proverb. Education will not; the world is full of educated derelicts. Persistence and determination alone are omnipotent. The slogan 'Press On' has solved and always will solve the problems of the human race.
> — Calvin Coolidge
> 30th president of the United States[303]

Equipped with the Model for Sustained Leadership Excellence, this chapter offers strategies for translating the model's principles into sustained leadership success. The chapter is organized into four sections. The first section recaps the model's three dimensions, highlighting how the core values, enabling attributes, and leadership process connect to support long-term leadership excellence.

The second section explores the relationship among these components, using scenarios to illustrate how they connect, reinforce one another, and empower leaders to achieve sustained leadership excellence. The third section offers practical guidance for leaders to operationalize the model's principles through journaling and self-assessment.

The final section presents a scenario to help leaders facilitate a strategic planning workshop designed to establish or revise a team's mission, vision, values, goals, objectives, priorities, and strategy—the Unifying Forces of the Leadership Process. A sample agenda is included in the scenario to support the effective planning and execution of the workshop.

By the end of this chapter, leaders will have actionable strategies to implement the model's principles and sustain their leadership impact. All scenarios presented are hypothetical and not intended to represent any specific person, organization, or event. Any similarity to actual individuals, organizations, or situations is purely coincidental.

Review of The Leadership Excellence Model

What is sustained leadership excellence? It is a leader's ability to safely and effectively achieve the correct mission results with their team over the long term. Drawing from research, literature, and leadership best practices explored in this book, the Model for Sustained Leadership Excellence was constructed to provide a framework for achieving this objective. The model affirms that the key to sustained leadership success—regardless of team size, profession, or mission—is to lead from a foundation of core values and enabling attributes.

Three dimensions of the model. As shown in Figure 7.1, the model is structured around three dimensions: a foundation of core values, pillars of enabling attributes, and a gabled capstone representing the leadership process.

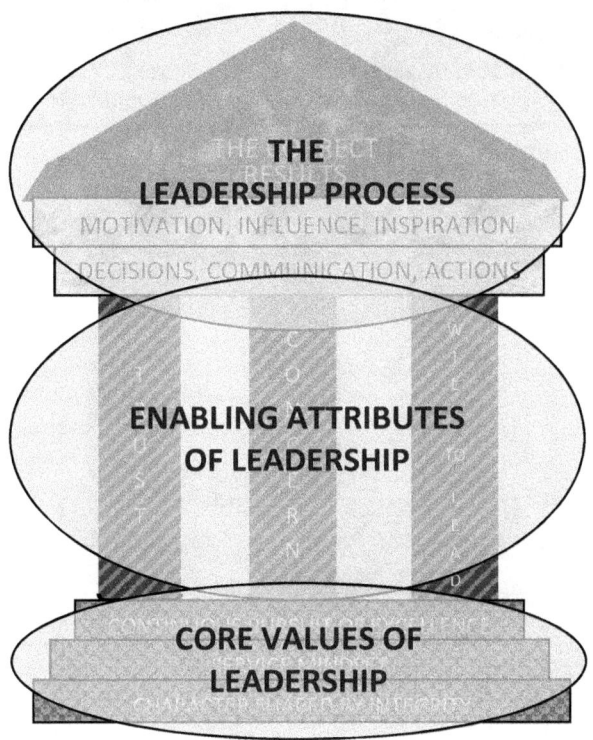

Figure 7.1. Three Dimensions of the Model for Sustained Leadership Excellence

Figure 7.2 depicts each element of the model's framework. Character Shaped by Integrity, a Service Mindset, and the Continuous Pursuit of Excellence form the model's foundational core values. Three pillars symbolize the model's enabling attributes of leadership: Trust, Concern, and the Will to Lead. The gabled capstone illustrates the inputs, outputs, and outcomes of the Leadership Process.

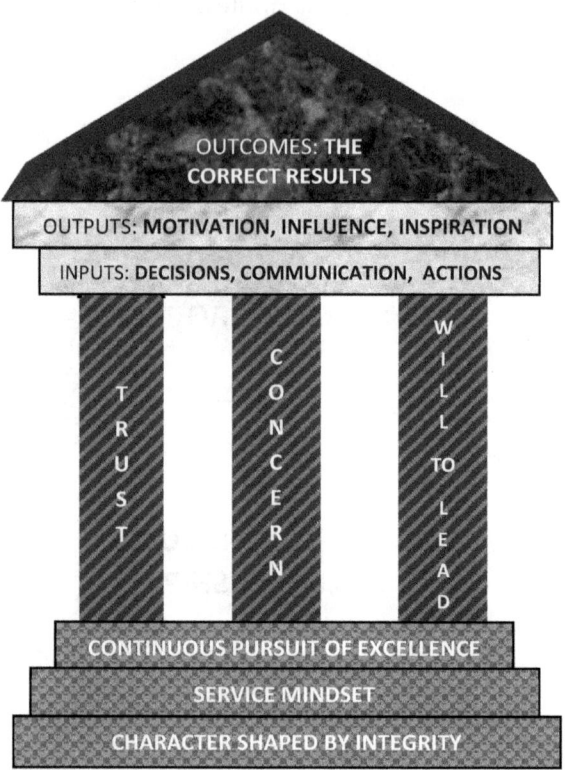

Figure 7.2. Model for Sustained Leadership Excellence

The leadership process. A leader's decisions, communication, and actions—referred to as the instruments of leadership—serve as the inputs of the leadership process. These instruments generate motivation, influence, and inspiration, which represent the model's outputs. Ultimately, these outputs drive the results achieved by a leader and their team—the outcomes of the leadership process.

Unifying forces. The leadership process requires unity of effort, achieved by steering a team's performance through a shared set of unifying forces, which include a team's mission, vision, values, goals, objectives, priorities, and strategy. Figure 7.3 illustrates the inputs, outputs, outcomes, and unifying forces of the leadership process. These unifying forces play a critical role in galvanizing, synchronizing, and steering a team's performance. The powerful influence of these forces on the leadership process is further emphasized in Figure 7.4.

Figure 7.3. The Leadership Process

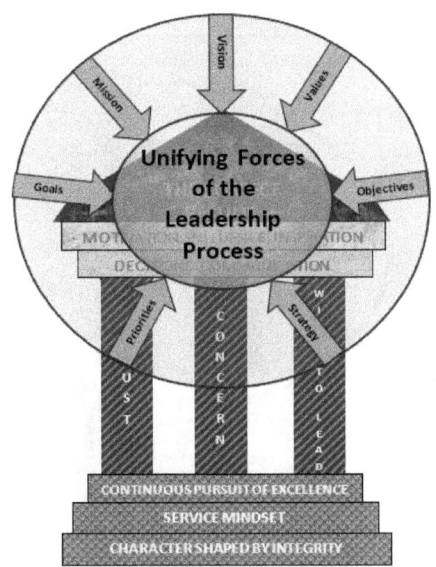

Figure 7.4. Influence of the Unifying Forces on the Leadership Process

Enabling attributes of leadership. Sustained success as a leader depends on the quality and harmony of the leadership instruments. This premise raises an important question: How can leaders consistently shape and guide their decisions, communication, and actions to effectively motivate, influence, and inspire their teams over the long term? The enabling attributes of Trust, Concern, and the Will to Lead, highlighted in Figure 7.5, are essential to shaping, informing, and harmonizing these leadership instruments. These attributes also enable the leadership capabilities outlined in Part I, which are essential to effectively fulfilling the leadership role.

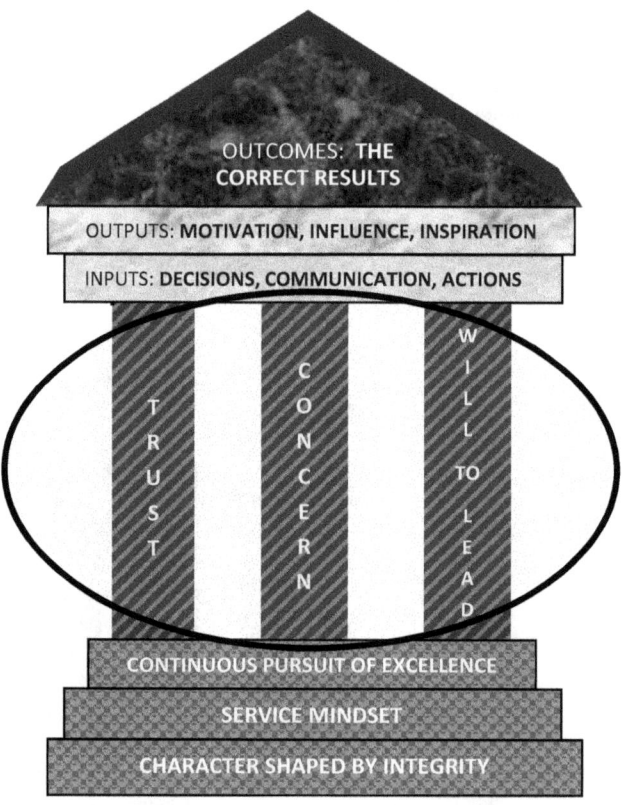

Figure 7.5. Enabling Attributes of Leadership Excellence

Core values of leadership. As illustrated in Figure 7.6, the model's core values—Character Shaped by Integrity, a Service Mindset, and the Continuous Pursuit of Excellence—are deeply held beliefs that remain constant, grounding leaders with a clear sense of identity and purpose.

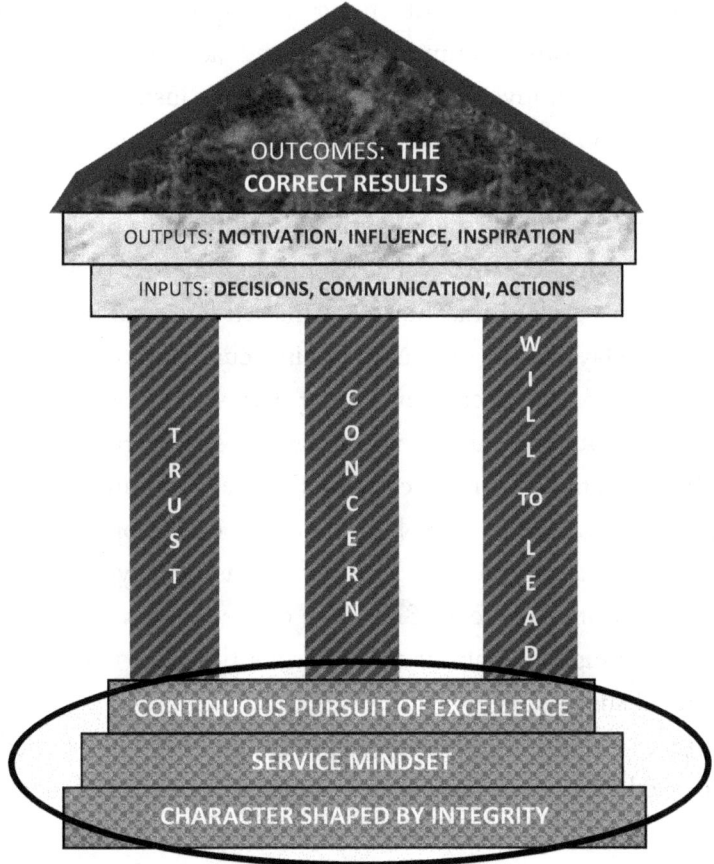

Figure 7.6. Core Values of Leadership Excellence

While the model's enabling attributes shape and inform the instruments of leadership, its foundational core values serve as the cognitive fuel that powers and sustains these attributes, which, in turn, drive the leadership process.

Integrated Framework

This section presents two scenarios that illustrate how the model's components interact to empower leadership excellence. The scenarios highlight the impact of the core values and enabling attributes on shaping and informing the inputs of the leadership process—decisions, communication, and actions—that generate the outputs—motivation, influence, and inspiration—driving teams to consistently achieve the desired outcomes of the process—the correct mission results.

Scenario 1: Teresa's leadership in addressing project delays. Teresa, a new mid-level product development leader at a pharmaceutical company, discovered that her team missed a critical project deadline. The delay had been caused by inaccurate status reporting, a problem that had been developing for several weeks without Teresa's knowledge. Upon investigating, she learned that team members hesitated to raise concerns or flag potential issues with the project's progress. They had feared repercussions from senior leadership, leading to a lack of transparency and honest communication. This fear of negative consequences contributed to missed warning signs about the project's timeline, which affected the overall success of the team's mission.

Inputs—decisions, communication, actions. Confronted with the missed deadline and its root cause, Teresa acted decisively. Instead of reacting with frustration, she recognized an opportunity to address the underlying issue of trust within the team. Teresa scheduled a team meeting and opened the conversation by acknowledging the missed deadline. She emphasized that mistakes were part of the learning process and encouraged her team to speak openly without fear of retaliation. Teresa made it clear that team members could voice concerns openly and without fear of repercussions, reinforcing that honest dialogue was essential to the team's product development mission.

To further address the root cause, Teresa collaborated with the team to examine the project's status reporting processes. Through a series of candid discussions, the team identified several inefficiencies, including manual data collection, inconsistent status updates, and a lack of accountability in the review process. Teresa facilitated a team decision to automate the data collection process, which would reduce human error and streamline reporting. Additionally, the team agreed to implement a more rigorous review process to ensure the accuracy of reports before they were shared with senior management.

Recognizing the urgency of getting the project back on track, Teresa worked with peer leaders in other departments to provide temporary staffing support. This collaborative approach helped alleviate some of the workload pressure on her team, allowing them to focus on correcting the inaccuracies and meeting revised deadlines.

Outputs—motivation, influence, inspiration. Teresa's approach had an inspirational impact on the team. By addressing the issue openly and focusing on solutions instead of assigning blame, she built a deeper sense of trust among her team members. Her transparency and support motivated the team to embrace the changes in reporting processes and feel empowered to speak up about potential issues in the future. Teresa's actions influenced the team to approach their work with a greater sense of accountability and pride in their performance.

The collaborative nature of her decisions, communication, and actions fostered a more engaged, problem-solving mindset. Teresa's involvement in working with peer leaders and ensuring the team received adequate support demonstrated her commitment to their success. The team became inspired by her willingness to actively help them overcome obstacles, which boosted morale and reinforced the importance of clear, honest communication.

By creating an environment where mistakes were seen as opportunities for improvement rather than reasons for punishment, Teresa fostered psychological safety within the team. This inspired greater transparency and initiative, ultimately driving the project's success.

Outcomes—results. Teresa's leadership resulted in the team getting the project back on schedule. The additional support from peer workgroups and the implementation of the new status reporting processes helped correct inaccuracies. The automated data collection system reduced errors, while the revised review process ensured that potential issues were flagged and addressed promptly.

Beyond just meeting the immediate deadline, Teresa's leadership brought about long-term improvements in the team's workflow management. The new practices were shared with other teams, contributing to broader organizational improvements. The team became more proactive in identifying potential risks and mitigating them before they impacted deadlines. Teresa's transparent approach also strengthened team cohesion. By fostering an environment of collaboration and open communication, she enhanced the overall culture of accountability and trust within the group.

Empowering leadership through the model's integrated framework. Teresa's decisions, communication, and actions were shaped by the model's enabling attributes of trust, concern, and the will to lead. She demonstrated key leadership capabilities such as emotional intelligence, interactive listening, engagement, coaching, courage, a commitment to learning, and resilience—fueled by the core values of character shaped by integrity, a service mindset, and the continuous pursuit of excellence. Through candid, transparent communication and a focus on continuous improvement, Teresa embodied the principles of the leadership model, enabling the team to overcome immediate challenges while laying a strong foundation for sustained success and growth.

Scenario 2: John's leadership in addressing a decline in team morale and productivity. John, the department head at a hospital, noticed a significant decline in staff morale. His teams were experiencing sustained pressure from heavy workloads and limited staffing resources, resulting in increased stress and frustration. The situation escalated when the first-shift team leader approached John with concerns about the second-shift leader's chronic lateness. The repeated tardiness placed added strain on both shifts, especially during shift changes and periods of heightened patient volume, adversely impacting the team's ability to deliver quality care.

As the issue persisted, tensions between the two team leaders grew, leading to strained communication, reduced collaboration, and declining productivity. John recognized that the drop in morale and fractured working relationships were undermining the broader department's ability to fulfill its core mission—delivering excellent patient care.

Inputs—decisions, communication, actions. To address the issues, John took a proactive and empathetic approach. He began by conducting one-on-one check-ins with each team leader. During these conversations, he listened to their concerns about workloads, resource limitations, and interpersonal tensions. John took care to create a safe environment for team members to express their frustrations and suggestions for improvement. By actively listening, he gained a deeper understanding of the issues undermining morale and performance.

He then convened a team-wide meeting to address the shared challenges. He encouraged open communication and collaborative problem-solving, inviting team members to share their thoughts and propose solutions. This inclusive approach fostered a sense of collective ownership of the solution. Among the suggestions, the team recommended adjusting work schedules and collaborating with other departments to share resources and reduce the workload burden.

While these team-wide efforts helped ease systemic pressures, John knew the interpersonal conflict between the two team leaders required attention. He met with them individually, applying the LEADERS Conflict Resolution Framework (Table 5.1) to guide respectful, honest conversations. Through this process, John learned that the tardy team leader had been caring for an aging neighbor, which accounted for the recurring lateness.

With empathy and professionalism, John acknowledged the personal challenges while explaining the impact the delays had on the department's effectiveness and patient care. Rather than assigning blame, he proposed a constructive solution: he recalled that the third-shift team leader had previously expressed interest in moving to the second shift. By facilitating a voluntary shift change, John addressed both the personal situation and the department's operational mission.

Outputs—motivation, influence, inspiration. John's approach to resolving the issue was well-received by both teams. His decision to listen and engage in open, honest communication motivated team members by making them feel valued and heard. They appreciated that he took their concerns seriously and collaborated with them to find solutions that served the entire team. By acknowledging their challenges and empowering them to contribute to the solution, John fostered a sense of ownership and accountability.

His empathy and willingness to address the difficult situation directly influenced how the team perceived him—as a leader who genuinely cared about their well-being. This transparency and concern strengthened trust and reinforced confidence in his leadership. As a result, John's actions not only resolved the immediate problem but also inspired greater collaboration, increased morale, and a spirit of mutual support to carry the team through future challenges.

Outcomes—results. As a result of John's leadership, patient care improved significantly, as reflected in rising patient satisfaction ratings. Team productivity and collaboration also saw marked improvement, based on feedback from the department's team survey. By addressing the root causes of low morale—workload, resources, and interpersonal conflict—John restored trust and strengthened teamwork.

The shift change between the two team leaders effectively addressed the performance concern, enabling smoother transitions and greater cohesion across shifts. Additionally, the broader initiatives to adjust work schedules and share resources helped alleviate some of the pressure on individual team members.

Overall, morale rebounded as team members felt more supported, understood, and valued by their leader. John's proactive and empathetic approach not only resolved the immediate challenges but also laid the groundwork for a more resilient, collaborative, and high-performing team culture—one centered on shared purpose and sustained excellence in patient care.

Empowering leadership through the model's integrated framework. John's decisions, communication, and actions were guided by the model's enabling attributes of trust, concern, and the will to lead. He demonstrated key leadership capabilities such as empathy, engagement, interactive listening, collaborative problem-solving, coaching, emotional intelligence, and a commitment to team success—each fueled by the core values of character shaped by integrity, a service mindset, and the continuous pursuit of excellence.

By addressing both interpersonal dynamics and systemic issues, John embodied the principles of the leadership model, restoring team cohesion and morale while strengthening the team's capacity to deliver high-quality patient care and navigate future challenges with resilience.

Operationalize the Model

The following section presents a two-part strategy leaders can use to operationalize the model's principles through journaling and self-assessments.

Part I. Journaling. Leaders are encouraged to reflect on the model's foundational core values and enabling attributes. They should assess how these values and attributes align with their personal beliefs, how they are expressed in their leadership behaviors, and how others may perceive them.

By maintaining a journal, written or audio, leaders can capture their thoughts on how each value and attribute influences their decisions, communication, and actions, as well as the outcomes of those behaviors. Journaling can also help identify specific instances where applying these principles positively motivated, influenced, or inspired their teams. The following scenario illustrates how reflection and journaling can help leaders internalize and apply the principles of the model in their leadership practice.

Scenario: Maria's team misses a key milestone. Maria, an entry-level leader overseeing a 14-member curriculum development team, faced a significant challenge when her team missed a key project milestone due to a team member's oversight. The delay disrupted the project's timeline and threatened to derail subsequent phases of development. As the leader, Maria felt a deep responsibility—not only for the missed deadline but also for its potential impact on the team's morale, performance, and reputation.

Inputs—decisions, communication, actions. Rather than conceal the error or deflect blame, Maria chose transparency. Recognizing her role in setting the tone for the team, she informed her supervisor of the oversight and explained her plan to address the issue.

Maria conducted a one-on-one conversation with the team member involved to understand the root cause. She learned the oversight stemmed from a misunderstanding about the milestone deadline. While she empathized with the situation, Maria clearly communicated the importance of attention to detail and accountability. Together, they identified corrective measures to prevent similar issues.

She then discussed the situation openly with the team during her weekly group meeting. Maria emphasized the importance of flagging issues early and encouraged team members to share lessons learned and strategies for improving milestone tracking. She reviewed the organization's project gate-review process and led a collaborative coaching session on refining the process for greater clarity and early detection of risks. She treated the discussion as an opportunity to learn from a mistake.

To strengthen team coordination, Maria shared her Operating Rhythm schedule (Table 4.3)—a tool she used to stay aligned with meetings, deliverables, and deadlines. She encouraged team members to adopt a similar approach to enhance situational awareness and alignment on key project milestones.

Outputs—motivation, influence, inspiration. Maria's transparency and willingness to take full responsibility for the oversight had an immediate positive effect on the team. Her approach demonstrated that she valued honesty, open communication, and learning from mistakes. This, in turn, motivated the team to be more proactive in raising potential issues or delays. Maria's actions inspired trust in her leadership because she showed that setbacks were opportunities for growth and improvement rather than moments for blame or punishment.

Her coaching session reinforced the importance of collaboration and continuous learning, further motivating the team to support each other and communicate more effectively. Team cohesion grew as members started to feel more comfortable raising concerns early, knowing they would not face backlash for doing so. Maria's initiative in facilitating the learning session showed her genuine concern for the development of her team members and the team's mission, which contributed to a stronger culture of collaboration.

By working with the team to brainstorm solutions, Maria's influence encouraged the group to accelerate the next phase of the project. The team missed the key milestone, but through their collaborative efforts and Maria's leadership, they met the project's overall internal customer timeline. Her approach demonstrated a commitment to mission timelines while maintaining a supportive and growth-oriented environment.

Outcomes—results. Thanks to Maria's leadership, the project milestone schedule was successfully adjusted, and the team ultimately delivered the final product on time. More importantly, the experience strengthened the team's understanding of the organization's milestone gate-review process, improving their ability to manage future projects with greater efficiency and precision—ultimately enhancing the value of the team's mission.

By introducing and modeling the use of her Operating Rhythm schedule, Maria helped the team improve their situational awareness and stay aligned on critical deadlines and priorities. Team members began to support one another more actively, reinforcing a shared sense of accountability.

What initially appeared to be a serious setback became a meaningful turning point. The experience highlighted the value of transparent communication, individual accountability, and continuous learning. Maria's approach not only brought the team back on track but also laid the groundwork for a more collaborative, resilient, and high-performing team culture.

Journal reflection. After the situation was resolved, Maria took time to reflect on how her decisions, communication, and actions aligned with the model's enabling attributes of trust, concern, and the will to lead. In her journal, she documented the impact of taking responsibility for the missed milestone. She noted how this decision and her associated communication and actions positively influenced team morale and reinforced their trust in her leadership. By modeling accountability instead of shifting blame, she noted that it fostered an environment where team members felt safe to communicate openly and offer constructive solutions.

She reflected on the positive feedback she received from team members after the coaching session. Maria recognized that her concern for the team's development not only improved job satisfaction but also conveyed genuine appreciation for their individual growth. She considered how fostering open dialogue and encouraging team members to share lessons learned helped build a more resilient, adaptive team culture—one better prepared to navigate future challenges.

Maria noted several process improvements that emerged from sharing her Operating Rhythm schedule. The tool proved valuable in helping the team maintain alignment, clarify expectations, and prevent future misunderstandings related to key deadlines and milestones.

In a subsequent quarterly team meeting, Maria also introduced the Model for Sustained Leadership Excellence to her team. She used the model's framework to recognize individuals who had exemplified its core values and enabling attributes. This not only helped the team understand the foundation of Maria's leadership approach but also underscored her commitment to cultivating future leaders who could apply the model to achieve long-term success.

By reflecting on and documenting these insights, Maria deepened her integration of the model's principles into her leadership practice. Her journaling reinforced the behaviors and mindset that would guide her leadership journey, ensuring sustained success over time.

Part II. Self-assessment. As discussed in Chapter Six, seeking feedback on leadership performance is essential for continuous improvement. Regular feedback from supervisors, team members, peers, customers, and other stakeholders helps leaders integrate and apply the model's principles in practice. It also provides valuable insight into how the model's framework enhances leadership effectiveness.

Performance feedback. Many organizations use performance management systems to provide performance reviews through a systematic review cycle. These reviews provide opportunities for self-reflection and candid feedback from supervisors, peers, and team members, providing insight into how well a leader's decisions, communication, and actions align with the leadership model's principles.

For example, consider the scenario in which Maria, the curriculum development leader, worked with her team to overcome a missed deadline for a key project milestone. During Maria's quarterly performance review, her supervisor provided positive feedback regarding how well her actions supported the team and the mission. During the meeting, Maria asked for feedback on *blind spots*, areas where she might lack awareness about how her performance was affecting the team and the team's mission.

Her supervisor identified one blind spot: the limited use of data analytics in her weekly reports. While Maria regularly reported project status on time and with thorough summaries, her supervisor encouraged her to provide deeper analysis, particularly when costs, schedules, or performance indicators signaled risk. She recommended including risk-mitigation strategies in future reports to support better decision-making and transparency.

Maria also invited feedback from her team. One team member acknowledged that her results-oriented leadership style did drive productivity and project momentum. However, they shared that her intense focus on outcomes—characterized by aggressive deadlines and frequent progress checks—sometimes made the team feel micromanaged or undervalued. This approach, while mission-driven, risked affecting morale and leading to stress or burnout over time.

The feedback helped Maria understand how her leadership style, though well-intentioned, could have unintended consequences.

It reinforced the importance of balancing a strong commitment to results with attentiveness to her team's well-being and morale. By acknowledging these insights, Maria took a critical step toward sustaining both team performance and trust—core outcomes of the leadership model in action.

Self-assessment tools. Self-assessment tools—including 360-degree feedback instruments—offer valuable insights into how others experience a leader's behaviors and decisions. These tools can also help leaders better understand how the model's core values and enabling attributes manifest in their daily leadership roles.

As introduced in Chapter Three, personality assessments such as the Big Five Personality Profile and the Myers-Briggs Type Indicator (MBTI) can enhance self-awareness and support personal development. The MBTI, in particular, helps leaders identify natural preferences, strengths, and areas for growth. Leaders are encouraged to take the MBTI through a qualified practitioner from The Myers-Briggs Company, which offers feedback sessions to deepen understanding and guide growth.[304]

Additionally, 360-degree assessments gather structured feedback from a wide range of sources, including a leader's supervisor, senior leaders, peers, team members, and other stakeholders. With some assessment tools, customers, suppliers, and external partners may also contribute, offering a broader perspective on leadership effectiveness.

Several providers offer these tools, including 360DegreeLeader, Lattice, Namely, and PerformYard.[305, 306, 307, 308] Platforms such as Qualtrics XM and SurveyMonkey also provide customizable 360-degree assessment solutions, along with templates, best practices, and implementation guides tailored to organizational needs.[309, 310]

Continuing with Maria's scenario: Later that year, following several key projects, Maria completed a 360-degree self-assessment to gain deeper insight into her leadership impact. The feedback consistently recognized her strong commitment to mission success and her ability to lead the team through challenges. However, it also revealed a recurring theme related to her communication style—specifically, the need to balance her results-driven approach with more frequent check-ins that supported team morale and emotional well-being. One team member noted that while Maria's high standards inspired strong performance, the pressure to meet ambitious goals sometimes limited open dialogue and created stress. This prompted Maria to reflect more intentionally on how to better align her leadership with the model's attribute of concern. In response, she committed to holding monthly one-on-one sessions focused not only on progress updates but also on individual development and the overall team climate.

Strategic Planning Workshop

This section presents a hypothetical strategic planning workshop scenario designed to help leaders establish or revise their team's mission, vision, values, goals, objectives, priorities, and strategy—the Unifying Forces of the Leadership Process (see Figure 7.7).

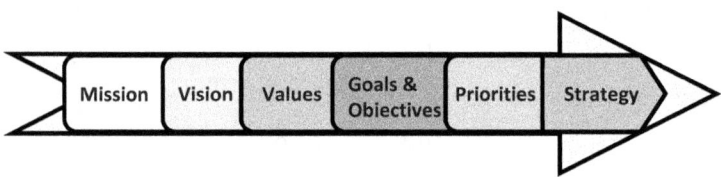

Figure 7.7. Unifying Forces of the Leadership Process

The scenario applies a five-module strategic planning framework to help guide leaders in organizing, facilitating, and leading a productive meeting. The aim is to promote collaboration, ensure alignment across strategic elements, and produce a unified plan that galvanizes and synchronizes team performance.

The workshop is structured around a six- to seven-hour agenda. The time allotted for each step should be adjusted to suit the organization's size, complexity, and operational context.

Scenario: FutureTech, a mid-sized technology organization specializing in cybersecurity, anticipates rapid growth and increased competition as it expands nationwide. They currently provide cybersecurity products and services in the eastern region of the United States. They plan to expand their business nationwide. Senior leaders recognize the need to revisit and refresh the team's mission, vision, values, goals, objectives, priorities, and strategy to maintain focus and a high-performing team culture. The company's senior officer, JoAnn, convenes a one-day strategic planning workshop with her leadership team to codify these strategic planning elements.

Participants: Ten leadership team members, including division and department heads from programs, business development, operations, information technology, systems management, human resources, finance, and product development.

Facilitator: JoAnn leads the workshop and guides the overall discussion. She invites her human resources partner to help manage meeting logistics, captures key decisions, actions, deliverables, timelines, and provides real-time process coaching.

Welcome, introductions, icebreaker (15-20 minutes):

Facilitator's Role: JoAnn sets the tone and articulates the purpose of the workshop, emphasizing open communication, respect for all perspectives, being curious before being critical, and the importance of staying focused and on time. JoAnn gives each team member an opportunity to introduce themselves and share one strategic challenge they are most eager to solve.

Explain objectives: JoAnn outlines the seven strategic elements to be defined and their role in aligning the team's direction and fostering a cohesive team culture. She quickly walks through each agenda step and time block, highlighting the deliverable for each.

Expected outcomes: All leaders feel welcomed and understand the rules of engagement. A clear, shared understanding of the day's purpose, structure, and outputs.

Module 1: Mission and vision (60-80 minutes)

Mission statement (30-40 minutes):

Purpose: Define FutureTech's fundamental purpose by articulating the team's core purpose.

Discussion: JoAnn opens the session by asking, "What is FutureTech's core purpose? Why do we exist?" The team agrees that the mission centers around "empowering businesses to thrive by providing innovative, secure, and reliable cybersecurity solutions."

Outcome: A mission statement that captures the team's purpose: "To empower organizations with innovative and secure cybersecurity solutions that protect their digital futures."

Vision statement (30-40 minutes):

Purpose: Articulate the team's aspirational future that inspires and aligns the team's efforts.

Discussion: JoAnn prompts, "What does success look like for FutureTech in five years?" Ideas include becoming an industry leader, expanding nationally, and creating cutting-edge cybersecurity solutions.

Outcome: A vision statement that defines the team's future aspirations: "To be the U.S. leader in cybersecurity, delivering cutting-edge innovation and unmatched trust to our clients."

Team break (15 minutes)

Module 2: Values (30-40 minutes)

Purpose: Identify the core values that will shape FutureTech's culture and guide decision-making in support of the mission and vision.

Discussion: JoAnn frames the conversation by asking, "What principles guide our decisions, communication, and interactions, even when no one is watching?" She then invites leaders to consider which three to five values underpin a culture of teamwork, innovation, resilience, excellence, and continuous improvement.

The team's HR partner shares a preliminary list—integrity, customer focus, innovation, accountability, learning, excellence, and respect—to spark ideas. Attendees pair up to brainstorm values that resonate most strongly with the mission and vision. When the full team reconvenes, each pair presents their top choices, generating a rich discussion about how values such as quality, productivity, innovation, integrity, and collaboration drive behavior and outcomes. JoAnn guides the group to refine and converge on the values that best reflect the organization's identity and aspirations.

Outcome: The team reaches consensus on three core values:

1. Integrity: We uphold the highest standards of honesty and trust.
2. Innovation: We are committed to pushing boundaries and embracing new ideas.
3. Collaboration: We believe in the power of teamwork to achieve sustained excellence.

Module 3: Goals, objectives, and priorities (100-130 minutes)

Goals (50-60 minutes):

Purpose: Define the team's broad, strategic goals in alignment with the mission, vision, and core values.

Discussion: JoAnn divides the group into pairs and asks each pair to draft SMART goals—specific, measurable, achievable, relevant, and time-bound—that will advance FutureTech's strategic direction. After 20 minutes of paired brainstorming, the team reconvenes. Each pair presents its proposed goals, and JoAnn facilitates a full-team discussion to identify common themes and eliminate overlap. The conversation centers on identifying which goals will have the greatest impact on customer satisfaction, innovation, and business expansion.

Outcome: Consensus on three overarching goals:
1. U.S. Market Expansion: Expand business across the U.S. market over the next twelve months.
2. Client Satisfaction: Achieve and maintain 95% client satisfaction by the end of Q4 (currently at 76%).
3. Product Innovation: Launch two new innovative cybersecurity products by the end of Q4.

Objectives (30-40 minutes):

Purpose: Break down each goal into one to three specific, actionable objectives. (Note: This scenario is illustrative and highlights only one objective for each goal. In practice, each goal would typically be supported by multiple objectives.)

Discussion: JoAnn guides the leadership team in translating each of the three agreed-upon goals into SMART objectives. Together, they clarify what needs to happen, by when, and who will be responsible. Leaders propose specific actions—such as conducting regional market research, launching a client relations program, and establishing a product development cadence. They debate timelines and success metrics to ensure each objective is both ambitious and achievable.

Outcome: The team defines objectives to support each goal:
1. Conduct market research across the Midwest and Western U.S. regions to target expansion opportunities, adding two new distributor partners in each region per quarter (supports Goal #1).

2. Implement a revamped client relations program designed to elevate client satisfaction (supports Goal 2).
3. Launch one new cybersecurity product every six months to sustain product-innovation momentum (supports Goal 3).

Priorities (20-30 minutes):

Purpose: Prioritize the team's goals to focus resources on the most critical initiatives over the next six–twelve months.

Discussion: JoAnn leads a prioritization exercise, inviting the leadership team to weigh each goal's strategic impact, resource requirements, and urgency. Through facilitated dialogue and a simple dot-voting method, the group prioritizes the three goals.

Outcome: The leadership team ranks its goals in order of priority:
1. Client satisfaction goal: Achieve and maintain 95% client satisfaction by the end of Q4.
2. Product innovation goal: Launch two new cybersecurity products by the end of Q4.
3. U.S. market expansion goal: Expand business across the U.S. market within the next twelve months.

Team lunch break: (60 minutes)

Module 4: Strategy (50-60 minutes)

Purpose: Establish clear strategies for achieving the previously defined goals and objectives.

Discussion: JoAnn invites the group to brainstorm on a whiteboard, asking, "What strategies will our team employ to safely and effectively accomplish our ambitious goals?" Leaders first work individually for a few minutes to jot down strategy ideas, focusing on actions, resources, and success metrics. They then share their proposals aloud, and the team's HR partner facilitates a collaborative discussion to refine each idea, assign ownership, set timelines, and define quantifiable measures of progress.

Outcome: The leadership team agrees on a set of targeted strategies and implementation schedules, each aligned with a specific goal and accountable leader:

1. Client Relations Program: Roll out a new client relations program to elevate client satisfaction from 76% to 95%, targeting a 5% increase each quarter.
   Primary owner: human resources.
   Supporting owners: program and operations leaders.
2. Product Innovation: Increase investment in AI-powered security solutions and launch two new cybersecurity products by Q4—one product every six months.
   Primary owner: product development.
   Supporting owners: information technology, systems management, program, operations, and finance leaders.
3. Market Expansion: Form partnerships with eight new local distributors—two per quarter—across the Midwest and Western U.S. regions by the end of Q4.
   Primary owner: business development.
   Supporting owners: program and finance leaders.

Module 5: Wrap-up and next steps (15-20 minutes)

Purpose: Consolidate all outputs, confirm strategy ownership, and establish a roadmap for implementation and ongoing review.

Discussion: JoAnn begins by recapping the finalized mission, vision, values, goals, objectives, priorities, and strategies—using the workshop's visual artifacts to reinforce alignment. She invites questions or clarifications to ensure every leader understands and agrees with each element. Next, the group confirms accountability, with each strategy owner restating their commitments and timelines. JoAnn then outlines the follow-up cadence, scheduling quarterly review meetings to monitor progress against goals. Finally, the team discusses communication plans for cascading the strategic elements to their respective teams through briefings, written reports, and divisional town halls.

Outcome: A comprehensive strategic plan is endorsed by all participants, with clear owners, milestones, and a quarterly review schedule. JoAnn and her leadership team leave the workshop prepared to communicate the plan across FutureTech, confident that the strategic elements of the unifying forces will guide sustained alignment and performance.

Quarterly progress reviews. At the end of Q1, JoAnn and the leadership team convene to evaluate progress using a digital dashboard populated with key performance indicators and data analytics. A "stoplight" assessment—red for off track, yellow for at risk, and green for on track—provides an at-a-glance view of each strategy's health against the goals. During the review, any yellow or red indicators prompt a focused discussion to diagnose root causes and agree on corrective actions. This structured cadence ensures that adjustments are made promptly, keeping the strategic plan aligned with FutureTech's objectives and maintaining momentum toward sustained success. Dashboard examples include:

Goal #1: Client satisfaction. Achieve and maintain a 95% client satisfaction rate by the end of Q4.

Status (**Red**): Q1 client satisfaction rate = 79%, 2% less than planned. The client relations training plan is behind schedule.

Strategy: To achieve and maintain a 95% client satisfaction rate by the end of Q4, FutureTech rolled out a new client relations program designed to boost satisfaction from its current 76% rate, targeting a 5% increase each quarter. At the end of Q1, however, satisfaction reached only 79%—2% below the planned 81%—placing this initiative in the red. (*Owners*: human resources, program, and operations leaders.)

Action: The team is negotiating a new training contract and expects to complete staff certification by mid-Q2 to get back on track.

Goal #2: Product innovation. Launch two new innovative cybersecurity products by Q4.

Status (**Green**): The product development team successfully tested its first new AI-powered product and is preparing to launch it by the end of Q2. The team is also testing its second new AI-powered product and is on track to launch it by Q4.

Strategy: The goal of launching two innovative cybersecurity products by Q4—one every six months—guides FutureTech's increased investment in AI-powered security solutions. Progress is strong: the product development team has successfully tested the first AI-driven solution and is preparing for its end-of-quarter 2 launch, while testing on the second product is proceeding on schedule for a quarter 4 release. (*Owners*: product development, information technology, systems management, program, operations, and finance leaders.)

Action: The steady progress keeps the strategy firmly in the green, with no corrective actions required.

Goal #3: U.S. market expansion. Expand business across the U.S. over the next twelve months.

Status (**Yellow**): The market expansion plan is behind schedule. Added two new distributors in the West, but only one new distributor in the Midwest, one less than planned for the Midwest region.

Strategy: FutureTech aims to expand nationally by partnering with eight new local distributors—two per quarter in the Midwest and Western regions. In Q1, the team secured two new distributors in the West but only one in the Midwest, placing this priority in yellow status as it falls short of the target of two per region. (*Owners*: business development, program, and finance leaders.)

Action: To get on track, the team plans to add three additional Midwest distributors by the end of Q2, in addition to the two additional distributors already planned for the West by the end of Q2, ensuring they align with the expansion timeline and support broader organizational growth.

Tips for a productive workshop:

Preparation: Communicate the workshop's purpose and desired outcomes well in advance. Share any pre-reading materials—such as market analyses, current performance dashboards, or key questions—to give participants time to reflect and arrive ready to contribute meaningfully. Clearly outline the agenda and send logistical details (location, tools, breaks) so everyone knows what to expect.

Facilitation: When possible, engage a neutral facilitator to guide discussions, manage the agenda, and ensure that all voices are heard. A facilitator can help keep the group focused, enforce time limits, and navigate any disagreements so the workshop stays constructive and on schedule.

Engagement: Leverage visual aids—whiteboards, sticky notes, flip charts, or digital collaboration platforms—to capture ideas in real time and make the conversation visible to all. Incorporate interactive techniques such as small-group brainstorming, dot-voting for consensus, and periodic "pulse checks" to maintain energy, foster ownership, and ensure alignment moving through each strategic element.

Follow-up: Within 24–48 hours of the workshop, distribute a draft summary document detailing decisions, action items, owners, and timelines. Invite participants to review and suggest edits before finalizing. Once approved, cascade the strategic plan to the broader organization through team briefings, reports, or town-hall meetings.

Sustained success depends on accountability—schedule regular progress reviews to monitor performance and make timely adjustments.

For additional insight into effective strategic planning, see Patrick Lencioni's *The Advantage: Why Organizational Health Trumps Everything Else in Business*.[311]

Moving Forward

The world needs skilled, capable, and ready leaders at every level, from entry-level to the top. To meet that need, this book introduced the Model for Sustained Leadership Excellence, derived from leadership practitioners, scholars, literature, research studies, and best practices. The model's singular purpose is to help develop, improve, and sustain the leadership capabilities of current and aspiring leaders.

While work cultures and missions vary across organizations, all leadership roles share a common aim: to consistently achieve the correct mission results safely and effectively with their team, regardless of an organization's mission or team. This premise led to the central question shaping the content of the book: Is there a leadership development framework that can fuel and sustain leadership excellence over the long term, regardless of the team, environment, or mission? The Model for Sustained Leadership Excellence was constructed to answer that question.

Designed for leaders across all fields and levels, the comprehensive and integrated model provides a coherent framework to sustain leadership performance over the long term.

As you reflect on the ideas, concepts, tools, and strategies introduced in this book, consider the possibilities they offer for your leadership journey. Whether you are guiding a small team or leading a global organization, I hope the research, best practices, and principles that shape the Model for Sustained Leadership Excellence empower you to lead with authenticity, courage, and a commitment to excellence.

Leadership excellence is not a destination—it is a lifelong journey. Embrace it with confidence, and let your decisions, communication, and actions inspire others to reach their full potential. With the Model for Sustained Leadership Excellence, you can build a leadership legacy that transforms teams, organizations, and communities for generations to come.

Acknowledgments

*

A leader's ability to motivate, influence, and inspire others to achieve the correct mission results is a fundamental aim of leadership. It can be said, therefore, that a leader's success is not entirely in their own hands but is often dependent on others. Similarly, writing a book requires collaboration and teamwork, with support from advisors, colleagues, family, and friends.

Throughout our lives, the people we meet, the places we go, and our interactions with the world around us shape our learning and development. As Tennyson declared in *Ulysses*, "I am a part of all that I have met."[312] This sentiment certainly applies to writing a book. And so, in that spirit of gratitude, I would like to thank the colleagues, mentors, family, and friends who directly contributed to completing this work.

I will start by thanking the great men and women in the United States armed forces and the armed forces of our international allies and partners, military and civilian, with whom I was honored to serve alongside during my military career. As members of the profession of arms, your courageous service and sacrifices taught me invaluable lessons about integrity, selflessness, and excellence. Your leadership, guidance, coaching, and mentorship played a significant role in my leadership development and inspired me to write this book.

I am especially grateful to Dr. Craig Brandt, professor emeritus at the Air Force Institute of Technology, for his insight, expertise, and mentorship. Dr. Brandt taught me how scholarly research and persistent editing contribute to organizing and developing effective written communication.

I also want to express my deep appreciation to retired Air Force Colonel Kent D. Williams, former dean at Air University's Air War College, for his wise counsel and confidence in my writing and research. His coaching greatly influenced my views on educating the next generation of military leaders and my personal leadership journey.

As a student of leadership, I owe a debt of gratitude to Dr. Donna W. Jorgensen, Professor of Education and Graduate Education Chair at Delaware Valley University. Dr. Jorgensen served as my dissertation committee chair, guiding and mentoring me through the research and writing process. Her professional expertise and sage advice were essential to the success of my research on the importance and value of leadership development programs for higher education leaders.

Thanks to Professor Dave Zimmer, Strategic Advisor for Change Management and Business Leadership, Pennsylvania State University Professor, noted speaker, and author, for his comprehensive review of draft manuscripts. Dave's feedback was instrumental in enhancing the value of the book's content.

I am also deeply grateful to my friends and doctoral cohort classmates, Gary Snyder, Jackie Royer, and Rich Hartwell. Their reviews of my manuscript were crucial to its completion, and their constructive feedback and professionalism inspired me.

Dennis Danko provided valuable insights and feedback during the final phase of the book review and editing process, for which I am very grateful. I enjoyed working with Dennis to bring the book-writing project across the finish line.

I want to express my appreciation to colleagues and partners across the aerospace industry for their coaching and mentorship and their steadfast dedication to our nation's aerospace industrial base, which remains vital to exploration and security.

A heartfelt thank you to my three amazing sons, Philip, Andre, and Stephen, who keep me young at heart and happy in spirit. Most importantly, I want to thank my wife, Maria, for her unwavering support throughout my journey in research, writing, and publishing. Her endless encouragement inspired me to complete this work. Her patience, strength, love, and genuine selflessness are extraordinary qualities she exemplifies daily. She continues to be a shining example for me and others to follow.

References

[1] Dowrick, L. (2019, September 16). *Jim's birthday* [video]. YouTube. September 16,.2019. https://www.youtube.com/watch?=b4754pfMs&t=27s

[2] Churchill, W. (1952). *Quote investigator: exploring the origins of quotations*, Winston Churchill made this remark on November 4, 1952, while speaking in the British House of Commons in London; his words were recorded in the *Hansard*, the official transcript record for the British Parliament. http://quoteinvestigator.com/2012/07/24/ready-to-learn/

[3] Development Dimensions International (DDI). (2025). *Global leadership forecast 2025: Insights and trends*. p. 3. DDI. https://media.ddiworld.com/research/global-leadership-forecast-2025-report.pdf?_gl=1*18by5ku*_gcl_au*MjAwMTk0NTg1NC4xNzM5NjQ5NjUw

[4] Development Dimensions International (DDI). (2025). *Global leadership forecast 2025: Insights and trends*. p. 3. DDI. https://media.ddiworld.com/research/global-leadership-forecast-2025-report.pdf?_gl=1*18by5ku*_gcl_au*MjAwMTk0NTg1NC4xNzM5NjQ5NjUw

[5] Development Dimensions International (DDI). (2025). *Global leadership forecast 2025: Insights and trends*. p. 5. DDI. https://media.ddiworld.com/research/global-leadership-forecast-2025-report.pdf?_gl=1*18by5ku*_gcl_au*MjAwMTk0NTg1NC4xNzM5NjQ5NjUw

[6] Development Dimensions International (DDI). (2025). *Global leadership forecast 2025: Insights and trends*. p. 19. DDI. https://media.ddiworld.com/research/global-leadership-forecast-2025-report.pdf?_gl=1*18by5ku*_gcl_au*MjAwMTk0NTg1NC4xNzM5NjQ5NjUw

[7] Howard, A., & Wellins, R. S. (2008). Overcoming the shortfalls in developing leaders. *Global leadership forecast 2008|2009 executive summary*. p. 1. Development Dimensions International, Inc. http://www.ddiworld.com/ddi/media/trend-research/globalleadershipforecast2008-2009_es_ddi.pdf

[8] Deloitte. (2023). *2023 Global human capital trends: Insights and trends*. Deloitte Insights. https://www2.deloitte.com/us/en/insights/focus/human-capital-trends/2023.html. "Leading in a boundaryless world" chapter link:

https://www2.deloitte.com/us/en/insights/focus/human-capital-trends/2023.html#read-the-chapter

[9] Deloitte. (2021). *2021 Deloitte global human capital trends—The social enterprise in a world disrupted* (2021). p. 20. Deloitte University Press. https://www2.deloitte.com/content/dam/insights/us/articles/6935_2021-HC-Trends/di_human-capital-trends.pdf

[10] Michaels, E., Handfield-Jones, H., & Axelrod, B. (2001), *The war for talent*. Harvard Business School Press. Sourced from Rothstein, Richard G., & Burke, Ronald J. (2010). *Self-management and leadership development*. p. 1. Edward Elgar Publishing Limited.

[11] Fulmer, R.M., & Conger, J.A. (2004), *Growing your Company's Leaders*, New York: AMACOM. Sourced from Rothstein, Richard G., & Burke, Ronald J. (2010). *Self-management and leadership development*. p. 1. Edward Elgar Publishing Limited.

[12] Hogan, R. and Hogan, J. (2001), Assessing leadership: A view of the dark side. *International Journal of Evaluation and Assessment*, 9, 40–51. Sourced from Rothstein, Richard G., & Burke, Ronald J. (2010). *Self-management and leadership development*. p. 1. Edward Elgar Publishing Limited.

[13] Burke, R.J. (2006). Why leaders fail: exploring the dark side. in R.J. Burke & C.L. Cooper (eds), *Inspiring Leaders*, London: Routledge, pp. 237–46. Sourced from Rothstein, Richard G., & Burke, Ronald J. (2010). *Self-management and leadership development*. p. 1. Edward Elgar Publishing Limited.

[14] Burke, R.J. (2006). Why leaders fail: exploring the dark side. In R.J. Burke & C.L. Cooper (eds), *Inspiring Leaders*, London: Routledge, pp. 237–46. Sourced from Rothstein, Richard G., & Burke, Ronald J. (2010). *Self-management and leadership development*. p. 1. Edward Elgar Publishing Limited.

[15] Rothstein, R. G., & Burke, R. J. (2010). *Self-management and leadership development*. p. 130. Edward Elgar Publishing Limited. Also, Barrett, A. & Beeson, J. (2002), *Developing business leaders for 2010*. New York Conference Board. Also, Buckingham, M. & Coffman, C. (1999). *First break all the rules: What the world's greatest managers do differently*. Simon and Schuster. Also, Kaiser, R.B., Hogan, R., & Craig, S.B. (2008). Leadership and the fate of organizations. *American Psychologist*, 63, 96-110. Also, Macey, W.H., & Schneider, B. (2008). The meaning of employee engagement. *Industrial and Organizational Psychology: Perspectives on Science and Practice*, 1, 3-30.

[16] U.S. Bureau of Labor Statistics. (2025). *Employed persons by detailed occupation and sex, 2024 annual averages* [Data table]. U.S. Department of Labor. https://www.bls.gov/cps/cpsaat11.htm.

[17] U.S. Bureau of Labor Statistics. (2024). *Employed persons by detailed occupation and sex, 2024 annual averages* [Data table]. U.S. Department of Labor. https://www.bls.gov/cps/cpsaat11.htm. Also, U.S. Bureau of Labor Statistics. (2016). *Spotlight on statistics: A look at the future of the U.S. labor force to 2060*. U.S. Department of Labor. https://www.bls.gov/spotlight/2016/a-look-at-the-future-of-the-us-labor-force-to-2060/home.htm. Also, Colby, S. L., & Ortman, J. M. (2015). Projections of the Size and Composition of the U.S. Population:

2014 to 2060, Population Estimates and Projections. pp. 25-1143. U.S. Department of Commerce Economics and Statistics Administration U.S. Census Bureau.
https://www.census.gov/content/dam/Census/library/publications/2015/demo/p25-1143.pdf.

[18] Rothstein, R. G., & Burke, R. J. (2010). *Self-management and leadership development.* p. 130. Edward Elgar Publishing Limited. Also, Bernhart, M. (2006). Preparing for a skills shortage and work intensification. *Employee Benefit News*, November. Also, Rappaport, Anna, Bancroft, Ed, & Okum, Lauren (2003), The aging workforce raises new talent management issues for employers. *Journal of Organizational Excellence*, 23(1), 55-66.

[19] Rothstein, R. G., & Burke, R. J. (2010). *Self-management and leadership development.* p. 130. Edward Elgar Publishing Limited.

[20] Rothstein, R. G., & Burke, R. J. (2010). *Self-management and leadership development.* p. 1. Edward Elgar Publishing Limited.

[21] Amazon.com (2025, February 9).
https://www.amazon.com/s?k=leadership+books&i=stripbooks&crid=30TY9F7OQD1I8&sprefix=leadership%2Cstripbooks%2C101&ref=nb_sb_ss_mvt-t4-ranker_1_10

[22] American Society for Training and Development (ASTD) Public Policy Counsel (2006). *Bridging the skills gap: how the skills shortage threatens growth and competitiveness . . . and what to do about it.* ASTD Publications.

[23] Iannuzzi, P. A., Jr. (2020). A phenomenological study of the importance, value, and need for leadership development training for academic department chairs. Doctoral research study. Delaware Valley University. ProQuest LLC. https://search.proquest.com/docview/2393750365?accountid=10488

[24] Rothstein, R. G., & Burke, R. J. (2010). *Self-management and leadership development.* p. 130. Edward Elgar Publishing Limited.

[25] Loew, L. (2015). Improving leadership development: The time to act is now. *Training Magazine.* https://trainingmag.com/improving-leadership-development-the-time-to-act-is-now/

[26] Hassan, F. (2011). "The frontline advantage." *Harvard Business Review.* https://hbr.org/2011/05/the-frontline-advantage

[27] Tichy, N. M. (1997). *The leadership engine: How winning companies build leaders at every level.* HarperCollins Publishers.

[28] Howard, A., & Wellins, R. S. (2008). Overcoming the shortfalls in developing leaders. *Global leadership forecast 2008|2009 executive summary.* p. 2. Development Dimensions International, Inc.

[29] Howard, A., & Wellins, R. S. (2008). Overcoming the shortfalls in developing leaders. Global leadership forecast 2008|2009 executive summary. p. 3. Development Dimensions International, Inc.

[30] Black, T. (2015, May 1). *Prezi.* https://prezi.com/bvhvvsslrzq7/study-the-past-if-you-would-define-the-future/

[31] Baines, J., & Malek, J. (2000). *The cultural atlas of ancient Egypt.* Facts on File.

[32] Bass, B. M. (1990). *Bass & Stogdill's handbook of leadership: Theory, research, and managerial applications*, 3rd ed. p. 3. Free Press.

[33] Griffith, S. B. (1963). *Sun Tzu: The art of war.* p. 63. Oxford University Press.

[34] Blanchard, K. (2013, May 22). Public forum presentation. American Society of Training and Development (ASTD) Conference and International Exposition, Dallas, Texas Convention Center.

[35] Blanchard, K., & Johnson, S. (1982). *The One Minute Manager.* William Morrow and Company.

[36] Leadership (2021, January 26). *Merriam-Webster.com.* http://www.merriam-webster.com/dictionary/ leadership.

[37] Gardner, J. W. (1990). *On leadership.* p. xvi. The Free Press.

[38] Gardner, J. W. (1990). *On leadership.* p xvi. The Free Press.

[39] Bennis, W. G., & Nanus, Burt (2003). *Leaders: Strategies for taking charge*, Second Ed. p. 207. Collins Business Essentials, HarperCollins Publishers Inc.

[40] Bennis, W. G., & Nanus, B. (2003). *Leaders: Strategies for taking charge*, Second Ed. p. 207. Collins Business Essentials, HarperCollins Publishers Inc.

[41] Puryear, E. F. (1988). *Nineteen stars: a study in military character and leadership.* Presidio Press.

[42] Drucker, P. F. (2002). *The effective executive.* p. 20. Harper Business Essentials, HarperCollins Publishers Inc.

[43] *The Officer's Guide*, 9th Edition (1943). p. 197. Military Service Publishing Company.

[44] Phillips, D. T. (1998). *Martin Luther King, Jr.: On leadership: Inspiration and wisdom for challenging times.* p. 33. Warner Books, A Time Warner Company.

[45] Gassner-Otting, L. (2024, December 18). *Bloomberg Business Week* interview. Available on Bloomberg podcast (13:00 minutes into 21:04 segment). Laura is a workplace expert and author of *Limitless: How to ignore everybody, carve your own path, and live your best life.* https://www.bloomberg.com/news/audio/2024-12-18/bloomberg-businessweek-trump-s-tariffs-and-taxes-podcast

[46] Tate, R., & While, J. (2005). *People leave managers . . . not organizations! Action-based leadership.* iUniverse.

[47] Burns, J. M. (1978). *Leadership.* p. 2. Perennial, an Imprint of HarperCollins Publishers.

[48] Szasz, F. M. (2005, December 26). *History news network.* http://historynewsnetwork.org/article/1328

[49] Gardner, J. W. (1990). *On leadership.* p. xix. The Free Press.

[50] *The Holy Bible* (1951). Catholic Press, Inc.

[51] Mahmoud, M., Rabi (1967). The political theory of Ibn Khaldun. Leiden: Brill. From Bass, B. M. (1990). *Bass & Stogdill's handbook of leadership: Theory, research, and managerial applications*, Third Ed. p. 5. Free Press.

[52] Nadkarni, M. V. (2016). *Ethics for our times: Essays in Gandhian perspective.* Oxford University Press.

[53] Baines, J., & Malek, J. (2000). *The cultural atlas of ancient Egypt.* Facts on File.

[54] Griffith, S. B. (1963). *Sun Tzu, the art of war.* p. 63. Oxford University Press.

55 Bass, B. M. (1990). *Bass & Stogdill's handbook of leadership: Theory, research, and managerial applications*, Third Ed. p. 6. Free Press.
56 Bonaparte, N. (n.d.). *Give me enough medals and I'll win you any war*. In *Napoleon's Art of War* [Quote]. Goodreads. Retrieved March 19, 2025, https://www.goodreads.com/quotes/580872-give-me-enough-medals-and-i-ll-win-you-any-war
57 Bonaparte, N. (2005). *Napoleon's art of war* (G. C. D'Aguilar, Trans.; B. De Toy, Intro.). Barnes & Noble, Incorporated.
58 *Wikipedia, The Free Encyclopedia* (2008, May 17). http://en.wikipedia.org/wiki/Frederick_Winslow_Taylor
59 Lussier, R. N., & Achua, C. F. (2013). *Leadership: Theory, application, & skill development*, Fifth Ed. p. 293. South-Western Cengage Learning.
60 Maslow, Abraham H. (1943). A theory of human motivation. *Psychological Review*. 50, 370-96.
61 Aitken, H. G. J. (1960). *Scientific management in action: Taylorism at Watertown Arsenal, 1908-1915*. Harvard University Press.
62 Maslow, A. H. (1943). A theory of human motivation. *Psychological Review*. 50, 370-96.
63 Drucker, P. F. (1973). *Management: Tasks, responsibilities, practices*. Harper & Row. Also *Wikipedia, The Free Encyclopedia* (2008). http://en.wikipedia.org/wiki/Frederick_Winslow_Taylor.
64 Maslow, A. H. (1943). A theory of human motivation. *Psychological Review*. 50, 370-96.
65 Maslow, A. H. (1943). A theory of human motivation. *Psychological Review*. 50, 370-96.
66 Maslow, A. H. (1943). A theory of human motivation. *Psychological Review*. 50, 370-96.
67 Maslow, A. H. (1943). A theory of human motivation. *Psychological Review*. 50, 370-96.
68 Lussier, R. N., & Achua, C. F. (2013). *Leadership: Theory, application, & skill development*, Fifth Ed. p. 84. South-Western Cengage Learning.
69 McGregor, D. (1960). *The human side of enterprise*. McGraw-Hill.
70 McGregor, D. (2015). Theory X Y. *Business Balls*. http://www.businessballs.com/mcgregor.htm.
71 McGregor, D. (2015). Theory X Y. *Business Balls*. http://www.businessballs.com/mcgregor.htm.
72 McGregor, D. (2015). Theory X Y. *Business Balls*. http://www.businessballs.com/mcgregor.htm.
73 Herzberg, F. I. (1987). One more time: How do you motivate employees? *Harvard Business Review*. Sep/Oct87, Vol. 65 Issue 5:109-120.
74 Lussier, R. N., & Achua, C. F. (2013). *Leadership: Theory, application, & skill development*, Fifth Ed. p. 84. South-Western Cengage Learning.
75 Lussier, R. N., & Achua, C. F. (2013). *Leadership: Theory, application, & skill development*, Fifth Ed. p. 82. South-Western Cengage Learning.
76 McCarney, R., Warner, J., Iliffe, S., van Haselen, R., Griffin, M., & Fisher, P. (2007). The Hawthorne effect: a randomised, controlled trial. *BMC Med Res Methodology* 7:30.
77 Landsberger, H. A. (1958). *Hawthorne Revisited*. Ithaca.

[78] Western Electric—a brief history (2017). The Porticus Centre. http://www.beatriceco.com/bti/porticus/bell/westernelectric_history.html#Western%20Electric%20-%20A%20Brief%20History. Also at https://en.wikipedia.org/wiki/Western_Electric

[79] Shewhart, W. A. (2017). *Wikipedia*. https://en.wikipedia.org/wiki/Walter_A._Shewhart#cite_ref-1

[80] Ross, J. E. (1999). *Total quality management, text, cases and readings.* Third Ed. p. 5. CRC Press LLC.

[81] Janakiraman, B., & Gopal, R.K. (2006). *Total quality management, text and case.* p. 145. Prentice-Hall of India.

[82] Deming, W. E. (1982). *Out of the crisis.* MIT Press.

[83] Written by the Mindtools Content Team (2014, February 16). Deming's 14-point philosophy: a recipe for total quality. From Deming, W. Edwards (2000). *Out of crisis.* IT Press. http://www.mindtools.com/pages/article/newSTR_75.htm

[84] Macht, J. (2016, June 24). *The management thinker we should never have forgotten.* Harvard Business Review. https://hbr.org/2016/06/the-management-thinker-we-should-never-have-forgotten

[85] Karekar, H. (2023, January 4). *Are 14 points of management from Dr. Deming in Out of the Crisis, 1982, still relevant in 2023?* Medium. https://hrishikeshkarekar.medium.com/are-14-points-of-management-from-dr-deming-in-out-of-the-crisis-1982-still-relevant-in-2023-d2b0582c899b

[86] Garnett, D. (2021, October 23). *W. Edwards Deming: The legacy he deserves is not the one he's usually given.* Doug Garnett's Blog. https://www.douggarnett.com/business-and-strategy/w-edwards-deming-the-legacy-he-deserves-is-not-one-of-metric-mania/

[87] Kissinger, H. A., & Mundie, C., & Schmidt, E. (2024). *Genesis: Artificial intelligence, hope, and the human spirit.* p. 5. Little, Brown and Company.

[88] Drucker, P. F. (2002). *The effective executive.* p. 169. Harper Business Essentials, HarperCollins Publishers Inc.

[89] Burns, J. M. (1978). *Leadership.* p. 3. Perennial, an Imprint of HarperCollins Publishers.

[90] Drucker, P. F. (2002). *The effective executive.* p. 4. Harper Business Essentials, HarperCollins Publishers Inc.

[91] Drucker, P. F. (1988, January 6). Leadership: More doing than dash. *The Wall Street Journal.* http://www.chariscorp-wordgems.com/leadership.drucker.html. Also available at https://rlaexp.com/studio/biz/conceptual_resources/authors/peter_drucker/managing-for-the-future/15-leadership-more-doing-than-dash.pdf

[92] Burns, J. M. (1978). *Leadership.* p. 19. Perennial, an Imprint of HarperCollins Publishers.

[93] Air Force Doctrine Document 1-1 (2004, February 18). Leadership and force development. p 1.

[94] Gardner, J. W. (1990). *On leadership.* p. ix. The Free Press.

⁹⁵ Hassan, F. (2013). The frontline advantage. The Forum Corporation. https://cdns3.trainingindustry.com/media/15448385/7_leadership_development_trends.pdf. Also available at https://hbr.org/2011/05/the-frontline-advantage.
⁹⁶ Lussier, R. N., & Achua, C. F. (2013). *Leadership: Theory, application, & skill development*, Fifth Ed. p. 11. South-Western Cengage Learning.
⁹⁷ Bennis, W. G., & Nanus, B. (2003). *Leaders: Strategies for taking charge*, Second Edition. p. 1. Collins Business Essentials, HarperCollins Publishers Inc.
⁹⁸ Bennis, W. G., & Nanus, B. (2003). *Leaders: Strategies for taking charge*, Second Edition. p. 1. Collins Business Essentials, HarperCollins Publishers Inc.
⁹⁹ Bennis, W. G. (2003). *On becoming a leader.* p. 39. Basic Books, Perseus Books Group.
¹⁰⁰ Bernstein, R. (2006). *America's coach: Life lessons and wisdom for gold medal success: a biographical journey of the late hockey icon Herb Brooks.* Adventure Publications, Inc.
¹⁰¹ Bernstein, R. (2006). *America's coach: Life lessons and wisdom for gold medal success: a biographical journey of the late hockey icon Herb Brooks.* Adventure Publications, Inc.
¹⁰² The Drucker Institute, Claremont Graduate University (2025, April 24). Drucker as guru. https://drucker.institute/about-peter-drucker/
¹⁰³ Drucker, P. F. (2002). *The effective executive.* p. 7. Harper Business Essentials, HarperCollins Publishers Inc.
¹⁰⁴ Creech, B. (1994). *The five pillars of TQM: How to make total quality management work for you.* p. 304. Truman Talley Books/Plume.
¹⁰⁵ Gardner, J. W. (1990). *On leadership.* p. 4. The Free Press.
¹⁰⁶ Gardner, J. W. (1990). *On leadership.* p. 4. The Free Press.
¹⁰⁷ Kotter, J. P. (2013). Management is (still) not leadership. *Harvard Business Review* Blog. http://blogs.hbr.org/2013/01/management-is-still-not-leadership/
¹⁰⁸ Kotter, J. P. (2013). Management is (still) not leadership. *Harvard Business Review* Blog. http://blogs.hbr.org/2013/01/management-is-still-not-leadership/
¹⁰⁹ Kotter, J. P. (2013). Management is (still) not leadership. *Harvard Business Review* Blog. http://blogs.hbr.org/2013/01/management-is-still-not-leadership/
¹¹⁰ Lussier, R. N., & Achua, C. F. (2013). *Leadership: Theory, application, & skill development*, Fifth Ed. p. 36. South-Western Cengage Learning.
¹¹¹ Lussier, R. N., & Achua, C. F. (2013). *Leadership: Theory, application, & skill development*, Fifth Ed. p. 36. South-Western Cengage Learning.
¹¹² Bennis, W. G., & Nanus, B. (2002). *Leaders: strategies for taking charge.* p. 207. Second Ed. Collins Business Essentials, HarperCollins Publishers Inc.
¹¹³ Bennis, W. G., & Nanus, B. (2002). *Leaders: strategies for taking charge.* p. 207. Second Ed. Collins Business Essentials, HarperCollins Publishers Inc.
¹¹⁴ Puryear, E. F. (1988). *Nineteen stars: a study in military character and leadership.* Presidio Press.
¹¹⁵ Gardner, J. W. (1990). *On leadership.* p. xix. The Free Press.
¹¹⁶ Gardner, J. W. (1990). *On leadership.* p. 157. The Free Press.
¹¹⁷ Drucker, P. F. (2002). *The effective executive.* p. 1. Harper Business Essentials, HarperCollins Publishers Inc.

[118] Tuchman, B. W. (1979, October 17). Library of Congress speech. http://www.qotd.org/search/single.html?qid=2201. Also at https://wist.info/tuchman-barbara/28912/.

[119] Bennis, W. G. (2002). *On becoming a leader.* p. v. Basic Books, Perseus Books Group.

[120] Bennis, W. G. (2002). *On becoming a leader.* pp. xxi-xxii. Basic Books, Perseus Books Group.

[121] Drucker, P. F. (2002). *The effective executive.* pp. 23-24. Harper Business Essentials, HarperCollins Publishers Inc.

[122] Phillips, D. T. (1998). *Martin Luther King, Jr.: on leadership: inspiration and wisdom for challenging times.* Warner Books, A Time Warner Company.

[123] Gardner, J. W. (1990). *On leadership.* pp. 48-54. The Free Press.

[124] World Economic Forum. (2016, September 29). *These are the leadership skills Harvard thinks you need.* World Economic Forum. https://www.weforum.org/stories/2016/09/these-traits-could-make-you-a-more-effective-leader/

[125] Lussier, R. N., & Achua, C. F. (2013). *Leadership: Theory, application, & skill development*, Fifth Ed. pp. 10-11. South-Western Cengage Learning.

[126] Maxwell, J. C. (1999). *The 21 indispensable qualities of a leader: Becoming the person others will want to follow.* Thomas Nelson Publishers Inc.

[127] Dalessandro, R. J., Colonel, U.S. Army (2009). *Army Officer's Guide*, 51st Ed. p. 285. Stackpole Books.

[128] Yukl, G. (2013). *Leadership in organizations.* Eighth Ed. Pearson. http://www.blackdiamond.dk/HDO/Organisation_Gary_Yukl_Leadership_in_Organizations.pdf. Original source: Yukl, G. (1998). *Leadership in organizations.* Prentice-Hall. Also at https://nibmehub.com/opac-service/pdf/read/Leadership%20in%20Organizations%20by%20Gary%20Yukl.pdf

[129] Zenger, J. H., & Folkman, J. (2002). *The extraordinary leader: Turning good managers into great leaders.* pp. 232-248. McGraw-Hill Companies Inc.

[130] *The officer's guide*, Ninth Ed. p. 197. (1943). Military Service Publishing Company.

[131] Drucker, P. F. (2002). *The effective executive.* p. 18. Harper Business Essentials, HarperCollins Publishers Inc.

[132] Lussier, R. N., & Achua, C. F. (2013). *Leadership: Theory, application, & skill development*, Fifth Ed. p. 36. South-Western Cengage Learning.

[133] Lussier, R. N., & Achua, C. F. (2013). *Leadership: Theory, application, & skill development*, Fifth Ed. p. 36. South-Western Cengage Learning.

[134] Bernstein, E. (2011, April 5). Do you get an A in personality? *The Wall Street Journal*: D1-D2.

[135] Wang, S. S. (2010, September 28). Why so many people can't make decisions. *The Wall Street Journal*. D1-D2.

[136] Hooiberg, R., & Lane, N. (2008). Using multisource feedback coaching effectively in executive education. *Academy of Management Learning & Education* 7(1) (2008): 108-123.

[137] Lussier, R. N., & Achua, C. F. (2013). *Leadership: Theory, application, & skill development*, Fifth Ed. p. 35. South-Western Cengage Learning.

[138] Kahnweiler, J. B. (2009). Why introverts can make the best leaders. *Forbes*: 8.
[139] Phillips, D. T. (1998). *Martin Luther King, Jr. on leadership: Inspiration and wisdom for challenging times.* p. 28. Warner Books, A Time Warner Company.
[140] Lussier, R. N., & Achua, C. F. (2013). *Leadership: Theory, application, & skill development,* Fifth Ed. p. 35. South-Western Cengage Learning.
[141] Lussier, R. N., & Achua, C. F. (2013). *Leadership: Theory, application, & skill development,* Fifth Ed. p. 37. South-Western Cengage Learning.
[142] Lussier, R. N., & Achua, C. F. (2013). *Leadership: Theory, application, & skill development,* Fifth Ed. p. 37. South-Western Cengage Learning.
[143] Lussier, R. N., & Achua, C. F. (2013). *Leadership: Theory, application, & skill development,* Fifth Ed. p. 37. South-Western Cengage Learning.
[144] Lussier, R. N., & Achua, C. F. (2013). *Leadership: Theory, application, & skill development,* Fifth Ed. p. 35. South-Western Cengage Learning.
[145] Lewin, K., L., R., & White, R. K. (1939). Patterns of aggressive behavior in experimentally created social climates. *Journal of Social Psychology*, 10 (1939), 271-301.
[146] Lussier, R. N., & Achua, C. F. (2013). *Leadership: Theory, application, & skill development,* Fifth Ed. p. 71. South-Western Cengage Learning.
[147] Lussier, R. N., & Achua, C. F. (2013). *Leadership: Theory, application, & skill development,* Fifth Ed. p. 71. South-Western Cengage Learning.
[148] Lussier, R. N., & Achua, C. F. (2013). *Leadership: Theory, application, & skill development,* Fifth Ed. p. 79. South-Western Cengage Learning.
[149] Lussier, R. N., & Achua, C. F. (2013). *Leadership: Theory, application, & skill development,* Fifth Ed. pp. 77-78. South-Western Cengage Learning.
[150] Drucker, P. F. (1988, January 6). Leadership: More doing than dash. *The Wall Street Journal.* http://www.chariscorp-wordgems.com/leadership.drucker.html
[151] Burns, J. M. (1978). *Leadership.* p. 20. Perennial, an Imprint of HarperCollins Publishers. Also at
https://rlaexp.com/studio/biz/conceptual_resources/authors/peter_drucker/managing-for-the-future/15-leadership-more-doing-than-dash.pdf
[152] Bennis, W. G., & Nanus, B. (2003). *Leaders: Strategies for taking charge,* Second Edition. p. 3. Collins Business Essentials, HarperCollins Publishers Inc.
[153] Slife, J. C., Lieutenant Colonel, U.S. Air Force (2004). *Creech blue: Gen Bill Creech and the reformation of the tactical air forces, 1978–1984.* p. 79. Air University Press in collaboration with the College of Aerospace Doctrine, Research and Education, Maxwell Air Force Base.
[154] Slife, J. C., Lieutenant Colonel, U.S. Air Force (2004). *Creech blue: Gen Bill Creech and the reformation of the tactical air forces, 1978–1984.* p. 79. Air University Press in collaboration with the College of Aerospace Doctrine, Research and Education, Maxwell Air Force Base.
[155] Slife, J. C., Lieutenant Colonel, U.S. Air Force (2004). *Creech blue: Gen Bill Creech and the reformation of the tactical air forces, 1978–1984.* p. 89. Air University Press in collaboration with the College of Aerospace Doctrine, Research and Education, Maxwell Air Force Base.

¹⁵⁶ Slife, J. C., Lieutenant Colonel, U.S. Air Force (2004). *Creech blue: Gen Bill Creech and the reformation of the tactical air forces, 1978–1984.* p. 82. Air University Press in collaboration with the College of Aerospace Doctrine, Research and Education, Maxwell Air Force Base.
¹⁵⁷ Creech, B. (1994). *The five pillars of TQM: How to make total quality management work for you.* p. 1 Introduction from Peter F. Drucker. Truman Talley Books/Plume.
¹⁵⁸ Gardner, J. W. (1990). *On leadership.* pp. 38-47. The Free Press.
¹⁵⁹ Zenger, J. H., & Folkman, J. (2002). *The extraordinary leader: Turning good managers into great leaders.* pp. 111-112. McGraw-Hill Companies Inc.
¹⁶⁰ Gardner, J. W. (1990). *On leadership.* p. 38. The Free Press.
¹⁶¹ Lussier, R. N., & Achua, C. F. (2013). *Leadership: Theory, application, & skill development,* Fifth Ed. p. 122. South-Western Cengage Learning.
¹⁶² Zenger, J. H., & Folkman, J. (2002). *The extraordinary leader: Turning good managers into great leaders.* McGraw-Hill Companies Inc.
¹⁶³ Cronin, T. E. (1989, February 1). *Chronicle of Higher Education.* B1-B2.
¹⁶⁴ Schwarzkopf, H. N., General, U.S. Army (1992). *The autobiography: It doesn't take a hero.* p 67. Linda Grey Bantam Books.
¹⁶⁵ Gardner, J. W. (1990). *On leadership.* p. 2. The Free Press.
¹⁶⁶ Pritchard, J. P. (2016, February 27). In a review of the book *Bill Gates: a biography.* HyperInk. http://www.hyperink.com/Conclusion-b1307a16. Also at https://www.inc.com/marcel-schwantes/bill-gates-explains-what-separates-successful-leaders-from-everyone-else-in-2-words.html
¹⁶⁷ Keegan, M. J. (2014, August 15). *IBM center for the business of government: connecting research to practice.* https://www.businessofgovernment.org/blog/leading-defense-health-agency-interview-lt-gen-dr-douglas-robb-director-defense-health-agency
¹⁶⁸ Quinn, M. (2017, December 6). Beyonce to Bill Gates: 24 millionaires reveal the hardest thing about being an entrepreneur. https://www.huffpost.com/entry/beyonce-to-bill-gates-24-millionaires-reveal-the-hardest-thing-about-being-an-entrepreneur_b_6866554
¹⁶⁹ Hassell, D. (2015). The awesome responsibility of leadership: an interview with Simon Sinek. https://www.linkedin.com/pulse/awesome-responsibility-leadershipan-interview-simon-sinek-hassell/
¹⁷⁰ Sinek, S. (2009). *Start with why: How great leaders inspire everyone to take action.* Penguin Group.
¹⁷¹ Tracy, B. (1993). *Maximum achievement.* pp 82-83. Fireside Books, Simon & Schuster.
¹⁷² Tracy, B. (1993). *Maximum achievement.* pp 82-83. Fireside Books, Simon & Schuster.
¹⁷³ Tracy, B. (1993). *Maximum achievement.* pp 82-83. Fireside Books, Simon & Schuster.
¹⁷⁴ Zimmer, D., MS, PMP, MCP, CCP (2017). Strategic Advisor for Change Management and Business Leadership. Professor, Pennsylvania State University. Speaker and author. Personal interview April 25, 2017.
¹⁷⁵ Jobs, S. P. (2024, November 11). *Steve Jobs on the most important job of a CEO* [Video]. YouTube. https://www.youtube.com/watch?v=HIpqbdxyypA

[176] Development Dimensions International (DDI). (2025). *Global leadership forecast 2025: Insights and trends.* p. 6. DDI. https://media.ddiworld.com/research/global-leadership-forecast-2025-report.pdf?_gl=1*18by5ku*_gcl_au*MjAwMTk0NTg1NC4xNzM5NjQ5NjUw

[177] Welch, J., & Welch, S. (2013, December 9). Five bosses you don't want (or want to be). http://www.linkedin.com/today/post/article/20131209210429-86541065-four-bosses-you-don-t-want-or-want-to-be?trk=tod-home-art-list-large_0

[178] Saks, A. M. (2006). Antecedents and consequences of employee engagement. Journal of Managerial Psychology, 21(7), 600–619. https://doi.org/10.1108/02683940610690169

[179] Jones, R. D., Major General, U.S. Army, (2016, February 27). *Family and MWR guide.* http://www.armymwr.com/userfiles/file/commander/travel_guide-5_4c.pdf

[180] Mehrabian, A. (1972). *Nonverbal communication.* New Brunswick: Aldine Transaction. University of Texas Permian Basin online communication portal https://online.utpb.edu/about-us/articles/communication/how-much-of-communication-is-nonverbal/#:~:text=The%2055%2F38%2F7%20Formula,%2C%20and%207%25%20words%20only.

[181] De Bono, E. (1990). *Lateral thinking: Creativity step by step.* First Perennial Ed. Perennial Library.

[182] LaVine, L. (2013). The power of giving back: How community involvement can boost your bottom line. https://www.entrepreneur.com/article/226974

[183] Tzu, L. (2016, February 27). ThinkExist.com. From *Tao Te Ching* (*The book of the way: 600 BC-531 BC*). http://thinkexist.com/quotation/to_lead_people-walk_beside_them-as_for_the_best/344532.html. Also at https://www.goodreads.com/quotes/10627-to-lead-people-walk-beside-them-as-for-the#:~:text=and%20meet%20your%20next%20favorite%20book!&text=As%20for%20the%20best%20leaders,We%20did%20it%20ourselves!&text=C.

[184] Kruse, K. (2012, October 16). 100 best quotes on leadership. *Forbes.com.* https://www.forbes.com/sites/kevinkruse/2012/10/16/quotes-on-leadership/#703305f72feb

[185] Northouse, P. G. (2022). *Leadership: Theory and practice.* Ninth Ed. Sage. pp. 15-16.

[186] Gardner, J. W. (1990). *On leadership.* p. 17. The Free Press.

[187] Kissinger, H. A., & Mundie, C., & Schmidt, E. (2024). *Genesis: Artificial intelligence, hope, and the human spirit.* pp. 27-28. Little, Brown and Company.

[188] Development Dimensions International (DDI). (2025). *Global leadership forecast 2025: Insights and trends.* p. 7. DDI. https://media.ddiworld.com/research/global-leadership-forecast-2025-report.pdf?_gl=1*18by5ku*_gcl_au*MjAwMTk0NTg1NC4xNzM5NjQ5NjUw

[189] Development Dimensions International (DDI). (2025). *Global leadership forecast 2025: Insights and trends.* p. 7. DDI. https://media.ddiworld.com/research/global-

leadership-forecast-2025-report.pdf?_gl=1*18by5ku*_gcl_au*MjAwMTk0NTg1NC4xNzM5NjQ5NjUw

[190] Kissinger, H. A., & Mundie, C., & Schmidt, E. (2024). *Genesis: Artificial intelligence, hope, and the human spirit.* pp. 27-28. Little, Brown and Company.

[191] Vince Lombardi Quotes (2015, December 27). http://www.vincelombardi.com/quotes.html

[192] United States Air Force Mission (2021). https://www.af.mil/News/Article-Display/Article/2565837/air-force-unveils-new-mission-statement/ Also at https://www.airforce.com/#:~:text=The%20mission%20of%20the%20United,helping%20us%20achieve%20mission%20success

[193] Welsh, M. A. III, General, U.S. Air Force Chief of Staff (2013, January 9). The world's greatest air force: Powered by airmen, fueled by innovation. *A Vision for the United States Air Force.* p 4. https://www.af.mil/Portals/1/images/airpower/GV_GR_GP_300DPI.pdf

[194] Schwantes, M. (2018, March 28). A young Steve Jobs once gave this priceless leadership lesson. Here it is in a few sentences. Inc.com. https://www.inc.com/marcel-schwantes/a-young-steve-jobs-once-gave-this-priceless-leadership-lesson-here-it-is-in-a-few-sentences.html

[195] Amorim, S. (2022). 10 quotes to empower your coaching questions. Erickson International. https://www.erickson.edu/resources/10-quotes-to-empower

[196] Covey, S. M. R. with Merrill, R. R. (2006). *The speed of trust: The one thing that changes everything.* P. 21. Free Press.

[197] Trust (2022, January 12). *Merriam-Webster.com.* http://www.merriam-webster.com/dictionary/trust

[198] Maxwell, J. C. (1999). *The 21 indispensable qualities of a leader: Becoming the person others will want to follow.* p. ix. Thomas Nelson Publishers Inc.

[199] Development Dimensions International (DDI). (2025). *Global leadership forecast 2025: Insights and trends.* p. 5. DDI. https://media.ddiworld.com/research/global-leadership-forecast-2025-report.pdf?_gl=1*18by5ku*_gcl_au*MjAwMTk0NTg1NC4xNzM5NjQ5NjUw

[200] Covey, S. M. R. with Merrill, R. R. (2006). *The speed of trust: The one thing that changes everything.* p. 21. Free Press.

[201] Covey, S. M. R. with Merrill, R. R. (2006). *The speed of trust: The one thing that changes everything.* p. 5. Free Press.

[202] *2024 Deloitte global human capital trends— Thriving beyond boundaries: Human performance in a boundaryless world* (2024). p. 41. Deloitte University Press. https://www2.deloitte.com/us/en/insights/focus/human-capital-trends.html

[203] Kouzes, J. M., & Posner, B. Z. (2017). *The leadership challenge.* Sixth Ed. John Wiley & Sons. https://nibmehub.com/opac-service/pdf/read/The%20Leadership%20Challenge_%20How%20to%20Make%20Extraordinary%20Things%20Happen%20in%20Organizations.pdf Also available at Also available in the *Innovative Leader*, #385, Volume 8, Number 2.

[204] Pritchard, J. P. (2016, February 27). In a review of the book *Bill Gates: a biography.* HyperInk. http://www.hyperink.com/Conclusion-b1307a16. Also at

https://www.inc.com/marcel-schwantes/bill-gates-explains-what-separates-successful-leaders-from-everyone-else-in-2-words.html

[205] DePree, M. (1992). *Leadership jazz, the art of conducting business through: Leadership-followership-teamwork-touch-voice.* pp 153-166. Dell Publishing.

[206] 3M (2015, December 28). http://www.3m.com/3M/en_US/company-us/

[207] Cronkite, W. (1997). *A reporter's life.* Ballantine Books. Also reference https://interviews.televisionacademy.com/interviews/walter-cronkite, and Parachin, V. M. (2015, December 28). Six ways to lead with compassion. *Perdido* magazine. http://www.perdidomagazine.com/articles/six-ways-lead-compassion

[208] Info Entrepreneurs (2009). *Manage risk.* Original document source Business Link UK. http://www.infoentrepreneurs.org/en/guides/manage-risk/

[209] *The Holy Bible.* King James Version (1814 A.D., stemming from 1769, 1611, and 1604 A.D. series). Matthew 5:37.

[210] Tracy, B. (2000). *The 100 absolutely unbreakable laws of business success.* Chapter 4, The Laws of Leadership, #34: The Law of Integrity. Berrett-Koehler Publishers, Inc. https://gthinkers.org/business_books/100LawsebookFINAL_BrianTracy.pd. Also available at https://brandautopsy.typepad.com/brandautopsy/2011/01/thomas-carlyle-on-treating-people.html

[211] Welch, J., & Welch, S. (2013, December 9). Five bosses you don't want (or want to be). http://www.linkedin.com/today/post/article/20131209210429-86541065-four-bosses-you-don-t-want-or-want-to-be?trk=tod-home-art-list-large_0

[212] Landry, L. (2019). Why emotional intelligence is important in leadership. Harvard Business School Online. https://online.hbs.edu/blog/post/emotional-intelligence-in-leadership

[213] Landry, L. (2019). Why emotional intelligence is important in leadership. Harvard Business School Online. https://online.hbs.edu/blog/post/emotional-intelligence-in-leadership

[214] Phillips, J. M., & Gully, S. M. (2014). *Organizational behavior: Tools for success,* Second Ed. p. 193. South-Western Cengage Learning.

[215] Drucker, P. F. (1988, January 6). Leadership: more doing than dash. *The Wall Street Journal.* http://www.chariscorp-wordgems.com/leadership.drucker.html. Also available at https://rlaexp.com/studio/biz/conceptual_resources/authors/peter_drucker/managing-for-the-future/15-leadership-more-doing-than-dash.pdf

[216] Kouzes, J. M., & Posner, B. Z. (1999). Without trust you cannot lead. #385 from Innovative Leader Volume 8, Number 2. http://www.winstonbrill.com/bril001/html/article_index/articles/351-400/article385_body.html

[217] Tracy, B. (1993). *Maximum achievement.* Pp. 82-83. Fireside Books, Simon & Schuster.

[218] Zimmer, D., MS, PMP, MCP, CCP (2017). Strategic Advisor for Change Management and Business Leadership, Professor, Pennsylvania State University, speaker, author, personal interview, April 25, 2017.

219 Angelou, M. (2012). Interview with *Beautifully Said* Magazine. https://hitherandthither.net/remembering-maya-angelou/

220 Concern. (2022, January 22). *Merriam-Webster.com*. http://www.merriam-webster.com/dictionary/concern

221 Grant, A. (2025, April 13). *America is learning the wrong lesson from Musk's success. The New York Times.* https://www.nytimes.com

222 Valade, D. (2024, August 24). Business leaders ask, what's next? Begin by listening. The Malabar Group Inc. https://malabargroup.ca/business-leaders-ask-whats-next-begin-by-listening/

223 Nulty, P. (1994). The National Business Hall of Fame. p. 118. *Fortune,* April 4, 1994. Also at Bower, Marvin (1997, November 1). Developing leaders in a business. Book excerpt. *McKinsey Quarterly.* https://www.mckinsey.com/featured-insights/leadership/developing-leaders-in-a-business

224 Welch, J., & Welch, S. (2013, December 9). Five bosses you don't want (or want to be). http://www.linkedin.com/today/post/article/20131209210429-86541065-four-bosses-you-don-t-want-or-want-to-be?trk=tod-home-art-list-large_0

225 Welch, J., & Welch, S. (2013, December 9). Five bosses you don't want (or want to be). http://www.linkedin.com/today/post/article/20131209210429-86541065-four-bosses-you-don-t-want-or-want-to-be?trk=tod-home-art-list-large_0Jack

226 Collins, J. (2001). *Good to great: Why some companies make the leap . . . and others don't.* p. 13. HarperCollins Publishers.

227 Development Dimensions International (DDI). (2025). *Global leadership forecast 2025: Insights and trends.* p. 6. DDI. https://media.ddiworld.com/research/global-leadership-forecast-2025-report.pdf?_gl=1*18by5ku*_gcl_au*MjAwMTk0NTg1NC4xNzM5NjQ5NjUw

228 Collins, J. (2001). *Good to great: Why some companies make the leap . . . and others don't.* p. 39 & 211. HarperCollins Publishers.

229 Parachin, V. M. (2015, December 28). Six ways to lead with compassion. *Perdido* magazine. http://www.perdidomagazine.com/articles/six-ways-lead-compassion

230 Sirota, D., Mischkind, L. A., & Meltzer, M. I. (2005). *The enthusiastic employee – how companies profit by giving workers what they want.* pp. 207-208. Pearson Education, Inc. publishing as Wharton School Publishing.

231 Development Dimensions International (DDI). (2025). *Global leadership forecast 2025: Insights and trends.* p. 6. DDI. https://media.ddiworld.com/research/global-leadership-forecast-2025-report.pdf?_gl=1*18by5ku*_gcl_au*MjAwMTk0NTg1NC4xNzM5NjQ5NjUw

232 Cleary, T. (1990). *The Book of leadership and strategy: Lessons of the Chinese masters.* p. 5. Shambhala Publications.

233 Bennis, W. G. (2003). *On becoming a leader.* p. xxxii. Basic Books, Perseus Books Group.

234 Will. (2022, January 24). *Merriam-Webster.com*. http://www.merriam-webster.com/dictionary/will

235 Gardner, J. W. (1990). *On leadership.* p. 19. The Free Press.

[236] Koestenbaum, P. (2002). *Do you have the will to lead?* Audiotapes published by Sounds True.
[237] Zack, D. (2012, September 26). How to manage when you hate being a manager. http://www.fastcompany.com/3001576/how-manage-when-you-hate-being-manager
[238] Zack, D. (2012, September 26). How to manage when you hate being a manager. http://www.fastcompany.com/3001576/how-manage-when-you-hate-being-manager
[239] Lussier, R. N., & Achua, C. F. (2013). *Leadership: Theory, application, & skill development*, Fifth Ed. p. 37. South-Western Cengage Learning.
[240] Thinkexist.com (2016). https://allauthor.com/quotes/154370/
[241] Quinn, M. (2017, December 6). Beyonce to Bill Gates: 24 millionaires reveal the hardest thing about being an entrepreneur. https://www.huffpost.com/entry/beyonce-to-bill-gates-24-millionaires-reveal-the-hardest-thing-about-being-an-entrepreneur_b_6866554
[242] Tichy, N. M. (1997). *The leadership engine: How winning companies build leaders at every level.* HarperCollins Publishers.
[243] Gardner, J. W. (1990). *On leadership.* p. 50. The Free Press.
[244] Quotio (2016, January 2). https://quotio.com/quote/If-I-had-to/475100
[245] Collins, J. (2001). *Good to great: Why some companies make the leap . . . and others don't.* p. 39. HarperCollins Publishers.
[246] Tracy, B. (2000). *21 great ways to become an outstanding manager: How to manage, motivate, delegate, supervise and build a high performance team.* Audio CD, Track 7, Develop a Great Character. Brian Tracy International.
[247] Kotter, J. P. (1996). *Leading change.* Harvard Business Review Press.
[248] Bridges, W. (2009). *Managing transitions: Making the most of change* (3rd ed.). Da Capo Lifelong Books.
[249] Bridges, W. (2009). *Managing transitions: Making the most of change* (3rd ed.). Da Capo Lifelong Books.
[250] Bridges, W. (2009). *Managing transitions: Making the most of change* (3rd ed.). Da Capo Lifelong Books.
[251] Tracy, B., & Stein, C. (2015). *Find your balance point: Clarify your priorities, simplify your life, and achieve more.* Berrett-Koehler Publishers, Inc., Oakland, CA. https://books.google.com/books?id=DpFzCQAAQBAJ&pg=PT64&dq=what+percent+of+decisions+people+make+will+be+wrong&hl=en&sa=X&ved=0ahUKEwj_spyZsOLOAhVL7CYKHaJhCs0Q6AEIHjAA#v=onepage&q=what%20percent%20of%20decisions%20people%20make%20will%20be%20wrong&f=false. For additional insight, reference Sibony, O. (2020). *You're about to make a terrible mistake: How biases distort decision-making—and what you can do to fight them.* Little, Brown Spark.
[252] Lencioni, P. (2012). *The advantage: why organizational health trumps everything else in business.* p. 35. Jossey-Bass.
[253] Lencioni, P. (2010, September 27). The most important leadership trait you shun. *The Wall Street Journal.* http://www.wsj.com/articles/SB10001424052748704895204575321380627619

388. From Patrick Lencioni's *The five dysfunctions of a team: a leadership fable* (2002). Jossey-Bass.
[254] Vince Lombardi Quotes (2025).http://www.vincelombardi.com/quotes.html
[255] Bower, M. (1997). *The will to lead: Running a business with a network of leaders.* Harvard Business School Press.
[256] Lencioni, Patrick (2012). *The advantage: Why organizational health trumps everything else in business.* p. 190. Jossey-Bass.
[257] Tracy, B. (n.d.). The power of positive thinking. Using stumbling blocks as stepping stones. http://www.briantracy.com/blog/personal-success/using-stumbling-blocks-as-stepping-stones/
[258] Einstein, A. (2017). Quote Investigator. https://quoteinvestigator.com/2017/11/20/value/ Also at *Philosiblog*. http://philosiblog.com/2015/10/29/try-not-to-become-a-man-of-success-but-rather-try-to-become-a-man-of-value/
[259] *A profession of arms: Our core values* (2022). https://www.airuniversity.af.edu/Portals/10/Foundational-Resources/Profession-of-Arms-Proof.pdf
[260] Lincoln, A. (2016, February 27). *BrainyQuote*. http://www.brainyquote.com/quotes/quotes/a/abrahamlin101343.html
[261] Bennis, W. G. (2003). *On becoming a leader.* p. xxiv. Basic Books, Perseus Books Group.
[262] Puryear, E. F. (2000). *American generalship, character is everything: The art of command.* p. ix. Presidio Press.
[263] Locke, E. A. (2006). Business ethics: a way out of morass. Academy of Management Learning & Education 5(3) (2006): 346-355.
[264] Lussier, R. N., & Achua, C. F. (2013). *Leadership: Theory, application, & skill development*, Fifth Ed. p. 39. South-Western Cengage Learning.
[265] Zenger, J. H., & Folkman, J. (2002). *The extraordinary leader: turning good managers into great leaders.* p. 24. McGraw-Hill Companies Inc.
[266] Zenger, J. H., & Folkman, J. (2002). *The extraordinary leader: turning good managers into great leaders.* p. 24. McGraw-Hill Companies Inc.
[267] Maxwell, J. C. (1999). *The 21 indispensable qualities of a leader: Becoming the person others will want to follow.* p. 7. Thomas Nelson Publishers Inc.
[268] Tracy, B. (2005). *Master strategies for higher achievement*, Gildan Audio Publishers, disc 1, track 7.
[269] Tracy, B. (2005). *Master strategies for higher achievement*, Gildan Audio Publishers, disc 1, track 7.
[270] Covey, S. M. R. (1989). *The seven habits of highly effective people: Restoring the character ethic.* p. 22. Fireside Books, Simon & Schuster Inc.
[271] Covey, S. M. R. (1989). *The seven habits of highly effective people: Restoring the character ethic.* p. 22. Fireside Books, Simon & Schuster Inc.
[272] Zimmerman, A. (2015, June). Seven keys to lasting leadership. http://drzimmerman.com/tuesdaytip/7-keys-to-lasting-leadership.php

[273] Landry, L. (2023, April 3). Why emotional intelligence is important in leadership. Harvard Business School Online. https://online.hbs.edu/blog/post/emotional-intelligence-in-leadership

[274] Landry, L. (2023, April 3). Why emotional intelligence is important in leadership. Harvard Business School Online. https://online.hbs.edu/blog/post/emotional-intelligence-in-leadership

[275] Sinek, S. (2014). *Leaders eat last: Why some teams pull together and others don't.* Penguin Group.

[276] Vargas, P. A., & Hanlon, J. (2007). Celebrating a profession: The servant leadership perspective. *Journal of Research Administration*, 38(2), 45-49.

[277] Sinek, S. (2014). *Leaders eat last: Why some teams pull together and others don't.* Penguin Group.

[278] Peters, T. J., & Waterman, R. H., Jr. (1982). *In search of excellence.* Harper & Row, New York.

[279] Kouzes, J. M., & Posner, B. Z. (2010). *The truth about leadership: The no-fads, heart-of-the-matter facts you need to know.* [Chapter: Leaders make a difference.] Jossey-Bass.

[280] Northouse, P. G. (2022). *Leadership: Theory and practice.* Ninth Ed. Sage. pp. 15-16.

[281] Greenleaf, R. K. (1977). *Servant leadership.* Paulist Press.

[282] Spurlock, K., Young, H., Henderson, M., & Hilburn, G. (2015, June 15). The concept of servant leadership (2015, June 15). *News-Star*, a Gannett Company. http://www.thenewsstar.com/story/opinion/editorials/2015/06/15/concept-servant-leadership/28781309/

[283] Spurlock, K., Young, H., Henderson, M., & Hilburn, G. (2015, June 15). The concept of servant leadership (2015, June 15). *News-Star*, a Gannett Company. http://www.thenewsstar.com/story/opinion/editorials/2015/06/15/concept-servant-leadership/28781309/

[284] Spurlock, K., Young, H., Henderson, M., & Hilburn, G. (2015, June 15). The concept of servant leadership (2015, June 15). *News-Star*, a Gannett Company. http://www.thenewsstar.com/story/opinion/editorials/2015/06/15/concept-servant-leadership/28781309/

[285] Greenleaf, R. K. (1970). The servant as leader. Essay, p 2. https://www.leadershiparlington.org/pdf/TheServantasLeader.pdf Also at Smith, C. (2005). *Servant leadership: The leadership theory of Robert K. Greenleaf.* https://www.boyden.com/media/just-what-the-doctor-ordered-15763495/Leadership%20%20Theory_Greenleaf%20Servant%20Leadership.pdf

[286] Greenleaf, R. K. (1977). *Servant leadership.* Paulist Press. Also at https://www.greenleaf.org/what-is-servant-leadership/

[287] Collins, J. (2001). *Good to great: Why some companies make the leap . . . and others don't.* p. 39. HarperCollins Publishers.

[288] Collins, J. (2001). *Good to great: Why some companies make the leap . . . and others don't.* p. 39. HarperCollins Publishers.

[289] Collins, J. (2001). *Good to great: Why some companies make the leap . . . and others don't.* p. 39. HarperCollins Publishers.

[290] Tan, C. M. (2012, September 11). Compassionate leaders are effective leaders. Greater Good Magazine. Greater Good Science Center, University of California, Berkeley. http://greatergood.berkeley.edu/article/item/compassionate_leaders_are_effective_leaders

[291] Collins, J. (2001). *Good to great: Why some companies make the leap . . . and others don't.* pp. 36-37. HarperCollins Publishers.

[292] The King Center (2013, April 9). http://www.thekingcenter.org/blog/mlk-quote-week-all-labor-uplifts-humanity-has-dignity-and-importance-and-should-be-undertaken. Also at https://mlkmpc.org/

[293] Senge, P. M. (2006). *The fifth discipline: The art and practice of the learning organization.* (Revised Edition). Doubleday.

[294] Zenger, J. & Folkman, J. (2016). Continuous learning: A key leadership capability. *Harvard Business Review.* https://hbr.org. Additional references include, Zenger, J., & Folkman, J. (2022, March 28). *The leadership skills needed at every level.* Zenger Folkman. https://zengerfolkman.com/articles/the-leadership-skills-needed-at-every-level/ and Zenger, J. H., & Folkman, J. (2019). *The extraordinary leader: Turning good managers into great leaders* (3rd ed.). McGraw-Hill.

[295] Stone, D. & Heen, S. (2014). *Thanks for the feedback: The science and art of receiving feedback well.* Viking.

[296] Scott, K. (2017). *Radical candor: Be a kick-ass boss without losing your humanity.* St. Martin's Press.

[297] Buckingham, M. & Goodall, A. (2019). The feedback fallacy. *Harvard Business Review.* https://hbr.org. Also at https://www.physicianleaders.org/articles/the-feedback-fallacy

[298] Christensen, C. M. (1997). *The innovator's dilemma: When new technologies cause great firms to fail.* Harvard Business Review Press.

[299] Camp, R. C. (1989). *Benchmarking: a signpost to excellence in quality and productivity.* Quality Press.

[300] Rarick, C. A. (2008). *Best practices: The ultimate guide to improving your company's performance.* CRC Press.

[301] Weinstein, B. (2010). *Ethical leadership: creating and sustaining an ethical business culture.* Business Expert Press.

[302] Quinn, M. (2017, December 6). Beyonce to Bill Gates: 24 millionaires reveal the hardest thing about being an entrepreneur. https://www.huffpost.com/entry/beyonce-to-bill-gates-24-millionaires-reveal-the-hardest-thing-about-being-an-entrepreneur_b_6866554

[303] Coolidge, C. (2024, May 4). *GoodReads.* https://www.goodreads.com/author/quotes/101882.Calvin_Coolidge

[304] The Myers-Briggs Company (2025, January 12). https://www.themyersbriggs.com/en-US/Products-and-Services/Myers-Briggs

[305] 360DegreeLeader (2025, January 4). 360DegreeLeader.com.

[306] Lattice (2025, January 4). Lattice.com.

[307] Namely (2025, January 4). Namely.com.

[308] PerformYard (2025, January 4). Performyard.com.
[309] Qualtrics (2025, January 6). Qualtrix.com.
[310] SurveyMonkey (2025, January 6). Surveymonkey.com.
[311] Lencioni, P. (2012). *The advantage: why organizational health trumps everything else in business.* pp. 73-10. Jossey-Bass.
[312] Tennyson, A. Lord (1842). *Ulysses.* Also, Tennyson, A. Lord. (1894). *The works of Alfred Lord Tennyson.* Edited by Charles Tennyson, Macmillan.

*Note: Manuscript reviewed for grammatical corrections and edits using Microsoft Word v2412 (2025), Grammarly Pro (2025), and OpenAI (2025) ChatGPT [Large language model].

*Note: Internet links in citations were reviewed and verified on May 2, 2025.

Index

A

Achua, Christopher F. 27, 33, 36, 60, 67, 74, 75, 80, 81, 82, 83, 84, 85, 90, 176, 193
American Society for Training and Development 4
artificial intelligence (AI) 53, 131, 132
autocratic leaders 83

B

Benchmarking: A Signpost to Excellence in Quality and Productivity 215
Bennis, Warren G. .. 8, 60, 61, 67, 68, 70, 71, 87, 175, 193
Berrett-Koehler 175
Best Practices: The Ultimate Guide to Improving Your Company's Performance 215
Blake, Robert 84
Blanchard, Ken 7
Bower, Marvin 188, 203
Brandon Hall Group 4
Bridges, William 183
Buckingham, Marcus 214

Building Trust 155
Burke, Ronald 3
Burns, James MacGregor 21, 55, 56, 59, 87

C

Camp, Robert 215
Carlisle, Thomas 153
character shaped by integrity 193
charismatic leaders 85
Christensen, Clayton 215
Collins, Jim 8, 60, 61, 67, 68, 87, 167, 168, 182, 206, 206
continuous pursuit of excellence 207
core values of leadership excellence 191
Covey, Stephen R. 141, 143, 199, 200
Creech, Bill, General, USAF 88
Cronin, Thomas 90
culture 98

D

Deming, W. Edwards 40, 41, 42, 44, 48, 88

democratic leaders 83
DeVos, Richard 181
diversity 72, 89, 119, 132, 160
Do You Have the Will to Lead? 175
Drucker, Peter F. ... 8, 29, 33, 55, 56, 57, 58, 61, 62, 68, 71, 72, 79, 85, 87, 89, 129, 155

E

emotional intelligence 200
enabling attribute of concern ... 160
enabling attribute of the will to lead 175
enabling attributes of leadership excellence 140
Ethical Leadership: Creating and Sustaining an Ethical Business Culture 215
Evans, M. G. 90

F

Folkman, Joseph. 77, 78, 89, 90, 195, 209
Fortune 500 206
Fourteen-Point Management Philosophy 42

G

Gardner, John W. 7, 8, 23, 59, 62, 63, 68, 73, 89, 90, 91, 129, 175, 181
Genesis: Artificial Intelligence, Hope, and the Human Spirit 53, 131
goals and objectives 135
Goleman, Daniel 154
Good to Great: Why Some Companies Make the Leap . . . and Others Don't 205
Goodall, Ashley 214

great man theory 201
Greenleaf, Robert 204

H

Harvard Business Review 154
Hawthorne Effect 38
Heen, Sheila 214
Herzberg, Frederick I. 27, 35, 36, 38, 39
Hesse, Hermann 205
House, Robert 90
Howard, Ann 2, 5

I

In Search of Excellence 203
Industrial Revolution 25
inputs, outputs, and outcomes of the leadership process 129

J

Japanese union of scientists and engineers 42
Jordan, William George 199
Journey to the East 205

K

key performance indicators 137
King, Martin Luther 10, 72
Kissinger, Henry A. 131
Koestenbaum, Peter 175
Kotter, John P. 63, 64, 182
Kouzes, James M. 145, 146, 155, 157, 204

L

Landry, Lauren 200
leader 9
leaders
    born or made? 67

LEADERS Conflict Resolution
    Framework 159
*Leaders Eat Last: Why Some Teams
    Pull Together and Others Don't*...203
leadership 10, 64
leadership capabilities 70
leadership focus areas 95
Leadership Grid 84
leadership styles 78
leading up 172
Lencioni, Patrick 186
Lewin, Kurt 83
Lussier, Robert N. 27, 33, 36, 60, 67, 74, 75, 80, 81, 82, 83, 84, 85, 90, 176, 193

M

Managerial Grid 84
*Managing Transitions: Making the
    Most of Change* 183
Maslow, Abraham H. .27, 28, 29, 30, 31, 32, 33, 35, 38, 39
Master Strategies for Higher Achievement
    195
Maxwell, John C. 75, 88, 89, 142, 143, 195
Mayer, John 154
McCanse, Anne Adams 84
McGregor, Douglas M. 27, 33, 34, 35, 38, 39, 83
McKinsey & Company 203
mission 134
mission focus areas 108
Model for Sustained Leadership
    Excellence 14, 126
Motivation-Hygiene Theory 36
Mouton, Jane 84
Mundie, Craig 131
Myers-Briggs Type Indicator 80

N

Nanus, Burt 8, 60, 61, 67, 68, 87
National Bureau of Economics 175

O

operating rhythm framework ... 118
Operation Desert Storm 203
operationalize the model's
    principles 232

P

Path-goal leadership theory 90
people focus areas 96
performance feedback 213
PerformYard 237
persona 80
Peters, Thomas J. 203
phases of the change management
    process 183
Posner Barry Z. ...145, 146, 155, 157, 204
practical leaders 85

R

*Radical Candor: Be a Kick-Ass Boss
    Without Losing Your Humanity* 214
Rarick, Charles 215
Rothstein, Mitchell 3
Rowling, J.K. 178

S

Salovey, Peter 154
Schmidt, Eric 131
Schwab, Charles 216
Schwarzkopf, Norman, General,
    U.S. Army 203
Scott, Kim 214
Servant Leadership 204

service mindset............................ 201
Shewhart, Walter A. 40
Sinek, Simon............ 96, 97, 201, 203
Sirota Consulting............................169
situational leaders 89
Stone, Douglas 214
strategic planning workshop 238
strategy..136
Sun Tzu 6, 24, 25
sustained leadership excellence 125

T

Tan, Chade-Meng........................ 205
Taylor, Frederick W.....27, 28, 29, 35, 38, 39, 55
Team leaders 84
tenets of concern............................174
Thanks for the Feedback: The Science and Art of Receiving Feedback Well 214
The Advantage: Why Organizational Health Trumps Everything Else in Business.. 186
The Art of War 6, 25
The Extraordinary Leader: Turning Good Managers into Great Leaders.........195
The Feedback Fallacy 214
The Fifth Discipline: The Art and Practice of the Learning Organization 209
The Five Dysfunctions of a Team.... 186
The Innovator's Dilemma: When New Technologies Cause Great Firms to Fail.. 215
The Leadership Engine 5, 179
the leadership process............. 15, 129
The Will to Lead: Running a Business with a Network of Leaders..........188

Theory of Human Motivation 29
Theory X and Theory Y.................33
Three Dimensions of the Model for Sustained Leadership Excellence 126
Tichy, Noel M. 5, 179
total quality management 41
Tracy, Brian.. 182, 99, 100, 153, 157, 182, 186, 190, 195, 199
transformational leaders 87

U

unifying forces of the leadership process 133

V

values 135
Vision 134

W

Warren Buffett's Management Secrets 169
Waterman, Robert H. 203
Weinstein, Bruce......................... 215
Welch, Jack and Suzy.....153, 165, 166
Wellins, Richard S. 2, 5

Y

Yukl, Gary.......................................76

Z

Zenger, John H....77, 78, 89, 90, 195, 209
Zimmer, Dave............ 100, 158, 252
Zimmerman, Alan.......................200
Zuckerberg, Mark.........................96

About the Author

Philip A. Iannuzzi, Jr., is an award-winning leader, author, and scholar with leadership experience across business, education, the military, and multi-national organizations. A retired U.S. Air Force colonel and pilot, he held key leadership roles in the Department of Defense, including Pentagon program manager, major command division chief, flying squadron commander, and director of NATO's Combined Joint Task Force Operations Center in Naples, Italy.

Following his military career, he joined The Boeing Company, where he led a regional C-17 Globemaster pilot, aircrew, and maintenance training center. He later served as a senior leader in Boeing's learning and development division providing workforce development solutions for the company's global Defense, Space & Security workforce.

He holds a doctoral degree in educational leadership from Delaware Valley University, along with a master of science degree in systems management from the University of Southern California, a master's degree in international strategic studies from Air War College, a master's degree in global air mobility logistics from the Air Force Institute of Technology, and a master's degree in joint military operations from Air Command and Staff College. He completed his bachelor of science degree at Penn State University. As an educator, he taught courses on leadership as an adjunct faculty member at Embry-Riddle Aeronautical University.

A prize-winning author, he is the recipient of the *National Defense Transportation Journal*'s Memorial Medal for Literary Merit and graduate school's Orvil Anderson Leadership Writing Award. His military honors and decorations include the Legion of Merit, Bronze Star, and Air Medal.

He lives in Doylestown, Pennsylvania, with his wife, Maria. They are proud parents of Philip, Andre, and Stephen. He now devotes his time to leadership development education through research, writing, teaching, and consulting. Outside of his professional work, he enjoys golf, travel, and spending time with family and friends.

Also by Philip A. Iannuzzi, Jr.

Importance, Value, and Need for Leadership Development Training for Academic Department Chairs

Evolution of the Expeditionary Aerospace Force and the Need to Develop Expeditionary Aerospace Commanders

Gathering of Eagles
A biography series featuring global aerospace pioneers
(with David L. McFarland)

www.ingramcontent.com/pod-product-compliance
Lightning Source LLC
Chambersburg PA
CBHW050517170426
43201CB00013B/1988